A London Life, 1930-1960:
Other Days, Other Ways

"God gave his children memory
That in life's garden there might be
June roses in December"
Studdart Kennedy

Doroth. _. īeague

SYNJON BOOKS

ISBN 0 904 373 10 X

Published by Synjon Books 2005

Synjon Books
5, Homestead View,
The Street, BORDEN,
Sittingbourne, Kent,
ME9 8JQ

For details of other publications see our website:
http://www.synjonbooks.co.uk

Dedication

Written with love to our son Tony, our daughter Helen and our grandchildren Della Judd, David Allinson and Simon Teague.

Acknowledgements

This book would not have been published without the encouragement and support of my son Tony and daughter, Helen Allinson.

My thanks are due also to Rebecca and especially to my husband John, for his patience and understanding.

CONTENTS

PREFACE

Geographically and geologically S.E. London is one and indivisible. It is for the most part a grandstand overlooking an area stretching to the Thames. Start at any point on the south bank of the river and walk southwards. First you will walk on level ground, maybe a few yards or perhaps a mile. Then almost suddenly the slope becomes a hill. The hills leading up to Blackheath are good examples, another is Pepys Hill, New Cross. Directories give "Pepys Road", but locally it was always Pepys Hill, pronounced PEP –IS. Roads parallel with this, Jerningham Road, Erlanger and Waller Roads all lead to the top of Telegraph Hill. To the east lies Hilly Fields, Shooters Hill. Whilst to the west rise Forest Hill, Denmark Hill and Sydenham Hill among others. From the top of these hills spreads a panoramic view of the Thames, winding its way through the vast amorphous spread of London and beyond to the hills of Hampstead and Highgate on the river's northern side.

This is the setting, then, for my own particular location; the space: the time – the 4th, 5th and 6th, decades of the 20th. Century. Sharply I recall setting out from the house with my aunt, early one spring morning over 70 years ago and walking to the crown of Telegraph Hill. Standing gazing into the distance she told me how 50 years before, when she was about 5, she too had climbed the hill to this very spot. "Dad was keen to show me the sunsets set off by the eruption of Krakatoa. People came from all around, Marvellous they were, I've never seen anything like it. The whole sky, brilliant, purple, gold, red, green. Of course there were no houses here; then it was called Plow Garlick Hill; just wild, grass, trees and bushes".

Unforgettable; unimaginable to me then; now, in early Spring, 2005, following the earthquake and tsunami of December 2004 in Indonesia, it is a solemn, poignant memory.

However, to us it was never known as anything but Telegraph Hill, from the telegraph station erected there during the Napoleonic Wars. When I wandered in the park there, at the summit, or looked out of our upstairs windows, I could see Tower Bridge, St. Paul's, tops of cranes in the docks and a number of power station chimneys, though all would often be clouded in mist and smoke.

So different today, shipping all gone, so no docks, St. Paul's and Tower Bridge dwarfed, scarcely visible, lost amid the towering new edifices of Canary Wharf, the Gherkin. All transformed; shining new, sharply defined in the clear smokeless air.   The old order changeth.

To recollect is not simply to recall memory, but to absorb in mystical contemplation.
Brian Redhead, 1992

BOOK 1 - The Thirties
Early days at Waller Road

My father never wanted children, he thought the world too terrible a place in which to bring them up. I once asked Mother whether she would have liked more. "I wouldn't have minded" she said, sounding lukewarm. The fact is that she was thirty-five when I was born, at that time considered an "elderly pregnancy" and I was a breach birth, the doctor only just saving me from strangling to death with my own umbilical cord. I was black in the face, it was a near thing they said; being feet first, Mum had a rotten time, the midwife sent for Dr. Govan after a few hours when she realised my position; it was all over by tea time on a Monday, I think.

Me aged 2 months

Peckham Rye was a favourite place for a walk, it seemed to me then a vast unending sea of grass; one bright sunny day Mother said, talking as we walked, "Everything you see, everything you do, everything you think and hear will become part of you and you will remember it forever, though you may not be aware of it". I thought this far-fetched and rather funny- "Do you mean I'll remember that toffee paper lying on the grass?". She laughed, saying she hadn't meant that, but as I stopped and pointed it out, I might. Now the whole incident remains clear to me; I can feel the light wind blowing across the Rye, see the distant trees and houses, see us there and hear our voices; I was seven years old.

Not my earliest memory then, so I'll dig back further. Our house had four floors, several of the rooms being let to lodgers, and when the two uppermost fell vacant, my parents thought it would be a good idea if they had one and I the little attic room next door to it, for until then I had shared theirs. These rooms were separated from all the others in the house by a small flight of stairs. To get up these stairs I had to pass *WILD ANIMALS*; there were Lions and indescribable others of terrible threat and immense power waiting to jump out from deep darknesses and tear me up. It was no problem getting up there, Mother came and tucked me up all clean and cosy, and when she left I dropped off to sleep, only to be woken by horrifying nightmares of fire. I screamed and screamed, but no-one could hear me, I was about thirty-six stairs up and could not go down because of the Wild Animal infested staircase. Of course Mother came up to see how I was faring in my new little bedroom - all freshly papered and nice - and was shocked to find me in such an awful state, and stayed with me until I was asleep again. Once they had gone to bed there was no trouble, they were next door, so I was all right. I think I was two or three at the time and it has always remained a real and vivid memory; I wonder why I reacted like that for I had no experience of dangerous fire, let alone wild animals.

I know that they persevered with me in that room for three nights, trying nightlights, all doors open, everything, but each night I had the same terrifying dreams, so in the end the plan was given up. I shared a room with Aunt Nell for several years then, that worked out well. Of course, these bedrooms were not heated; in very cold weather the inside of the windows would be covered in ice and pretty ferny frost patterns, and ice formed on the cup of water placed by my bed. We did not have hot-water bottles, they were thought to be dangerous, the bed was warmed with a brick which had been heated by the fire for an hour or so, then wrapped in a piece of thick old blanket, done up with two big safetypins. If it had become too hot, a strong smell of scorching arose and it was undone to cool off a bit. It was an excellent way of heating a bed, put in well before I climbed in, and then pushed down by my feet; it kept warm all night. The others had flat irons. Aunt's room was only six stairs up from the living room and a large brightly patterned cretonne-covered screen divided my corner of the room from the rest. As well as our beds, our room contained a large old mahogany chest-of-drawers and our wardrobe was a curtained-off alcove; pretty basic, a wooden shelf set down from the ceiling a couple of feet, the edge of which supported a curtain rail; a rod at the back was placed several inches from the floor to take our shoes, all everyday stuff. As Aunt and I were in tune from the beginning - the difference in our ages was as nothing - this arrangement worked well, but it did not prevent my fears from surfacing now and again.

The window of this room faced a sharply rising side road, and when the infrequent car drove down it in the dark, it's lights shone brightly, running across the walls and ceiling. For some unknown reason I knew these as the "Bull's Eyes" and was stricken with dread. Poor Mother!. However I managed to overcome this phenomenon and other very real fears I had about the house, those concerning the basement. Being built about halfway up Telegraph Hill, the front was lower than the back, so that the basement was not below ground in the front - it had a downstairs front door and low-set front windows - but the garden door at it's far end was set into the hillside. Both front doors were "grained"; that upstairs had shining brass letterbox and knocker, but downstairs the "tradesmen's" door fittings were painted black and so didn't have to be polished each week.

The trouble was that the basement had large coal cellars leading off it at either end. One could, if under say, three feet six inches tall, just walk into these endless dark caverns, peering round their cobwebby low brick pillars. It was at the entrance to one of these that my father charged the wireless batteries, I'd stand and watch him fixing on the coloured wires. "Never touch", he'd say, "Stand just there, it's acid". I tried never to have to open the door to the basement stairs at night on my own; of course there was no electric light there until Dad had it put in in 1933, so one had to carry a little oil lamp or candle to see to light the gas. Cars drove very fast down that hilly side street (Arbuthnot Road), and as their number increased, so did the collisions with those using Waller Road.

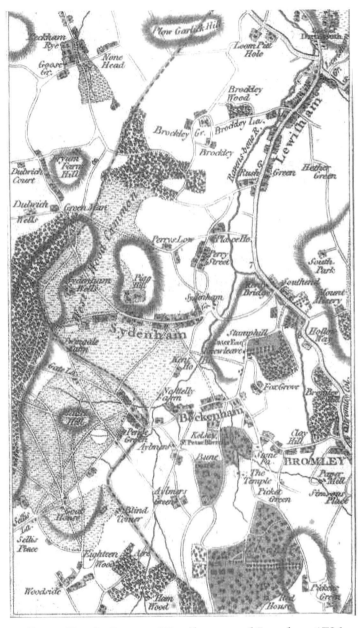

From Cary's Survey 15 miles round London, 1786

13

Frequently there would be a loud crash, and we took the casualties into our basement (scullery) and tended them there, mopped up blood, wrapped them in blankets, gave them tea while we waited for the policeman. Mother organised a petition to have a warning "+ Crossroads" sign put up. This was done about 1936 and the accidents ceased from then on.

Houses at New Cross Gate, New Cross Road

This house that I was born in in the spring of 1927 was large and well built. My Mother's two sisters had bought the lease with money saved from their dress-making business which gradually folded up during the early 1920's as more and more clothes were mass produced and after the First World War sewing hands were harder to get. They moved there from Ansdell Road, Peckham, early in 1925; all previous houses they lived in had been rented; this was the time when home ownership first became general and leasehold properties were common.

The land was owned by the Haberdashers Company and the houses on the estate were built to specific requirements. We were required to paint the outside of the house every five years, as set out in the lease, this often extended to seven years and a company inspector would call to remind us. The whole neighbourhood, therefore, looked attractive and well kept. Large plane trees lined the roads, each little front garden had its well clipped hedge, nicely painted iron railings and gate and the back gardens were long.

In common with other houses built at the turn of the century, the living room windows on the ground floor faced those of the next door house, thus although they were large bays, they received but little light. We were fortunate, being on a corner site, this window faced due south and there was nothing to impede the sunlight, it was lovely, and as Mother said, it saved pounds in fuel bills, and enabled her to keep scarlet flowering geraniums on the widened windowsill all year round. As the sun moved round, it shone through the bay windows at the front of the house, it was all light and sunny and marvellous for watching sunsets, too. I always loved thunderstorms; Mum and I would stand at the window and watch, excited and thrilling to the noise, blackness, wind and rain and shriek at the lightning; Nell was afraid and went down into the scullery (basement). The big front door in the hall had jewel coloured glass windows; tiny oblongs and larger diamonds of ruby, sapphire, emerald and amber surrounding the central circle of opaque white glass, painted with a design of flowers and leaves in sepia. The sunlight made coloured patterns on the hall mats and linoleum; I touched them they were so pretty. These windows were blown out during the blitz in 1940, and eventually replaced with arctic glass, which at the time I considered to be *Better*, so much more modern!.

15

A flight of about eleven stairs led up from the hall, and a shallow flight of six led down to the dining room, the door of which also had coloured glass panels. There were two, similar, each depicting a man in Elizabethan dress - puffed, beribboned sleeves, large feathered hat, slashed doublet and hose, sword and elaborate gauntlets. I never liked them; we called them *Gog & Magog*; very early on I thought them old fashioned, as I did the whole house, I wanted to live in something small and new; the house had about forty stairs in all, so I would have liked a little house, the sort that were being built in the surrounding countryside in vast numbers at that time, but which were dismissed by the adults around me as "Jerry built".

I cannot recall any of my childhood without thinking of war. Born eight years after the signing of the Treaty of Versailles, the aftermath of the Great War was all about me from the first. Current talk was of the Sino-Japanese War, soon followed by the fighting, killing and distress of the Spanish Civil War; with the bombing by the Germans of Guernica in 1937; I remember helping to do up parcels sent to the relief of refugees. The nazis were already in power in Germany when Mussolini invaded Ethiopia, then came Munich, the issuing of gas masks and finally the outbreak of World War Two. But I am going much too fast, leaving my earliest memories behind too quickly. At the very bottom of our road stood the corner house in Queens Road, these were older, larger houses, already long since divided into flats. We walked that way every Saturday morning to buy the Sunday joint at *Chalk & Cox*, never more than 2/6d., and the vegetables at *Kingston's* at New Cross Gate, also when getting a bus or tram to Rye Lane, Peckham, or London, or maybe the opposite way to Lewisham or Greenwich. We therefore frequently walked past the house whose large brick side wall abutted immediately onto the pavement opposite New Cross Fire

Station; fixed to this wall, high above my head, was, what appeared to me then, a large wooden overmantle composed of three panels, with a boxed-in shelf at the base.

It was newest and brightest when I was youngest, it deteriorated badly towards 1939 and was finally taken down. It was a World War One memorial, a sort of shrine; looking up at the fancy gold letters in the centre panel, I asked Mother what it said? "To the Memory of our Glorious Dead", she replied, "1914-1918", and she tried to explain. On the shelf there were three jam jars filled with fresh garden flowers, except on Armistice Day when they were bright with artificial poppies. I soon knew what that meant - complete silence at two minutes to 11 a.m. on the eleventh day of the eleventh month. When I was at school we stood to attention; cars, horses, everybody. everything was still and silent; then the guns went off and we sat down again. It was awesome and made an impression; we tried to feel sad and tragic, because we knew that we should, but failed because we did not, could not, know what it all meant. As I grew older, I suppose about 9 or 10, and saw the gold paint peel off the little shrine, the wood begin to rot, the jam jars left to go green with mould, the flowers long since withered shrivelled and dead and never now replaced, I thought, "aren't the dead glorious *now* then? When did they stop? and that made me very sad and uncertain. I wondered about the person who had placed the memorial there...

Me aged 2 years (1929)

Until I started school when I was five, I lived totally in the company of adults: warm, caring, loving people, but not of my generation. As I said, Mother was thirty-five when I was born, and being a strong personality, had a great influence over me; she brought me up; my father was happy to remain a shadowy, kindly figure in the background. Indeed, he never spoke a cross word to me nor reprimanded me in any way - which I noticed and felt was a bit odd. Perhaps he thought Mother's discipline enough for two; whatever the reason, he left it all to her, and she accepted the responsibility with enthusiasm. I had no option but to toe the line - for a long time she kept a chart on the wall on which a red tick or a black cross was entered each night according to the way I had behaved during the day - no room for liberal self-expression where she was concerned - *Mother knew best* and never doubted it. She did not believe in corporal punishment, but her anger could be frightening. She admitted to me much later that she had always had a very quick temper and thought I would be the same and was surprised to discover that I did not. So, how was I punished?. Once I ate some salted peanuts that had been given to me, but had been told to keep until after dinner (midday), Mother threw the whole lot in the dustbin - she knew that was wrong as soon as she'd done it, and there we were, both bawling and screaming our heads off!. But I didn't forget it and realised from then on that she too had feet of clay. It made me secretive and rather reserved; she never did anything like that again. I did pretty well as I was told, but frequently was rude and had to apologise: "say you're sorry", it went on and on. "I can say *sorry*, but won't mean it". So I would shout out the word "sorry" and really not mean it at all, but it seemed to go down all right.

I believe that I remember the dark, unpleasant moments of my childhood so clearly because they so contrast with the everyday content and happiness that was my lot. I was indeed fortunate, my upbringing was stable and imaginative too. Mother's eldest sister, as I've said, lived in the house; when I think of fairy stories now, and hear of good fairies and bad at a baby's Christening, I think of Aunt Nell as being one of my good fairies (they are limited in number), but she was Mother's too; I'll explain as we go along. Mum, as her mother and both her grandmothers before her, undertook the task of running a home with competence, it came first with her, it never occurred to her to go out to work, the idea never arose. The household tasks were performed regularly, no skipping, Jobs were allotted to each day of the week, others monthly, some annually. One must remember that before, say 1936, we had no vacuum cleaner, so the mats were shaken every day, the lino swept and mopped and the carpets sprinkled with moist tea leaves, then swept on hands and knees with a dustpan and brush, as were the stairs. In winter, coal fires had to be cleared out each day and re-laid, they were wonderful to sit by, but, invariably, only one room had one lit, and that had a trivet in front and a hob at the side, with kettles always kept on them for hot water. Being thrifty, orange peel was always put in a tin dish inside the fender to dry - used for kindling, it flared up sparkling and spluttering. There was also a string tied right round the mantelpiece with bits of washing drying throughout the winter weeks; and on winter Mondays you couldn't see the fire for the steaming three-sided horse of washing.

Nothing has changed more in the last seventy years than the way we do our washing. It was an ancient ritual; the copper, an integral part of the house, stood out from a wall in the scullery (the basement), built of rendered brick. The fire would be laid early Monday morning, a fiddly job, as the aperture was quite small and low down. Laid as any fire, with crushed newspaper, sticks and coal, the latter broken small to fit in, the washing was then put into the copper itself. With lodgers it amounted to an enormous wash. Soiled, stained garments had been scrubbed beforehand with a rough bar of harsh, green household soap and soaked well. Woollens and silks, if any, had to be washed separately, by hand, another day, also rayon, the only man-made fibre then. If you hadn't got a copper, the washing would be boiled up in a bucket on the gas-stove or range.

The copper was filled with water from a large white enamelled jug, how much it held I've no idea, but several gallons; a handful of soda added to soften our hard water (2d. a big blue bag full) and when all the laundry was safely submerged, the whole lot was clamped down with the heavy round wooden lid as it came to the boil, it was necessary for it to actually boil - it took over an hour or more - it was stirred about frequently with a great wooden copper stick, the fire stoked up, the trap door closed, the ash falling to the ground beneath. When beginning to boil it would make the familiar, unmistakable sound, bubble, bubble, thump, thump, bubble, faster and faster, an unforgettable smell arose amid the warm billowing steam and down in the dark basement the fire glinted and I danced about in atavistic ceremony. "O do get out of the way, Girlie, do, it's boiling - get out of the way - *quick*". The lid was raised, the dripping clothes lifted with the copperstick into the galvanised bath or tub. The fire died down, and it seemed over.

Not for Mum and Aunt it wasn't. There was scrubbing on the scrubbing board, working the dolly up and down in the tub, then the rinsing, the bluing, the starching and the hanging up to dry - if at all possible out of doors. The ashes had to be riddled out and swept up and some of the hot suds bailed out with a little, metal-handled bowl and used to mop up the messy floor, then left to dry. No wonder it was always cold meat off Sunday's joint for dinner and a bit of cold pie, for after that there was all the folding with some items rolled up for damp ironing. The whole process took lots of time and energy but gave much satisfaction too, piles of fresh, creaseless, sweet-smelling laundry, lots of tea and chatter. A job well done.

Meanwhile, their middle sister, Mill, used a Dulwich local laundry for sheets, tablecloths and especially Tom's shirts. You can imagine that didn't go down very well with those at Waller.

On Fridays and Saturday afternoons, the coke boiler in the kitchen was lit, Mum did more washing then, especially for the lodgers, drying it near the boiler when the weather was bad. One day I remarked that I wished Mother didn't have all their washing to do - a cold wet day, she was tired, and I wanted her to do something with *me*, "Well", she said, eyeing me positively, "If I didn't do this for them, I don't know how we'd manage to go on holiday this year". I hadn't realised things were so tight and never mentioned it again. People worked very hard then, for little reward. It was lovely when the washing was hung out in the garden. I often helped with that, I liked the flapping of the garments in the wind and the fresh scent of them when they were dry. "Keep your weather eye open", Nell would tell me, "There's clouds coming up". She regarded the North anxiously, "It won't rain yet, look, there's a blue eye in the north". I could see it too, curtains of dark, heavy, rain cloud had opened to reveal a patch of clearest blue.

The boiler was lit two days running to enable everyone in the house (seven or eight people), to take a bath - the lodgers were given an allotted time. Everyone had a bath once a week, and Mother was very strict about washing. "Wash neck, face, hands, under your arms, feet and bottom every day, down as far as possible - and don't forget *possible* otherwise you'll smell". The lodgers had use of the bathroom, so I used the kitchen sink, Dad shaved in the scullery. The water was heated in kettles on the gas stove in the morning, in the evening in winter by the fire. We never had bath salts, just a pinch of soda to soften the water, and once a week we washed our hair in rainwater and soft soap made up from ends of tablets. It was dried by the fire in winter, there were no hair driers, and outdoors in the sun in summer - if it was cool we just wrapped it in a towel for about fifteen minutes, like a turban, and it dried naturally quite quickly. Mother always cut my hair, once a month on the waxing moon, and would singe it with a taper, which I hated, it sizzled and smelt awful, so I yelled and jerked about and was told to "Stand still you little donkey, how can I make a good job of it with you jivering about like that?" Her own hair was long, not cut until W.W.II., and she would swing it over her shoulder and singe it with skill and determination; I watched fascinated to see the ends melting and the curls of acrid smoke rise up. "Why do you do it?" I wanted to know. "Mother always did it", she would answer, "It stops split ends and keeps it healthy"; perhaps she was right.

There was no guilt because Mother hadn't a career, running the home was her job, most of the married women who went out to work did so from necessity, not choice. But she was not cut out to be a *hausfrau* and instinctively I knew that her "causes" meant nearly as much to her as I did. Having Aunt Nell living in the house set her free to attend various Quaker committees - she was a newly converted Friend, having become a member of the Society in 1930. She was an active member of the Peace Pledge Union, headquarters in Queens Road, and was a leader of the Adult School classes held every Thursday afternoon at Peckham Meeting House where she also played the hymns. Aunt Nell would have tea ready for me when I came home from school, bread and butter, home made jam and one rock cake - Mum baked a batch every Friday to last the week and it was usual for us to sit by the fire on winter evenings and wait for darkness to fall. "Don't put the light on yet" she'd say, "Let us sit in the gloaming, it's nice and it'll save a penny or two". I grew up to appreciate those quiet, harmonious times very much. And so you may picture us, she gazing into the warm red glowing coals, aware of the present but seeing the past, and me equally aware of the present and wondering if it were true that pictures of the future could be seen within it's fiery depths.

Spring-cleaning was an event, all bustling efficiency. Mother and Aunt were so full of achievement - and so they should be, cleaning about thirty brass stair rods, washing innumerable venetian blinds and clearing up after the chimney sweep, not to mention washing the paintwork which became unbelievably dirty in days of open fires. I remember coming in from school one such day and Aunt giving me 2d. to go and buy a 2 oz. bar of Cadbury's milk chocolate or, better still, Rowntree's Motoring chocolate (launched in 1923 at a shilling for half a pound), a rare treat, full of fruit and nuts, they had earned it, and we shared it together.

The coming of the warm, sunny days of Spring awoke the dormant flies, blue-bottles were quite common then. Once or twice a "fly-paper" was hung up near to where

24

cooking went on, a sticky, brown strip about a foot long. Attracted to this, the flies, unable to get away, died a lingering fidgety death. Horrid. Nell preferred swotting, grimly chasing the offending creature with a rolled newspaper she would chant, "Do you love God little fly? Then go to God little fly". Wallop, wallop. Or maybe, "Wretched buzzing thing – Go to Perdition!" Whack. Quickly dispatched, over and done with, no messing. Nell was full of these colourful turns of phrase, they fascinated me. Another, used to vent her feelings after several days cold, dark and dismal was grimly said, "Ugh, I hate this horrid *cut throat* weather", Pause. I queried, found it unknowable. Only she used them; now they echo strongly in my mind through the intervening years. Where, from whom, had she got them? And so, as with all lives, influences of past generations lingered, were alive and well, informing the present. Turns of phrase uttered without thought, used as everyday speech, especially by Nell. If I grizzled a bit, "Turn off that tap", she'd say, and Mother would add in no uncertain terms, "You've got a face like a donkey's baby". When a miserable old neighbour once called and left smiling, Nell remembered, "She soon perked up, like an old hat in a shower of rain". Lively, spontaneous, meaningful.

Mother was a passionate woman with strong likes and dislikes and one of the greatest loves all her life long was her garden. My father was very clever at making excellent paths, erecting stout fences, and he even took a water pipe from the house to near the end of the garden to make it easier for Mother to do the watering, but it was she who grew things, flowers, vegetables and fruit. The garden was one of my earliest joys too and my greatest delight on a warm summer's day was to be allowed to play with water on the lawn. I'd have a pail, bowls and a tin cup, I loved the feel of the hot wet grass blades and the soft black soil on my feet, and wiggled my toes: I was very little. I remember staring up into the darkness of a large sycamore tree, and standing watching the never ending columns of ants running up and down. Later, I'd pick random bunches of flowers and search for skeleton leaves to press in an old book; the scent of the flowering currant, like tom cats, in the corner by the outside lavatory was very strong.

I was paid 1d. a jam jar to collect snails and caterpillars off the cabbages and watched them foam as they drowned in the strong salt water; if the snail collecting was a bit slow I'd get some from the old rockery at the end of the garden, where great clusters of them lived unmolested under swags of snow-in-summer, beneath the boundary line of old acacias. One fine summer's day Dad urgently rushed me up the garden, "Look, look up there" he said, and there above the tall trees floated a silent and majestic monster, large black letters on its great silver belly. "That says R101" he said; I think the airship was destroyed soon after.

Among regular traders at the weekend was the muffin man, striding purposefully, a tray covered with a clean white cloth held balanced on his head with one hand while swinging a large hand-bell with the other. Then also came the shout, "Shrimps and Winkles!" Shrimps, a nice treat for Sunday tea, but so fiddley, picking the meat from out of the shell; fresh, distinctive sea-smell. We never bought winkles!

Between our fence and next door grew a line of mature cordon red currants; I doted on these, so glowing and translucent, and ate as many as I could when no-one was looking. We grew gooseberries and bought two good apple trees, a Bramley and a Rev. Wilkes. Vegetables grew well too, for Mother was an early compost fan, and if we saw any horse dung (there were still a number of horse-drawn vehicles around), within shovelling distance, she'd rush out with a pail and return as though with a trophy.

The grim skeleton of the R101 on the Beauvais hillside

I saw this from garden before crash.

Airship medals sold for £6,050

By Godfrey Barker

MEDALS awarded posthumously to the crew of the R101 airship which crashed in flames on a Beauvais hillside, fetched prices up to £6,050 at Glendinings in London yesterday.

The R101 set off for India on Oct 4, 1930. The excitement aroused by the maiden flight of Britain's answer to Germany's Zeppelin may have caused the captain, C H Irwin, to ignore a falling barometer.

His craft was in trouble within minutes of rising when her nose dipped sharply over the Chilterns and water had to be dumped. By the time she reached London, she was dangerously low in the sky.

Henry Leech

Her skin was sodden with rain as she passed over the French coast at 11.36pm. It was at 2am that a French poacher saw the R101 pitching and rolling over Beauvais before the blast plunged her into a hill. The crew medals sold yesterday came from the descendants of engineer Henry Leech of Cardington, Beds.

Capt Irwin's AFC group made £5,500. The Albert Medal awarded to Henry Leech for acts of gallantry fetched £6,050. Leech — who later reported "a surprisingly mild shock" as the airship hit the hill, "followed by a brilliant flash" — crawled back into the wreckage to help workmates.

Although badly burned himself, he hauled one to safety. It was Leech who called the Air Ministry in London at 4am with news of the disaster.

The AFM awarded to Chief Engineer William Gent fetched £4,400.

Postscript to the R101 disaster *(Daily Telegraph 14.6.1990)*

27

It is difficult to write of everyday things in childhood for only really nasty or surprisingly good things come to mind, so much has happened since, but I shall always remember the music on Sunday evenings, Nell joined us for that, otherwise she was not in with Mum and Dad when dad was in. We all wore our Sunday best, tea was over, we relaxed in a happy harmonious atmosphere. Mum and Dad had met at Morley (Adult Education) College in the choir and loved singing together, Mother was a competent accompanist and we would all sing away from the *News Chronicle Community Song Book,* and Mum would play tunes such as, "The Robin's Return" or "Happy Darkies", then they'd sing duets such as "The Gypsy Countess", Barcarole, and those from operetta, "The Maid of the Mountains" or "A Tale of Old Japan". Both had good voices, Mother's high soprano, she could easily reach top G, Dad's a very pleasant and tuneful baritone. I loved his songs - "In Cellar Cool" - he'd go so low he could hardly reach the note and we'd die of laughing. Then "The Bandelliero" and the "Demon King", so dramatic, "Excelsior", "Son of the Desert", "Trumpeter","The Diver" and we'd have lots of Gilbert and Sullivan.

I would sing too, possibly from *The Fellowship Hymn Book,* Dad somehow didn't mind *me* singing a hymn, (I was a child, religion was for such, he'd beam at me in encouragement) or something from *The Fellowship Song Book,* both Adult School publications. There was a rich collection of old sheet music with illustrated covers; on the rare occasions that Dad bought a modern song that had caught his fancy - 6d. from Woolworths - Mother rarely approved, her taste was good, but narrow. I enjoyed it all, always liked singing, but never advanced beyond *Ezra Read's Pianoforte Tutor* in my feeble attempts to learn that instrument.

Close Relations

The lives of Helen, Millicent and Maude Blundell never really diverged. The relationship of the eldest and youngest was harmonious and flourished; between Mill and the other two there was frequent friction and disagreement. I could never see any facial resemblance between them, they said that Nell's eyes were like her Mother's - she called them "gooseberry", Mill's several shades darker, hazel, whilst Mother's were almost black, sparkling and full of expression. Mill had left home the year I was born, and I felt no attachment to her; she lived in East Dulwich Road with Tom Harrison, whom I knew as Uncle Tom. It was typical of the time that I was led to assume that they were married, no one ever hinted otherwise, such was the climate of opinion, so rigid the standards of those days. How very surprising then, it is to me now, to know that she of all people could break that rule of conduct and go, at the age of forty-eight, to live with a married man. I write, "she of all people", because her attitude to me as a child was authoritarian, patronising and superior, full of rectitude. She disapproved of my speech, I spoke slang, she said, "Not CAN I, but MAY I" --- she waited while I corrected the phrase. "A cardinal rule for you to remember", she would pronounce, "Is NEVER ASK for anything". "Never let me hear you say Posh, Swanky, O.K., etc, etc, or SHUT UP". But language is a living thing, never static, though it was to her; it had not changed since her childhood - or would ever, she thought.

Tom was a sales representative for a sugar company and therefore ran a car. They went away for Easter and travelled to Scotland, Wales, The Lakes for an annual holiday, always there was a rare to do getting her clothes ready. Nell was always dragged in to help make a new tweed costume, light weight coat, dresses and so on, they had to be "just right". What a palaver. I felt their life style to be a cut above ours, that certainly was the impression given. Mill sported a fox fur slung round her shoulders, a fashion of the time: fascinated me; weird, tiny glistening eyes and little manufactured nose. There was a cord, but it also fastened by biting its own tail on your bosom. Mum and Nell were scathing.

She had a joke - suddenly, when I was engrossed in something - "You'll die after that". Grim faced. Horrid. "Well you haven't died *before* it have you?". Self-satisfied smile. My grudgingly written "Thank you" letters were handed back spelling corrected. I was only an average knitter, whereas she at 12 years had knitted "Maudie" a complete outfit when she was born. "You look so disagreeable", she said "You could look quite nice if you'd only *smile*" "You can't help your face as you are only six, but if you continue to scowl you'll be hideous by the time you're sixty", and such like endearing remarks. When I was about seven, I was told that I was to stay with her for the night as a treat.

Mum took me over on the 37 bus, and there I was, she seemed delighted to have me, and gave me a dripping cake - nice, made with mutton fat. Then I had to help pick out tiny bones from a (cold) mutton stew, "Not one fragment must remain", after that I was allowed to polish the knives on a grinder, that was fun. There was Billy Boy, a canary in a cage hanging in the window, we sang to him and he responded; the lady next door wept when Aunt showed me off, her only child, little Donnie, had just died from measles. Uncle Tom, when he came in, said nothing much, but showed me his small boxes of samples of pretty coloured sugar flowers and decoration - he worked for Burtons, a sugar company. I looked at the telephone, we had nothing like that, at the elegant Queen Anne dining room furniture (Maples), at the expensive settee and comfortable, new armchairs, (draped with old sheets to prevent fading), the beautiful pictures, fine canteen of cutlery, and I wanted to go home.

Me aged 6 (1933)

Poor Mill, she tried, I know now, in her own way, to make a fuss of me, but we didn't "click". Put into a high, large, shining brass bedstead, into stiff cold linen sheets, tucked in so tight I could hardly move, I wept, silently. After some time Mill came in with a candle to look at me, there I was, miserable, wet faced and cold. She was upset then and sat with me singing jolly songs, so after a while I cheered up and went to sleep. I visited the house quite often, much later once or twice on my own, but I never slept there again. It was not until more than a quarter of a century later that we were reconciled and became good friends. By then our circumstances were quite changed, we each accepted the other for what we were, but I never really understood this complex, many sided woman.

Being taken by Nell, more than once, well before the war, when I was seven or eight to a "Special Evening" at "The Ethical" (Society), (this was held on Sunday evenings at, I think, the Oliver Goldsmith School on the corner of Southampton Way, Camberwell), Mill and one or two others would rush to welcome me. I was the only person in the room under 40 and I didn't like it at all. The dreary old Board School Hall, the rickety chairs, the ancient (to me) solemn congregation of, I suppose 20, the lecture as boring as could be. Out came the "Ethical Hymn Book", a thin lady drabbly dressed, long cardigan, longer skirt, flat buttoned shoes, dark cloche hat with drooping feathers plonked out a melody on an untuned piano. "To Mercy, Pity, Peace and Love" they muttered uncertainly together. (William Blake: The Divine Image), or "England Arise, the long, long night is over!" (Shelley, I think). Another floats through my mind, as enigmatic then as now:-

"Lives of great men still remind us,
We can make our lives sublime
And departing leave behind us

Footprints in the sands of time".
(Longfellow: "Resignation")

A dim realization dawned on me that these Free Thinking Humanist Radicals were *fossils*. All passion spent: how perceptive children are, how cruel, because unknowing.

Considering that Aunt Nell was just on fifty when I was born, we got on remarkably well. She was totally unassuming, but self-assured, she seemed to work all the time, but was never soured by it, indeed she enjoyed being fully occupied. I watched her tidying her grey hair before the mirror one day. "Look at my saggy old face", she said, "You'd never think now that my skin was once fresh and young like yours". I stared at her in bewilderment, what was wrong with her face?, that was *HER*, that's how she is, I thought, how was she ever anything else?, I was intrigued, it stuck in my mind, and slowly, over the years, I came to realise that far from *Nothing was before ME*, Aunt Nell had lived a full and interesting half century before I arrived on the scene. (I've written about that already). She was short, like her mother, about five foot one, but had inherited her father's "Blundell" nose; "Alright on the Duke of Wellington", she would say, "but not on me".

I remember she would have a cat-nap after mid-day dinner, then wash and tidy herself and be as lively as a flea until evening. Then, whatever the weather, about nine o'clock, she would go for her *constitutional*, as she put it, not saying anything, just going; coming in after twenty minutes or so, she would say, "Ah, that was lovely, I needed a blow, I'll sleep well tonight". It worked for her, she had done it all her life; she'd say "Good if you're needleworking all day". It was a lifelong routine, there was no thought of mugging in those days.

She and Mother did the housework - or shopping - in the morning, and it was while they worked together that they would talk of their family and of the past. It sounded so wonderful, a golden age; obviously their parents were an evenly matched and happily married couple, and their high days and holidays were re-lived over and over again and odd family failings and funny incidents recalled with immediacy and delight. It was this love and affection for their parents which opened for me the doors of the past; I felt I knew Grandma and Grandpa Blundell and their many relations as well as anyone I'd really met.

When young, Nell had loved dancing, they all went to the Royal Horticultural Hall and had splendid times. We had a gramophone and she bought a record of *Sir Roger de Coverly,* "Come on", she'd say, "Let's dance", and taught me *Sir Roger,* and we'd dance and dance until we had no more breath. She taught me the polka too and the gay Viennese waltz - what fun we had!.

She liked to get up early, even in winter, and it was on such a morning, that, alone in the bedroom, instead of cleaning the hair out of my comb in the usual way, I thought I would burn it out in the flame of the candle. To my terror, it immediately burst into flame, ...ZZZZ zzz ZZZ - the comb was celluloid and became a veritable torch. I screamed, Aunt was there in a flash and grabbing the flaring object from my paralysed grasp, flung it to the floor and stamped right on it, immediately the flames were extinguished. A thick cloud of pungent smoke hung in the air, I sobbed, Nell showed me the charred remains of the comb, the burnt hole in the linoleum and the marks on her shoes; I'd learnt my lesson and thereafter treated fire with great respect. Dad fitted a diamond shaped patch neatly into the lino, which was still visible when they moved away in 1960.

I think I was about four when it happened, and for a number of years, about that time, Nell and I would get up early on several Sundays in summer and go out before anyone else was up. How I loved those occasions!. Nell always had a cup of tea in the scullery, we would close the door so as not to waken anyone, and have a slice of bread and dripping each, beef if possible, deliciously grainy, with juice. I remember pulling on my socks and sipping the tea, all eager excitement we were -- that was Nell -- each day was fresh, activities, however simple, an adventure. Looking at the clock, it was nearly seven; hurry now!. Out we'd go, walking up the hill, through the warm, green, dewy empty park. We went then in a loop, back towards home, but one day we walked over the top of Telegraph Hill, past St. Catherine's church and a little down Vesta Road. She held me up over a wall, "Look", she said, "They are building nice new flats for the people to live in instead of the slums". That was Honor Oak Park Estate.

Every day, Monday to Friday, Dad had lunch at Lyons at Camberwell Green – how *lucky* I thought. On arriving home at about 6 o'clock he sat down to the tea Mum had ready for him; if it was a small smoked haddock, his favourite, I'd stand patiently by his chair and he'd hand me a bit on a fork. Sometimes, funds running low, Mother bought tiny cheap Polish eggs – then flooding the market. I don't know why, but Dad took exception to them, if fried, of course, he didn't know, but if boiled, a problem arose, for each was clearly stamped "Polski". Nell came to the rescue with a dab of "Thawpit" (cleaning fluid), Mother was tickled pink, although she knew it was cheating. "Oh well" muttered Nell, "What the eye don't see, the heart don't grieve over". I liked that.

On rare occasions, Dad had to go in on a Sunday morning, I think it was twice he took me along with him. It's a long time ago, but I remember standing beside a canal (a branch of the Grand Union?) watching salt being unloaded from a barge and being told it had come all the way from Middlewich, Cheshire. Dad worked Saturdays until one o'clock, getting in about one thirty and we had our dinner then. Sometimes it was tripe and onions which I would not eat, so I had the sauce with potato and onions. When I was old enough, I'd go down Waller Road to meet him off the tram, and once a fortnight we would go to Kennington in the afternoon to see his parents and Grace and Lily. It is sad in a way, but I never got to know Dad's people or to feel comfortable with them; I always felt a barrier there, an atmosphere. Certainly the Barkers and the Blundells did not mix, whether there had ever been a quarrel, I shall never know; they were cast in different moulds.

This anecdote may have a bearing on the situation; my father's sister Emily had married one, Joseph Hoare, who for the last ten years of his life was kept alive by continual medication - injections, tablets and long periods in hospital. He was forced to work part-time and finally to retire before he could claim a pension. Mother would say things like, "No more than he deserves", or, "That is just retribution", not normally a vindictive creature, her attitude shocked me and I asked her what she meant. Her answers were obscure, but by degrees I got from her that to avoid active service in the Great War, he had regularly drunk a lot of soapy water. "Yes", she said, "It was an old trick, you drank it just before your medical, it made your heart beat faster and you were given three months to recover and then another medical and so on. He did this all the time, too cowardly to fight and too cowardly to be a conscientious objector - was frightened of being put in prison. Well, you can't sink much lower than that, can you? What a worm, I told him so". I bet she did. When he died in 1957, both my parents were of the opinion that his faking of heart trouble had in fact caused it. I feel that in all probability that caused the rift, Joe would have been vulnerable to criticism of his prolonged action, and hated Mother for speaking out truly.

Sundays: Quaker, Methodist and Secular

Friends Meeting House, Peckham circa 1933

I have always been aware of God, and known that I was, in some inexplicable way, part of His creation. I was not a religious child however, I never read the Bible to myself, but enjoyed going to Peckham Meeting on alternate Sunday mornings with Mother. I must say a word about the building, which is in Highshore Road, off Rye Lane, Peckham. First constructed in 1823, in what was then a rural area, by 1843, due to the immense popularity of one of the Women Ministers, enlargement became essential. The Meeting Room itself, rectangular in shape, lit by a series of small-paned windows placed high up in the walls, could easily hold 150 people. Running across the far end of this stark, wood-panelled room, facing the entrance doors, rose a high darkly polished bent-wood sounding board, below which, on a raised platform was set the hard, upright Ministers' bench. The Elder's benches stood in front of this, the Clerk's seat in the middle, whilst the long unadorned benches for those attending were placed to form the other three sides of the square.

There were of course the usual offices, and behind lay the green and peaceful Burial Ground, set about with simple flat tombstones, shrubs, trees and a bird-bath given by Friends Bryant & May. The Victorian pegs, on which the women once hung their bonnets, stuck out in a neat row, and the bench on which Peter the Great of Russia had sat when attending Meeting at Deptford stood in the lobby, bearing a brass plate which stated this fact. The Czar was at that time, 1698, staying with John Evelyn at Sayes Court in order to study ship building at Deptford. The office of Minister was discontinued sometime in the twenties, and so, in my days, those especially designed seats remained empty. The building, now listed, was sold to the Ministry of Works in 1960. We children sat in Meeting for the first quarter of an hour's silence, which I found boring and I was glad to go out to a class with about eight other children, where we heard stories of, for instance, Quaker saints, David Livingstone or Albert Schweitzer, and drew pictures.

Peckham Meeting had a regular congregation of about forty and infrequent dramatic events enlivened the proceedings; two of the male members would occasionally burst into song, one a full dramatic tenor, the other a tuneless bass (Peter Cauldwell) - no preamble, just this sudden, loud shock of song into the palpable silence. A different sort of dramatic event occurred when the current caretaker, a woman, opened the door to the gasman stark naked. He took to his heels, rushed back to report it and George Edwards was visited by the police. A proper huha ensued, George concluding that caretakers were more trouble than they were worth; that is why we never had one at Bromley. Peckham Meeting was composed of many active Friends, there was Doctor Alfred Salter, M.P. for Bermondsey, who with his wife Ada, had instigated the planting of trees in the streets of that borough, and Sidney Pierpoint, who on being told he was terminally ill, vowed that if by a miracle his life be spared, he would on his approaching retirement, devote the remainder of his life to the Lord's work. During the thirties this took the form of running an evangelical Sunday School in the Meeting House every Sunday afternoon without fail, and dozens of local children took advantage of this service. Ada was his loyal helpmeet, they organised the teachers, the classes, a summer outing and a Christmas party.

A women's branch of the Adult School Union was held there every Thursday afternoon, well attended, not all Quakers. In those years, many Meetings held Adult School classes, a movement that had been started by certain Friends at the turn of the century. Meetings began and ended with a hymn and Mum played the piano and was occasionally secretary. I was taken along, infrequently. These classes ended on the outbreak of war and were never restarted. As if this were not enough, a Monday afternoon Women's Meeting was also held, with numbers running to well over a hundred. I got involved with helping Mother at their Christmas Dinner, it seemed an enormous affair, the women began queuing up outside ages before they were let in. In their dark po hats, which they kept on throughout the proceedings, and their ill-fitting clothes, they stood talking eagerly, full of anticipation. They would experience nothing new today, they knew it all, but therein lay its charm; their hard lives had toughened, not embittered them - the recruits of communism lay elsewhere. Long trestle tables were erected the whole length of the hall, which was decorated with greenery; great urns filled with boiling tea, fitted with little taps which I was never allowed to operate. The meal itself always consisted of cold boiled ham or beef, boiled potatoes and hot beetroot, both the latter being boiled in huge coppers filling the place with steam. The meats were given annually by the Edwards family.

A word about them; they had made a comfortable income from building up a mutton pie business, started by their grand-parents in Bermondsey during the 1860's, by this time they had six flourishing shops in South East London. They bought the meat in Smithfield, their Mother boiled it, skimming off the fat with which the pastry was made, the pies were filled with the meat and were then cooked and sold in their Dining Rooms. Before I was born they had lived as a family in a large house in Jerningham Road; a number of them, although now living separately, continued to be involved in the business. At this time, George (born 1892) and his wife Irene (nee Lloyd – the bankers), lived in Colyton Road, Dulwich. The first thing that met your eyes on entering their house was a large beautifully illuminated text:- "Christ is the Unseen Guest in this house". A child, I was at first startled to read it. Awesome, not to me comforting, but powerful, meaningful, unforgettable. Reminiscent of *Advices and Queries 2:-* "Bring the whole of your life under the ordering of the Spirit of Christ"

This is the setting, then, for my earliest memory of George Edwards, concentrating in the steam, dexterously cutting slice after slice and slipping them on to the plates as they were held out to him, great fresh joints continually being brought in. Then as the hundred and more plates passed along, potatoes and beetroot were ladled on, a dollop of pickle added - great care being taken to ensure an equal helping was on each plate to avoid a riot. These were then carried into the hall by more willing helpers to the avid participants within. Oh, the bustle and confusion, the finding of a missing fork, the righting of miscalculations, the loud excited hum of conversation. As the piles of dirty plates and cutlery were brought out, the endless washing up began in the scullery, while in the hall cups of strong tea were passed round with bowls overflowing with sugar and plates piled high with home-made cakes, all agreed, - it was a blow-out!. These proceedings were followed by a sing-song and a shadowgraph put on by members of the Meeting, but the climax came at the end, with Sidney Pierpoint singing, as he always did, in his high, resonant tenor, in contrapuntal style, *Count Your Blessings,* his face shining with fervent and unadulterated joy. Ada thumped away on the old piano, *And They All Joined In,* with gusto - it brought the house down.

Friends in those days prayed with urgency and passion, and, falling on their knees would beg the Almighty for forgiveness, support and charity, or offer praise for His love, His goodness and His bounty. None doubted then that the way to Him was through Christ the Son, and none doubted that His way was narrow, but knew, too, that His yoke was easy and His burden light.

Sometimes we would walk home after Meeting, through Brayards Road past Gordon Road Workhouse, it seemed a long way to me. I remember the Sunday roast dinner smells emanating from the houses we passed, and when at last we reached home, there was a smell equally delicious to greet us, Nell had the dinner all ready, and we did it justice. Even medium sized joints of silverside or aitchbone of beef in those days were sold on the bone, and perhaps next day when it was all finished, I was allowed to have the marrow, which I scooped out with a large hairpin, sitting up on the scullery table. We had

42

thick gravy, but when she had carved the joint, whatever its nature, Nell would ask, "Who's for the blood gravy? ME". There was no competition as with a big smile she poured the liquor from the carving plate over her dinner. Obviously it was not very well done; *horrid*, I thought.

Mother was a naturally religious person, taking after neither of her parents. Her father was a liberal agnostic, her mother never went to church or read the Bible, yet she was not an atheist. Her God was stern, and she was a God fearing woman, finding little comfort in her belief and rarely speaking of it. A sentence from *Quaker Quarterly* fits in here, "In the mid-nineteenth century a theory of God as wrathful and of man as hopelessly sinful was being taught which revolted many sensitive and thoughtful people. Some turned away altogether from what was offered to them as religion". Both of my Blundell grandparents, Aunt Nell, her grandma Cole, my father and his own father come into this category. When my parents met they were both open about their beliefs and were active members of the Labour Party, but whereas Mother's faith grew and flourished, my Father's never did.

Years later she said that it was she who had changed, my father had remained the same. Whether any spark of spiritual recognition was blotted out by his painful childhood experiences, followed by those of the Great War, I cannot know. Certainly my earliest childhood memories of him are as a communist, disclaiming any God and denying the reality of Jesus. He ranted slogans, "It's the System", he would say, the workers will rise up and distribute the wealth of the *toffs* and the *Upper Crust* among themselves - everyone would be equal he told me. Mother had come to realise that the world's problems could never be solved by politicians, only by a change of heart within man himself, by prayer and trying to follow the will of Christ; she was an ardent pacifist. "The world will only be put right by revolution", was his motto; "The people will rise up against the bosses". I was fascinated as though by a snake. "But people might be killed", I said, "Yes, if necessary", "Where, in this street?", I asked. "Anywhere, everywhere, we can't fail to win, We'll put the world right, it will be a bloody revolution". These words sank into my soul; I can see us now, standing there, by the scullery sink, looking up at him, yet seeing people in my mind's eye running screaming, blood streaming. I believe he had no idea of my true reaction: I was appalled and amazed that he, my kind father, should hold such violent and destructive beliefs.

Every other Sunday morning, then, dressed for Sunday, including hat and gloves, as for Meeting, my father took me out. Our favourite place was Greenwich. We took the 53 bus up Blackheath Hill to the "Green Man" and there, in this ancient, historic pub, occasionally, Dad would indulge in half a pint of bitter and bring me out lemonade and a hard round arrowroot biscuit. We'd stand in the sun and refresh ourselves; but this was the exception to the rule. No trace of "The Green Man" remains today. Best of all I enjoyed going on the pier and walking beside the Thames, it was busy then, with ships of all nations and Dad had a little book of flags and funnels and would work out which country they came from and we always bought a penny bag of peanuts from an old man stationed there.

On other occasions we would visit Greenwich Park, see the deer, and if it was one o'clock watch the ball come down on the observatory dome. We walked on Blackheath and looked at the model boating pond or went to Brockwell Park and saw hundreds of cyclists, and, sometimes we walked to Peckham Park taking in a narrow, ancient footpath known as "Solomon's Passage". That pretty park with its whalebone arches, its greedy ducks, its rose gardens, arboretum and dog pond. I have never seen such a pond anywhere else, but here dogs were brought to swim, and there they'd be, dozens of them in every shape, colour and size, yapping and snarling as they leapt in and out of the water - some were excellent swimmers. I loved it, jumping about on the muddy verge to dodge them as they came out of the water, violently shaking themselves from nose to tail, tiny droplets of water flying out in all directions. Other times we took a bus to London, and once, in the Adelphi, a poor man appeared from the shadows and asked whether Dad had a cup of tea on him?. He gave him a copper or two and dragged me away, as I was remarking that, "He must be very stupid to think that you carried cups of tea about". It was explained to me that it was unlawful to beg for money, but that some people had not enough to buy food; that sobered me up. The Adelphi with its dark cavernous arches was pulled down soon after that.

The Adelphi; demolished in 1936

Another day crossing Westminster Bridge we'd gaze at the Houses of Parliament, watch the shipping, look up at Boadicea charging with those wildly bladed wheels, see the great Brewery lion and the Shot Tower, where the Hayward Gallery now stands. These are among the landmarks all Londoners knew and loved. If we went to London on a 53 bus by way of the Old Kent Road, we'd pass the great church of St. George the Martyr, "Look, Look", he'd say, pointing urgently, "That's little Dorrit's church". Not understood.

St George the Martyr church, c 1925.

On many occasions we visited Hyde Park and the Serpentine, the Thames bridges, the Embankment and other sights familiar to him and a favourite jaunt was to take that 53 bus from New Cross Gate to Waterloo, from there it was but a short way to the River. The area was quiet on a Sunday, the Thames-side wharves, so busy in the week, were in the main closed up and still. Reaching all along the south bank there was then no access to the waterfront, save for a spot close to Hungerford Bridge. We stood by some worn stone steps, leading down to a patch of sand scattered with flotsam, lapped by the flowing waters. "We used to play down there", Dad said, "me and some other boys, it was *good*; Mother never found out, it was forbidden. No, no, not far. Oh, no, not when *little*, like you".

Then up high stone steps on to Hungerford Bridge, and walking there, last week (July, 1999) looking down river I saw St. Paul's Cathedral, dominated now by numbers of sky-scrapers, then, in the 30's, it rose in majesty above all London. Turning, I looked across to the Embankment Gardens and saw, as I saw then, Cleopatra's Needle, could feel my hand tightly clutching his glove, the rigid, rough leatherseams, was aware of his dark grey winter coat - it was a winter Sunday. Knowing we would go to see the "Needle", harken while he read the inscription to me (too young to read it myself), and explain the circumstance of this strange stone pillar being floated all the way across the sea from Egypt. Listening to the warmth and wonder in his voice, trying to feel just a little of the enthusiasm he felt. No. I did not, then preferring to run in the gardens and to feel the fresh wind off the busy river; but I remember it. Yes, I remember it well.

It is easy to see that living in close proximity, tensions were prone to develop between my Mother, Father and

Aunt. Aunt's outlook on life was similar to Mother's, but she was neither as religious nor as idealistic, more practical and pragmatic. The varying principles of my parents' convictions led to many unresolved arguments, bitter and acrimonious. Aunt kept out of the way. I was used to it and kept quiet, listening, but often I wished they'd shut up, with one glorifying Karl Marx and Russia, the other George Fox and the *Kingdom of Heaven*, I knew that their quarreling was futile and that they never would agree.

Of my own volition, I attended Kitto Road Methodist Sunday School with several of my school friends in the road: it was interesting, cosy and friendly and it was here, when I was seven or eight that a special *Teetotal Service* was held, denouncing *The Horrors of Drink*. At the end of the service, each of us was urged to sign a fancy certificate, vowing that alcohol would never, ever pass our lips. Suddenly I refused, saying that I did not know what I might want to do when I was grown up. They were somewhat put out, but I was adamant; my parents were as surprised at my reaction as I was myself.

Every summer we were taken on a Sunday School Treat, for which we paid very little, to Allhallows-on-sea. We went by coach, taking a picnic, paddled and played organised games, it was good fun except when it rained, as it was very exposed there, and undeveloped, only a few caravans and a little general store. Normal Sunday afternoons, however, followed a happy blend of hymns, for example:-

"Jesus wants me for a sunbeam
To shine for Him each day,
In every way try to please Him
At home, at school, at play"
Chorus

"A sunbeam, a sunbeam
I'll be a sunbeam for Jesus
A sunbeam, a sunbeam
I'll be a sunbeam for Him".
"Though sun or moon I cannot be
To make the whole world bright
I'll find some little, cheerless spot
And shine with all my might"

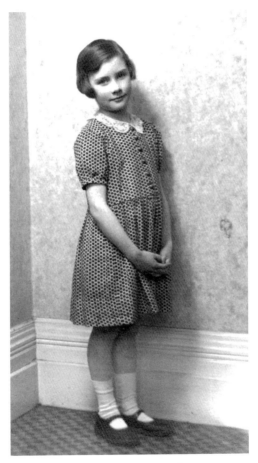

Me aged 8 (1935)

Then the lessons and Bible readings; it was their custom to distribute pretty texts to take home, and, after collecting them for several years, my Bible became so fat that it would not shut, so full was it of these colourful texts, all inserted in the right place; *Be of Good Cheer, Blessed are the Pure in Heart, I am the True Vine,* and so on, all with appropriate illustrations - I wish I had not thrown them all away. Filing round in a crocodile, we put our halfpennies into the collecting box:-

Hear the pennies dropping, listen how they fall,
Every one for Jesus, He will get them all.
Dropping, dropping, dropping, hear the pennies fall,
They are all for Jesus, He shall have them all.

Not inspired words, perhaps, but sincere, dedicated and generous people; *If you have a kindness shown, pass it on,* simple words which have remained with me all my life.

Lodgers

A Waller Road house

We always had lodgers, that was quite usual, indeed all
the houses in my road were lived in by more than one
family. Waller Road was part of the Haberdashers' Estate,
built about 1900 to house lower-middle class families
who were expected to keep a live-in servant and employ
a *daily*. After the Great War, with the servant supply
dried up, these families moved out to places like
Bromley, where smaller, more easily run homes were
being built. We were the first owners of 131, Waller Road
not to have servants, the white porcelain bell pushes were

still in place when I was little, the row of bells still fixed high on the scullery wall, although by then they had been disconnected. I can faintly remember three of the lodgers who were in the house when I was born. One was Mahdi, an Egyptian student at L.S.E., a devout Mohammedan who lent Mother the *Koran* which she read and discussed with him. He was said to have been of a cultured family and when his course ended he returned to Africa. At the same time two ladies lodged with us, one was Dorothea Sharpe, daughter of Cecil Sharpe the English Folk Song collector, who had died in 1924. The other, her friend Miss Kendle, who wore shirts and ties and had her hair cut like a man. They moved away about 1930 and bought a bungalow to share.

Then there was Mr. O'Sullivan, an emotional, warm-hearted Irishman, the London reporter on a Dublin newspaper. When I was born he asked if my eyes were open yet?. He thought humans were born blind, like kittens; he always called me *Baby*. An unquestioning Roman Catholic, he plucked up enough courage to borrow our copy of Kingsley's *Westward Ho!*, which he thoroughly enjoyed in spite of its being on the forbidden index. His pay was gradually reduced and he was always poor and shabby and when in 1932 his job came to an end, he had no option but to return penniless to Dublin. The night before he left they did his washing, mended his socks and Aunt sat turning in the frayed cuffs of his old tweed greatcoat. We got up early next morning and gave him a cooked breakfast, he went to get his battered old trunk, and when he bent to kiss me goodbye, placed a silver crucifix in my hand. "God Bless you Baby", he said. Aunt shoved two packets of sandwiches into his hand and he put one into each side pocket of his too large coat. The door closed behind him in the cold early morning light; Mother and Aunty had a good cry. "Oh dear, we're in the doldrums" muttered Nell dabbing her eyes. We never knew what became of him; the slump was very bad then and things generally pretty grim; but the house missed the warmth and humorous spontaneity of this sincere little man. I never wore the crucifix, my Father would have been very put out and Mother told me that Quakers did not believe in outward symbols (they had been thrown out with candles, music, stained glass windows and other evidences of artistic beauty). I kept it in a little box on a bed of cotton wool, and one day I picked out the three nails which held the body, and buried this tiny tortured figure in the rockery; it was better that way. The engraved design on the cross was thus revealed, and still, if you hold it up, the light shines through the minute holes pierced by those tiny, long lost nails.

Aunt Mill disliked Nell calling them *lodgers*. They are *Paying Guests*, she would say, *P.G's.* Nell could see no difference, to her, and to me they remained lodgers. Mr. Reid was with us the longest, he was there before I was born and did not leave until W.W.II, Thin and slightly hunch-backed, this quiet, reserved, rather sad Scot, with little hair, a sharp nose and thin turned down mouth, remained in the house until bombing forced us all to move out in 1941. His rent book stated that he had bed, seven breakfasts, five evening meals, lunch and tea on Saturdays, breakfast only on Sundays. For this he paid 25/- per week (£1.25), and this included not only cleaning his room, but making his bed and *emptying his chamber pot every morning* - into a white enamel slop pail, with a lid, which Nell carried round for that purpose. Frequently it was I who carried up his jug of hot shaving water at 7.30a.m., on the dot; knock on the door, "Your shaving water Mr. Reid". A weekly bath was also included, but he had his own gas meter for the fire and laundry was extra, billed separately. The upstairs toilet was used by the lodgers, we used the outdoor one by the back door. In those days any paper was used for the lavatory, the best was the butcher's paper; my job was to fold it and cut it into squares, pierce a hole in it with a stiletto, thread it with string and hang it on the appropriate hook; lodgers provided their own toilet rolls if they wished.

Mr. Reid's name was Ninian, which I found screamingly funny, no use Mother telling me it was the name of a Scottish saint, that was beside the point. He worked as a tally man for a firm of tailors and led a most monotonous life. Apart from spending every Sunday with a married sister at Croydon, come rain or shine, and going to work each day, he never went anywhere or met anyone, but returning home in the evening, stumped up to his room and stayed there with the evening paper. It was a very pleasant room, large, with bay windows, from which, on a clear day, you could see St. Paul's and Tower Bridge and the outline of the distant Hampstead Hills beyond - no tower blocks then. I suppose he was contented enough, he read a little; I remember Aunt lending him *Pendennis* and asking how he was getting on with it?. It was rather a tease, he read a page a day. Every summer he spent a week in Torquay; he also drank half a bottle of *White Horse whisky* a week, smoked a foul pipe and told me that his father beat all his children regularly with a tawse. With equal regularity, Mr. Reid gave me a small tube of Nestle's Milk Chocolate "rounds" every Saturday, and Mother allowed me to eat one every day - one of her greatest concerns was that I should not be spoiled; she went to considerable lengths to achieve this aim.

The little semi-attic room where I once had nightmares was turned into a kitchenette about 1934/5, fitted up with a white china sink, draining board and modern little gas stove. (I liked this, our gas stove downstairs was ancient, heavy and black, our shallow stone sink had no draining board). That and two adjoining rooms were let as a self-contained unfurnished flat, no service, although Mum took in their washing, and it was she who let the flat; Nell then had only two lodgers, but received weekly payments off the house from Dad. At one time this flat was let to a Mrs. Morgan, a solid ordinary woman from the north, but she took in her daughter, *Bim,* and son-in-law *Brooke Sheldon,* and their dog!. Such a charming, beautifully dressed couple, in their late thirties. His family were Macclesfield silk manufacturers, well-off, but he had a severe drink problem which his family tried to control by giving him a very small weekly allowance. They settled in with Mrs. Morgan for several weeks, but finally Mother had to give them notice and they returned to Macclesfield. I was sorry, they were so courteous and kind to me; on one occasion Bim noticed me having a tea party in the garden with some friends and, seeing us using old bits of china, brought down her newly purchased *breakfast set,* all we could wish for, *art deco,* two cups and saucers, jug and teapot all to match. Mother was worried we would break something, and sure enough, we did - a cup, which is why I remember the incident so well. We were heartbroken and contrite, but Bim calmed us down, saying, truly that it was a calculated risk, it was only a cup, and maybe she could replace it; I hope she did.

One Christmas they invited me into their smartly furnished sitting room and gave me a manicure set in a soft blue case complete with pretty file and nail buffer, they always offered me delicious titbits to eat. Another year they gave me a most elegant pair of fine, lined, kid gloves, edged with soft grey fur. I prized them greatly and was desolated when, a year or so later I couldn't get them on. As Mother said, "Too good for you, fancy buying gloves like that for a child, a complete waste of money". She and Nell were given thick, pure silk scarves, long with sharply pointed ends, art-deco in design, Mother's varying shades of blue and Nell's warm tones of autumn, brown and gold; unheard of luxury, they lasted many years.

When Mrs. Morgan left - to become concierge at a superior block of flats in Kensington, a Mr. and Mrs. Tom Leonard, from Bermondsey, took the flat. He was a stevadore at Surrey Docks, as were a number of men in our road, and she worked as a packer at *Peak Freans* in Bermondsey. At one time she thought of leaving because:- "The Bedders Boys are in, timing every move you make, even if it's a pee". (Beddows - a mechanised, conveyor belt type of production, eliminating hand-made processes, typical of the times). Sometimes she brought us a large bag of broken biscuits and Tom got us loose desiccated coconut, remarkably cheap, and then Mum would make a tray of pink and white coconut-ice, very special. Early in 1939, she had a severe haemorrhage and went to see Dr. Frost; when she got in she came down to Mother and collapsed in a chair. I had just come in from school and was told to get some strong tea, quick, and put plenty of sugar in it. She was crying, "It was dreadful, he kept saying, *You've done something to yourself, haven't you?*, and didn't want to give me anything, but call the police - *it's an abortion,* he said, but I told him, *It's just a miscarriage*". She was very distressed, Mum helped her upstairs and got her to bed. Naturally I was curious; *miscarriage and abortion* were explained to me, and the difference between them. Such things were never spoken of, nor mentioned in the papers then and if a woman became pregnant it was a criminal offence to stop it yourself, there were ways, but you could be put in prison for attempting it. I felt a flash of anger - how dare anyone make you have a baby if you did not want one?. I was told in no uncertain terms that it was highly dangerous to try to destroy an embryo, and the likelihood of dying frightfully from bleeding to death or blood poisoning gave me food for thought. It is interesting that I was not told that it was either a sin or murder.

I remember. a week or so later, Mrs. Leonard felt in need of cheering up and asked me to go with her to buy a frock. Rather flattered, I thought it would be fun, not realising that the shop was in the Old Kent Road, near Canal Bridge, about two miles away. It was lively then, with little shops all the way, but hot and dusty, and noisy with all the traffic. The dresses were very smart, Hollywood style, it seemed she tried on dozens, it was interminable and I got bored. I thought her extremely smart, though, and up-to-date, and wished that I could have ready-made frocks too, instead of the ones Aunt Nell made for me. They were beautifully made - always tried on at least twice, so tedious - but were always plenty big, with a deep hem to let down and tucks to let out, and I thought very tame and homespun in appearance; I would have liked something a bit more stylish and flashy. Mrs. Leonard plucked her eyebrows and dyed her hair; she wore high-heeled shoes and used make-up which Mother considered *wrong* and quite unnecessary. Once she came home with her hair a blazing mahogany: opening the door to her, "My God, girl", her husband shouted, "you'd have your bum hennaed if you could". I remember them well, they left us while I was in hospital early in 1940 and bought a house in Pickhurst Lane.

You will notice that we were all comparatively formal; *Mr. and Mrs.*, and I should mention that the lodgers always knocked on our door when they wanted us, ensuring a degree of privacy essential with so many living under one roof. I have written about them in some detail as they represent a fair cross-section of society and a way of life which is gone for ever.

Friends & Neighbours

We did not really know most of our neighbours well, just their names and faces, those we were closer to appear elsewhere. One old man whose face I knew well was a tramp in tattered rags. I used to watch him out of the front room window, as at certain times of the year he'd shuffle up to the large plane tree outside our house. Cough, hawk, spit and splutter – "There's old Gobbo-duck and his oysters". Then putting his hand to his nose he blew out strips of mucous on to the loose bark, then rubbing his fingers against the tree, he'd scuff his feet and move on. This for a number of years in the early 30's, same tramp, same tree. Everyone knew him. You may say he wasn't a *neighbour*! but I recognised him as well as some of those who were, and on now to a few of them. Several houses down lived a somewhat crippled man, as a boy stricken with infantile paralysis. He had never worked, but "had means" - walked like his feet were, "flat irons on a string". Remarks in those days were blunt, picturesque, not over kindly, yet if the necessity arose, anyone would have helped him out. Always well dressed in loud plusfours, he took his beautiful red setter out walking each day.

At number 123 lived the Eliases, whose life is fully described in "On Sundays we wore white", by Eileen Elias, who was about 17 when I was born. I remember that Mr. Elias, a keen astronomer, had set up a telescope in his garden, and when Dad was busy fixing a trellis fence all along the top of our wall bordering Arbuthnot Road, he bellowed at him in barking Welsh accents, "You have no right to put that screen up there, it will obscure my view of the stars". Dad fair bristled with anger and muttered crossly to himself, but refused to respond, took no notice whatever, for of course it did no such thing. For us the trellis proved to be a great improvement situated as we were, for on rare occasions kids threw odd items of rubbish over; but they had not reckoned with Mum. I remember vividly, as a small silent witness I stood by appalled, for several times filled with boiling rage she flung open the great door in the wall and appeared before them like an avenging angel. Taken totally by surprise, the group scattered, ran for their lives, but Mum chased after them, blood up, called them back loud and clear; "Come here, I am going to talk to you, yes *you boys*" (nearly always boys). Amazed, they stopped, sheepish, sullen, struck dumb, shuffling while she confronted them with scorching but controlled, intimidating disgust. Satisfied, a winged fury, eyes still blazing with a certain pleasure, she would come back, lock the great door and report victory. She'd told them they were really good, sensible boys, not the oafish louts they appeared to be --- etc., etc. It would not work nowadays, then it did, for to our certain knowledge the same boys never did it again. Dad never rose to the bait, he was usually at work when this happened, but when it occurred one Saturday he was so thoroughly put out by the whole incident that he decided to put up a trellis the whole length of the wall.

Later an aunt and her niece came to live at 123, the Sowerbutts, quiet and pleasant; funny name, I thought. They were teachers who took in students from Goldsmiths College. In September, 1949, two months after I had left 131, Joan Livermore, later our friend, had digs at 123. By the way, the Edwards family, Quakers referred to earlier, lived in the 20's at 47, Jerningham Road and Margaret Jones at 63 in the 50's.

The only neighbours who made any impression on my early childhood were those who lived next door. Downstairs lived a middle-aged couple named

Shuttleworth, ordinary enough, while upstairs lived her parents, brimming with hatred for each other and the world at large. The fountainhead of the hate was the lady, her husband told Dad that snake's venom ran in her veins instead of blood. I remember upsetting sounds of screaming, uncontrolled temper, coming through the walls, and of furniture being thrown about; on one occasion we were told that a settee had been thrown at Mr. Shuttleworth and I wondered with silent amazement how one set about such a feat, tried to visualise it. It all ended in tragedy; came a knock at the door, a hasty running to and fro, subdued, terrified whispers; I was put in the front room and told to stay there. I felt lucky to have been put in there, for I stood with my face glued to the window, watching the police come and go, windows being flung open, an ambulance arrive and a body covered with a white sheet carried out on a stretcher from the upstairs door, right down the ten front steps and into the waiting vehicle. I could not help but learn that Mr. Cook had committed suicide by lying down in front of his unlit gas fire with the tap fully turned on. I was about three at the time, in a year or two old Mrs. Cook herself was dead, the Shuttleworths retired and moved to St. John's Road, Tunbridge Wells. Aunt Nell visited them several times, twice she took me with her, on the *Green Line Coach*, but as I was sick each time on the journey, I was never taken again.

It was expected that I should either mix with adult friends of the family, (mainly on a seen but not heard basis), go into the garden or sit quietly and read or draw. Most of these people were agreeable, but one frightened me and no-one could understand why, so I remember her very well; she is the only person that I have ever spoken to who was born in the early 1840's, dying when I was about seven and she 92. Most of Mother's friends I called

"Auntie", as was the custom then, but Miss Walker was always given that title. She was four foot ten, tiny, dressed completely in rustling black with a small black straw bonnet and boots; her skirts reached to her ankles and she wore a black patch over one eye; she always carried a large walking stick. She lived in rooms in Southampton Street, Peckham, cosily, if darkly furnished; I was taken there once or twice. However, it was her coming to tea with us that I dreaded, knowing that she would want to walk up to the park and that she would require me to accompany her. Mother was adamant; - I loved the park and it was such a small thing to do for a nearly blind old lady; but behind that blacked out lens I could discern the sewn-down eyelid, deeply sunken, red, and frequently watering, while the other eye studied me watchfully through the thick, oval wire-framed glass. So there was no way out; up the hill we went, I walking at a funereal pace to keep up with her, hoping that no-one saw us together, yet attempting to appear normal. Fifty and more years on, now, I would be interested to hear her life story; for many years she had been governess to a wealthy family in St. Petersburg, but had been forced to return home to look after her widowed father; she could still speak French. But then, it was the sightless eye which fascinated me, and I would try to look at it without her noticing my doing so; it never occurred to me to find out how she came by her disability.

I was not rubbing an old lamp, but dusting some old china recently when a genie of the past arose, clinging, shadowy. Jessie Lovelace was the elder sister of Olive, who had been employed by my Aunts before the First World War as a sewing hand. The family had lived on the hill in Gibbon Road, for as long as anyone could remember, a treeless somewhat run-down road, which led up the hill from Evelina Road to the station. At the bottom of the road on the corner, past the dreaded stink-pipe, stood a large, old-fashioned chemist's shop, and running along the top of its plate glass windows was a shelf, on which stood five great translucent "flagons" of jewel coloured liquid, emerald, sapphire, ruby, gold and deepest indigo, wonderful, fascinating; the ancient sign of a chemist, never seen today.

Jessie's mother was long since dead, but she still kept house for her father, old by then, but still the faded barber's pole stuck out at an angle from their seedy abode, and still he plied his trade. Next to their narrow front door, the grubby shop window, with its indecipherable lettering, was hung about with dingy lace curtains, aspidistra on the sill. Dad never had his hair cut there, "Wouldn't go near the place". I was with Nell once when she knocked and spoke to Jessie on the step, tried to peer in, only a stale air of neglect. Poor Jessie, she came round to us for a cup of tea, often. Knock, knock. "Oh Lord, it's Jessie again". Always "on spec". She'd sit down at the table, bits of grey hair straggling from her shapeless old hat, never taken off, neither was the rusty, worn coat. They didn't mind *her*, just the length of time it took for her to go, sidling slowly out backwards, jawing all the time, "Too much of what the cat licks his arse with, as Dad would say" - Nell. I could see her loose, hopeless mouth, her pale, bulbous eyes, stricken, habitually filled with anxiety. Once she brought Olive with her, "Out from Epsom", attempting to live at home after 20 years in the institution. I was very young, my mind unencumbered by lurid tales of "the Mad-house", which I would hear at school later. I stared at her, I remember, curious, for I had heard hushed, guarded talk of her, but there she sat, staring at the tea table, the pretty best rosy china got out for the occasion, silent, like me, crumbling a little cake to fragments while the others indulged in deliberate, cheery conversation. Small, her dark shingled hair closely covered with a battered felt hat, her coat - which had seen better days - clutched about her; black inscrutable eyes - staring, gazing at nothing. A few days later, unable to cope with the outside world, she returned voluntarily, to Epsom, there to remain for at least another 20 years and more.

Me aged 10 (1937)

I was a little older when Jessie arrived carrying a broken cardboard box full of china. Would Nell give her five shillings for it? A crude pock-marked old teaset, lots of cups, more saucers, no plates but teapot, jug and sugar

64

basin. Nell certainly did not want it, we'd enough old china already, and in the depression, say 1934, 5/- was not readily spared. Jessie was desperate, now they'd nothing to eat, she said. The china was her family's, local made in Dorset, her family were connected with one of the Tolpuddle Martyrs. Nell, put out, relented, grumbling, stowed it away in a cupboard. There it is, *there,* in my china cabinet. I always liked it, simply because it was *old,* no-one else ever did. How old is it?. Where made? If only it could speak. So many questions remain. What happened to the Lovelaces, they were bombed out in 1940; but thereafter? We shall never know.

Clothes

You can see from photos, on previous pages, how we dressed, Mum knitted my 1929 outfit in deep pink. In the photo taken at Carisbrook Castle in 1933 the dress is of mauve and white check gingham, and in the bottom photo, taken aged 8 the dress is of crepon, cream with dark red spots and matching wooden buttons; both Nell made from bits. Leggings were popular for little girls, later I had a pair in soft leather, elastic under the instep, tiny buttons up the side. I hated them, it took so long to have them buttoned up, you had to keep perfectly still and like most children of that age I was a fidget.

All women wore aprons, removed only after clearing up the evening meal, or socialising. From my earliest youth I was obliged to wear one too, on approaching the meal table it was – "Girlie, where's your pinny ?"

We dressed far more formally than today, for us there were no "Leisure Clothes", for leisure, such as it was, old garments were worn. However, everyone had "Sunday Best", to be worn irrespective of the occasion, be it church or chapel, a walk in the park or visiting relatives. It was normal for things to be mended, altered, darned, girls frocks to be "let out" or "let down", boy's trousers to be patched, for clothes to be passed on in the family and between neighbours. People generally were meticulously careful, "Wanton Waste brings Woeful Want", we were told; things were worn until they wore out. When I was disappointed I'd be told sharply, "not to pull that long jib". Sheets were turned sides-to-middle for women generally were clever with their needles!. I never knew one who could not knit, often they could crochet too. Many sewed excellently, with pleasure, usually while chatting or listening to the wireless. Companionable, relaxing, creative, costing very little, and useful.

Everyone wore hats, men like Dad a trilby, others a bowler, the upper classes sported toppers, the lower classes caps. Women's hats were cloche, I called them "Po hats", felt, shaped like a basin with very little brim, if any. Gloves were always worn, cotton in summer, knitted, often on 4 thin needles (Mill) in winter - or of finely shaped kid leather if you could afford them. Seventy or so years ago we were much more wary of the weather, however warm, if there was the least chance of rain we would take a "Mac", in wet weather everyone wore one, old and young alike. Made of strong rubberised cotton fabric, called MacIntoshes after the inventor, always dark in colour, of classic cut, they lasted for years. They certainly kept the rain out, but got rather uncomfortable as the skin couldn't breath and you got sweaty. In those days umbrellas were commonly called "Gamps", after Dickens's Sairy Gamp; they were always dark in colour, made of cotton, so took time to dry out. Drying wet clothes was always a job, as heating in the home was so limited, which is possibly why in very wet or snowy weather some people, Aunt Nell was one, wore galoshes, that is thick rubber overshoes. They kept your feet dry, but were clumsy and ungainly and an awful nuisance to pull on and off, fitting so tightly, as they had to, over your ordinary shoes.

Now for an odd item of clothing; searching through a drawer the other day I came across a relic of Mill's and startlingly the past touched the present. This "relic" is a pretty sateen bag in which Mill had for decades kept the moleskin muff which she was given by an aunt, as a girl. She loved it, and I can just imagine her gaily tripping along wearing it 100 years ago. Being a hoarder she had kept it, then, having shortened the cord by which it hung from the neck, gave it to me, I suppose I was about 6, fully expecting me to *wear* it. A shining, velvety, black thing, warm and cosy and although the padding grinned through the red silk lining here and there, it did not notice at all. I had never seen it before; she herself would never have been "found dead" wearing anything so dated. I certainly never would, although it intrigued me, it was romantic, pretty, good for dressing up games. But that she would not countenance.

Up to the time when I was 11 and went to Honor Oak School, Aunt Nell made all my clothes; frocks, blouses and skirts, most of the skirts with a cotton bodice to button on to, also coats and nighties. She was a dab hand at cutting out, three or four times when I was very little, (4-6 years old) making a frock for me from Mum's dress length. I remember two of these very clearly: one was of crepe de chine, mainly deep blues, reds and amethyst, all over paisley type design, quite plain with "cap" sleeves and tiny white lace collar. The other was bracken-coloured voile, blotched orange and yellow flowers, Magyar style with sleeve and yoke cut in one, popular then, with a two inch frill at the bottom. The fabric was very fine, so the yoke was lined cotton and there was a bit of ecru lace at the neck. Mum and I both liked this, it was not unique, as it would be today, quite fun. Another thing, if the material was suitable - cotton - Nell made me knickers to match my dresses - very smart I thought - better than the usual interlock navy, though I always wore these for school. But I wanted to be like the other girls, not always to have my clothes made for me; just to go out to a shop, choose something and buy it ready-made, off the peg. I never appreciated the care and skill which went into the making of my clothes, nor the fine fabrics of which they were made. I hated the trying on -

Nell even noticed that my right hip was bigger than the left, that's how precise the cutting out was. Mum knitted all cardigans, vests, gloves, etc. But I always loved *shoes*, all kinds, sandals, lace-ups, anklestraps - *because* these were the one item of clothing apart from knickers and socks which *couldn't* be home made - we had to go out and *buy* them.

During the mid-1930s there was a severe slump in the Manchester cotton mills and it was suggested that if every woman in England bought a dress length (about 3 yards), it would be over. Mother couldn't really afford it, but after much humming and ha-ing she did.

Medical

Smells have affected me strongly all my life; now and
again Nell would buy herself a quarter of gorgonzola
cheese and I would kick and cry to get down from the
table because I couldn't stand the smell of it. However, I
was addicted to tarry smells and would stand in the
street watching the majestic steam rollers belch clouds of
steam and gladly take in great breaths of tar fumes,
which it was believed were of benefit to the lungs. I so
doted on the smell of paraffin, (always kept in the house
for the little stove), that one day when I was three I drank
some from a bottle, which caused a frightful commotion.
I had no idea what was wrong, and was forced to drink
warm salt water, at which I was violently sick and every
thing returned to normal; disliking the cure so much, I
never drank it again. Scotts Emulsion was another thing
which made me sick; this popular tonic was bought for
me once when I was run down. The label on the bottle
depicted a sailor in a sou'wester with an enormous fish
draped over his shoulder, its tail down at his feet. As
Mother poured the thick white slime into a dessert spoon,
the most horrible smell of rotten fish filled the room.
"Open your mouth", she'd say, and shove the spoon in at
which I started to heave. She tried pinching my nose, that
ruse was worse than useless, the filthy stuff spilled all
over the place and we had to change our clothes, it was
awful. But she was not easily beaten; "Look", she said,
"I'll take some myself". "Go on then", I thought, and I
really did then try to get some down, but my stomach
revolted and up it came again and Mother admitted
defeat. Later, Mum considering that, "I looked white
round the gills", that is run-down, decided on Virol, a
brand of malt extract, which was quite pleasant, but
cludged up one's mouth and was difficult to swallow.

The roads were kept tarred and gravelled at that time and falling down and getting a gravel rash was a common and painful business. Usually on knees or elbows, the wounds were thoroughly cleansed and dabbed with iodine, which seemed to sear to the bone. I had no serious illnesses when I was little, just the usual childish complaints, but these were taken seriously, the days of heavy infant mortality had only just receded. Having measles meant that a fire was lit in the bedroom and I luxuriated in the warmth and attention I received. A bowl of hot water to wash my face and hands, fresh sheets after the fever had broken; lying there being read to while drowsily watching the flickering shadows from the fire dance endlessly on the ceiling, lighting up the ornate plaster rose around the light fixture, and illuminating the elaborate cornices and moulded coving. I gazed too at the pictures hung about the room, "The Boyhood of Raleigh" (Millais), "Mrs. Siddons", Raphael's Madonna, all familiar and dear, whilst facing my bed hung a print of a manuscript in rich colour and Victorian Gothic lettering with the following lines:-

"Adrift on Time's returnless Tide,
Like Wave that follows Wave, we glide,
God grant I leave upon the Shore
Some wrack of Good it lacked before.
Some sign of Grace, some Hope to make
This sad World happier for its sake
(possibly Whittier).

The room I shared with Aunt was divided from the front room by tall folding doors, and on the sitting room side stood the piano, which Mother would play to me, and more than once Dad brought me grapes, a rare treat.

If I caught a cold, my chest was first rubbed with a concoction of tallow and wonderfully aromatic camphorated oil, and then covered with an itchy piece of flannel. Nell would bring me a steaming cup – "Here's a nice joram, ease your chest in no time". By the mid thirties both my parents were nature cure addicts and became hooked on the idea of drawing warm salt water up through the nostrils daily. The idea being to rid the membranes of bacteria, prevent colds, and if you got one, cure it rapidly. Mum and Dad both practised this, it became a morning ritual, like cleaning the teeth, but I never managed it, though pressed very hard to try. "Like this", Mum would dip her nose resolutely into a large steaming mug, breath in purposefully, and seconds later disgorge it all out of her mouth into the sink. It was worse if we actually had colds; "This gets rid of all the phlegm - go on do try, it'll clear your nose in a twinkling". But no, I preferred sniffing and being bunged up any day to that revolting practice.

Talking of revolting practices, enemas were then in fashion, in those days people seemed addicted to constipation. Once I found out what happened if I told them, in answer to their query, that I had not "been", I made very sure always to say that I had. Lying nearly bare on a bed, with your behind on a towel, with tepid soapy water pouring into a funnel, down through a pipe with a nozzle stuck well into your bum is no joke; once was enough, after that, yes I'd always "been". Jane Blundell had learnt from her nursemaid Ma, that the way to get young children to open their bowels was to cut off a long thin slice of soap and insert it gently and gradually two or three times into the afflicted's anus. Don't know if it worked, horrible.

Sometimes "wind" was a problem, "Oh well" Mum would say, "Rub your stomach round, firmly, like this" –

display, "if that's no good do some bicycles" i.e. lie on the floor, raise both legs in the air and pedal. It worked!

People suffered from boils and whitlows, kaolin poultices were in common use to bring out the poison, help bring them to a "head". Kaolin was heated up as hot as could be borne, then whacked on the painful spot and tied tightly on; I understand it was incredibly painful but stoically endured – this was the cure- hopefully the pus would run.

The "Medicine Chest" was kept on a shelf in the kitchen, (in the back – off the dining room), made by Mum's father years before. Still used now in the garage to store bits and pieces. Always well supplied, it generally held a bottle of Syrup of figs, (constipation), Parishes Food (anaemia) as also Iron Jelloids capsules, Friar's Balsam- for congested head cold and sinuses. Drops of this dark brown fluid were sprinkled into a basin of very hot water, one then sat up to the table with a towel draped over one's head and inhaled the fragrant steam as deeply as possible. It helped, but after five minutes or so, one emerged with a face like a boiled beetroot. One time Nell became addicted to a disgusting cough linctus called "Tutti Frutti", just the smell made you heave.

Many well-known, popular items spring to mind, "Golden Eye Ointment", a most efficacious unguent for styes or any inflammation in that region. "White Horse Oils", embellished with a picture of a noble shire horse on the label, used for all and every rheumatic pain – with a wonderfully comforting smell into the bargain. There would be "Snowfire" cream for chilblains, a tube of "Glymiel Jelly" for chapped hands – so common in those days; Epsom salts, "Fynnon Salts". What else? , of course a pack of lint, a roll of cotton wool and various bandages.

I was not acquainted with death as were children of a previous generation; the first one to make an impression on me was that of the young woman next door-but-one, she died of T.B., still quite a scourge in the early 1930's. Aunt Nell was putting on her coat and best hat; "Where are you going?" I wanted to know. Very quietly Nell replied, "To see Mrs. Eliot". "Oh, but I thought she was dead!" I exclaimed in my ignorance. "We've drawn the curtains", Mother took over, explaining that it was the custom to visit the dead, to see the body and say goodbye. How strange, I thought, curious, yet knowing that I could not go. Nell returned a little later, experience written on her face. "I shan't go" said Mother, "It's an outworn custom". Silence, a look: "I think you should" Nell said. Mother went.

I think it was shortly after this, in early spring that Mother took me to Nunhead Cemetery to see where her parents were buried. I liked it there it was remote and peaceful, tall trees swayed, it was green and wild, like the country. Startled birds flew up as we walked the grassy paths seeing many strange memorials. "Does it make you sad?" I asked, "Oh no not now", she answered. I knelt down and patted the fresh springing turf. "Why haven't they got a stone?", I wanted to know. "We hadn't much money and they would not have wanted one", she said. "I know their spirits are free and with me always, it was only their bodies that died, you know. (Behold, I tell you a mystery). We don't need a memorial to remind us of them, and when we are gone, what would their names carved on a stone mean to anyone else?" What, indeed?

Christmas Time

Preparations for Christmas meant more to me than the day itself. As the days became darker and the evenings drew in earlier, extra food of various kinds was purchased - mainly in the form of dried fruit. Towards the end of November a clean white cloth would be spread on the large living room table - solidly made of deal - what a table! I must digress a moment and sing its praises; it was in use all day and every day, usually covered with a brown chenille cloth with a vase of flowers set in the middle, but you could cover it with an old blanket and iron on it, clamp a mincer on it, hammer on it, stand on it, chop and cut on it - it remained unmarked and resilient always. I can remember a coverlet being thrown over it and me using it as a little house, sitting on a low stool in there with my bits and pieces, putting my hand up and picking tiny balls of glue that adhered to the joints of nine inch planks that formed its top; its smooth, rounded edges, its brown painted lathe-turned solid legs, its still lightly perfumed smell; no-one could see me there (I don't suppose they wanted to), it was as secret and enclosing as any lovely garden bower.

But that is beside the point; Christmas was fast approaching and with the puddings and mincemeat to be made, Mother and Aunt got busy. Ingredients were set on the table and jobs allocated, I always helped to stone the raisins and thereby managed to eat some, but it was tedious, I preferred, when old enough, chopping up the large sections of candied peel, removing the delicious sediment of flavoured sugar and sharing it to eat, skinning the lumps of suet, chopping them finely, and chewing bits of that too. Rubbing up the bread crumbs, weighing each item, tipping all the ingredients for the pudding into a huge old earthenware crock. What was it moistened with? Eggs, milk and beer. "We haven't any ", said Mother. "I'll go", said Nell, pulling on her coat and hat and picking up a large blue-flowered jug, Mother demurring loudly. "It'll only take five minutes to the "Golden Anchor" - Nell. "Can I come?", I asked. "Oh no", Nell answered, "But if you stand at the front room window, you'll see me go and in five minutes come back again", and that is what I did. I found it intriguing; Mother would not go, but Nell did, considering it rather a lark, walking home with a jug of foaming stout.

Christmas was, is and should always be a time of ritual, symbolism, reflection, wonder and rejoicing. Everyone in the house, including the lodgers, was invited in to stir the pudding, three stirs for three wishes (don't tell anybody what you wished), and everybody came. Four large puddings were made, one for New Year's Day, which was also Dad's birthday, one for Mother's birthday, one for Nell's, both in February, and they even kept one for mine; we were never too full up to enjoy them then and they were marvellous; not one for Christmas Day, you notice.

Dad and I made paper-chains from packets of bright coloured strips of paper, gummed at one end, and now and again he would buy a large festive paper bell or ball, which opened to reveal rainbow colours, and closed again for storing; we treasured these from year to year. Once he brought home a bright red fuzzy chain, ornamented with silver bells, another year it was fairy lights, big, clumsy and crudely painted by today's standards, but wonderfully new then. When, in about 1935, he bought a small, artificial Christmas tree, I really thought we had arrived. Only the front room was decorated and you will notice that this was Dad's province, he and I did it together. Mum liked what we had done, but basically disapproved of money being spent on such geegaws; in true Quaker fashion she believed that Christmas should be alive in your heart everyday, and the Day itself no different from any other.

Ah! but it was. This was how it went; waking early in the cold dark, finding one of Dad's socks at the foot of my bed, containing perhaps a new pencil and notebook, some sweets, a few nuts, a tangerine wrapped in silver paper. Nice, normal, average, nothing to go crazy over; I had always been told the truth about the holy St. Nicholas and his worldly shadow Father Christmas; for weeks we had sung carols at school, at home and at Sunday school, and now the long promised day had arrived; we switched on the wireless, heard more carols and listened to the bells. We all greeted one another with, "Happy Christmas" and Mr. Reid gave us presents, Aunt and Mother each a box containing two pairs of thick, fully fashioned silk stockings with seams, gussets, clocks, and me a large size packet of the usual Nestles chocolate that he always gave me. Nell made me a new dress, that was nice, (handsome is as handsome does) and some years I was given a really good present from my parents, a doll's pram, a scooter or a little tricycle, from Gamages.

Then we would get ready to spend the day with Aunt Mill and Uncle Tom at Dulwich, going on the 37 bus. The roasting turkey smelt delicious, I could hardly wait to begin it; it was an excellent meal, finishing up with Mill's famous mince pies. To me, the afternoon dragged somewhat, I expect they were all sleepy after the rich food and unaccustomed glass of sherry. Mill always gave me "something suitable"; frequently a box of Reeve's paints with a brush and plenty of instructions on how to care for it. Uncle Tom gave me a £1 note, he gave Nell a present too. "Where's your present and Dad's?" I wanted to know. "Ssshhh", whispered Mother, "The dinner is his present to us; his firm give him the turkey, so he shares it with us." I ruminated on that; everyone was reticent there, always, all the time.

I liked Uncle Tom to talk, he had a Leicestershire accent and said "wan" instead of "one"; he asked if I played a game he had played when a boy, "Seedy here I come" I didn't understand; he was a man of few words, so the conversation dwindled and died. Years later I discovered he had meant, "See thee here I come", an old game played in the Midlands. At three o'clock he switched the wireless on for the King's speech, we sat silent and solemn out of politeness. When they woke up a bit, we played records on the gramophone, taking it in turns to wind it up. There was for instance young Ernest Luff singing "O, for the wings of a dove", "Drages" (an 8 inch record advertising the furnishing firm) and Sandy Powell's monologue, "Building a chicken house", you got to know them by heart; and quite a few more.

Dad and Tom always smoked one cigar each and I would be asked to recite. That being over we played paper games - consequences, birds, beasts, funny people and pass the rhyme - I was very fond of that sort of thing, and there was a game where I hid something while others waited outside the door, then I would chant, "Hot boiled beans and very good butter, Ladies and gentlemen come to supper." We took it in turns to hide an object, the rhyme remains a puzzle. I remember clearly sitting at tea one year and Uncle telling us that he'd heard through his firm, Burton, Son & Sanders, that Cadbury's were about to put "filled blocks" on the market, describing them as filled with peppermint, coffee cream, Turkish delight, or caramel, etc., and saying how much more profitable they would be than solid chocolate. Mill and Tom had no decorations, but I liked the lamp hanging over the elegant, oval Queen Anne dining table - with its six chairs and two carvers - which lowered on a pulley and lit up the graciously laid table; its gathered orange silk shade and deep glass bead fringe glowing prettily.

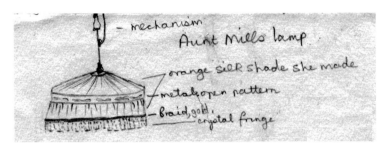

Later, but not very late, we would cross the road to the 37 bus stop to wait as we always waited on ordinary days - but no longer, for it to arrive; to drop into bed, tired but satisfied enough; too sleepy to wonder about tomorrow, No, try as one might, Christmas Day is never quite the same as any other.

The tomorrow I knew I could not escape was Boxing Day; there was little variation, it went like this; Mum and Dad fussing, he humming busily, she straight-faced, determined. Nell, helping to get me ready, "Don't look so Pofaced" - "Now, you're going to enjoy yourself". (Oh no I'm not), I didn't.

We took a bus to Liverpool Street Station, the noisiest, filthiest station I ever remember, the air thick with sulphuric fumes; from there we took the underground to Leytonstone; an interminable journey, altogether about an hour and a half each way, with a ten minute walk to the house at the end. Entering, it was full of people I had mostly not seen for a year, who had slept there all night, fourteen in all and Bruce, a dog. (Joe and Em, Joan, Lou, Grace and Lily, Harry and Ivor, Sue and Ernest Bullcrag, Ada and Charlie Hoare, plus little Charlie and young Jimmy). I was slightly acquainted with some of them, Joseph Hoare, Emily his wife, Joan, Grace, Lily and Lou. Harry was Joe's printer apprentice (d.1991) and Ivor, his wife (d.1995), Sue was Joe's sister and Ernest her husband, Jimmy their son. Charlie Hoare, Joe's brother, his wife, Ada and son little Charlie. The whole place was choked with heavy, faded, dusty garlands, enormous balls and bells, from the narrow hall, right up the stairs and through into the kitchen. Tarted up here and there with brash sparkling red nosed reindeer and a huge, unsteady row of Santas. There was no room to BE.

Everyone talked all the time, interspersed with horrid practical jokes and a few unseemly anecdotes and jests. Don't misunderstand me, no one was unkind, or deliberately hurtful or rude, it was just that I felt alien and out of place. I was regarded with detachment and felt at ease with no-one; my cousin, three years my senior, kept with her own two older cousins, they were intimate. For several years running, the men, Dad included of course, went off to a football match in the afternoon, not making it easier for me. I believe Dad enjoyed himself, I hope so, but Mother did not, and being her, never laid low, un-noticed in a corner. As soon as we had arrived and she'd sat down, she would fan her face and ask for a window to be opened, (people caught one another's eyes). The air, to say the least, was stagnant, a posh gas fire full on, no one had bathed properly the night before, the atmosphere redolent of talc, smoke and the effects of eating too much stuffing, Brussel sprouts, turkey, Christmas pudding, mince pies, nuts and so on. On at least one occasion she plonked a collection box on to the middle of the ravaged meal table saying, "Now we've eaten this splendid meal, how about remembering those who never get enough to eat?. A silence; to do them justice they did put something into the box; she certainly had the courage of her convictions - but the assembled company were more open to sentiment than straightforward appeal. I knew Dad was embarrassed, and me? I wanted to crawl under the table.

Liverpool Street Station 1927 – 29 *(from an engraving by Edward Bawden)*

There was the inevitable sing-song, mellowed by a generous supply of beer and port; they waxed so mellow it made me cringe, especially; "If you were the only girl in the world", Aunt Em - of all people! And "My old Dutch", what woman could stand being called that? even once. But it went on and on, year after year. Their gramophone records were different from ours, contemporary efforts such as, "Sunny side of the street", "Deep purple", "Blues in the night", "I'm forever blowing bubbles", selections from "White Horse Inn" and the "Inkspots" and Flanagan and Allen were played continuously while people talked, laughed, smoked and coughed. Mother couldn't stand, "All this rubbish I have to listen to. Pity they can't spend their money on something worthwhile". Joe was a printer at Lloyd's on night work, so they were better off than we were. They were not ungenerous, their presents were bright and gaudy, and I appreciated them.

A clique of women always gathered in the kitchen conversing about I know not what, and snapped into silence when I went in there; they would stare at me the interloper, with cold, dark brown eyes. Without exception they were enormous, large boned women, broad in the beam, and more than once I was sent flying by a sudden swipe from one of their buttocks, encased as they were in rigid, armour plated corsets.

The last to arrive and the first to depart, they always gave me a balloon on a string to take home, and I felt quite a lift as I took it, knowing that Boxing Day was over for another year and that now life could return to normal again; it was never discussed (in my hearing) afterwards, it just happened. The war put a stop to this ritual and except for Grace and Lily, for whom, over the years, I developed respect and affection, I never saw any of them again apart from Joan, briefly, a couple of times. It would be interesting to read a description of these celebrations, that ended in 1938, from someone else's pen (but those others are now all dead) and to compare the two; maybe they were the highlight of some people's lives.

That is enough of the festive season; quite simply, it was secular; it lacked for me that which lies at the heart of the true celebration of the birth of Jesus, although I could not have expressed it so then.

I feel like a traveller, who, pausing on his way, turns to look back at the place where his journey began; it isn't a bad thing, to stop, take a deep breath and a backward glance; it is surprising how sharp and clear some things appear, whilst others are enshrouded in mist; but it swirls about and suddenly all manner of things are revealed which you'd think were gone for ever.

Special Days

Apart from Christmas there were "special days" which I recall either because they were especially good, or because they so contrast with things today. For instance:- "The sweep's coming" - he always arrived very early, soon after seven o'clock; everything had to be moved out of the room that could be, immoveables draped with dust sheets. He came in May, so it was fully daylight and I was sent down the garden to see the brush emerge from the chimney and cry out accordingly. Mother always paid him to leave the soot, in a neat heap, for the garden, and we'd go and give his horse, small, neat and dark brown, a piece of sugar, held out bravely on the open palm of my hand, quite an effort on my part, but I didn't want to miss him, and patted his drum-like sides.

Sweeps brush.

I remember the evening of 30th November, 1936 very clearly. Dad came home from work full of the fact that there was a dreadful red glow in the sky, hadn't we seen it? He was afraid there was a serious fire somewhere not far away. We all went out in the front to look, by then a lot of neighbours were out staring too and soon rumour ran around that it was the Crystal Palace. At first this was treated with disbelief, for how could such a superb building, constructed completely of glass and iron, catch fire and *burn* ? Never before had I seen the whole sky lit up with such an eerie glow. Four years later I was to recognise that fearful light when the City and Docks were bombed, but in 1936 it was utterly new, strange and frightening to me. Compared with those of an earlier generation, "The Palace" to me meant little, it had lost its sparkle, become rundown. When taken there, only two or three times, I would wonder at my parents nostalgia for earlier days. To them, indeed to many South Londoners of their generation the Crystal Palace was a place of magic, excitement and beauty, filled with exotic rare delights. Within easy reach (transport was excellent), affordable, the hours spent there fired their imaginations, relaxed yet stimulated too.That is why I remember standing there on that chill November evening, detached, yet feeling the upset of loss ebb and flow around me, the disbelief that such a thing could happen.

Christmas being followed by New Year, I should have mentioned that first, but no-one I knew celebrated it. Several times I was awakened by the banging of tin trays at nearby front doors, and could hear the ship's sirens down on the river go "Cock-adoodle-dooo". That was all; it was also Dad's birthday, but he preferred it to go un-noticed; he had cards and little presents, nothing more. All our birthdays were rather like that, I thought it rather a flat day, not remembering being born, nor a time when I was not here, nor feeling it to be different from any other day, it seemed rather forced. I always have felt that a child's birthday means more to the parents than the individual concerned. We always had a really nice cake and I was given small presents, but nothing I specially remember.

First days of the month were certainly special, to ensure "Good Luck", the first word you spoke that morning had to be "Rabbits". "Have you said Rabbits?", they asked anxiously. And if you wanted Extra Good Luck it must be White Rabbits. When and where this pagan practice originated, I've no idea. I still do it, sadly though it doesn't seem to work. In contrast, the 13th. of the month, usually considered unlucky, was by them never mentioned. Strange how old habits die hard - I still most carefully crush all egg shells – for as I was told, if you throw them out whole, witches use them as boats and bring evil to the house. Again, where did that idea come from?

By today's standards we were poor, but not by the standards of that time. I think one man up the road owned a car, you could see it - there were no garages. Being a travelling salesman, Uncle Tom had one - it was said to be the reason he took the job, otherwise he was a qualified pharmacist, owned a number of text books on the subject. It was this skill that enabled him to make up a bottle of "pink" every year on the annual occasion of his taking us (Nell separately), out. It would be to Richmond Park or Hampton Court, or similar, and I had to drink a small medicine glass of it before we set out, to prevent me being sick and it certainly did the trick; it was not nasty, rather ether-ish, I don't know what was in it.

The car had a folding roof, a short rounded back with a boot, a dicky, a running board, leather upholstery, a horn and bright yellow body. In the later 1930's this was changed to an ordinary black Morris. Uncle Tom never came to our house for tea or to visit, just Mill every Tuesday afternoon; we never had people for a meal with us, Dad couldn't stand it, but Mum and Nell sometimes had a friend to tea: never anyone with children, Mother was not "child-oriented" at all, said that if she asked so and so along, she'd have to bring her "appendages".

Mother was always harking back to the golden age of her youth, and I found this irksome in the extreme. "Ah, but you should have seen it twenty years ago" or "It was so lovely when I was young" - staring tragically into the past _ "It will never be the same again", or "It's a pity you can't see it as it used to be", great sigh, "It's completely ruined now". I seemed to have come along at the wrong moment, but looking at my small world, I saw that it was good; luckily I had nothing with which to compare it. When I was older, about ten, I told her that the reason she infinitely preferred the past to the present, was that the greater part of her life was over, while I found the present all absorbing and delighted in looking to the future because I had so much more of it before me. I think, now, that I was angry that I was not part of her happiest years, as I believe most children are of their Mother's. Startled, she reflected a moment, "Yes", she answered quietly, "I expect you are right".

Mother got into the way of taking me to Bromley for the day, during the school summer holidays, and I found this pure joy; this seems quite extraordinary now, in 1987, but it was so; half a century has passed and the few green fields which separated Bromley from London have long since been built on, but I can be there, putting some sandwiches in a bag and walking up Gibbbon Road to Nunhead Station. Arriving at Bromley South she would wax nostalgic about walks they used to go on to Hayes - she could not resist it, they meant so much to her, but this was nothing to me, as we, hand in hand, like birds freed from a cage, walked excitedly up the familiar old High

Street, the street that exists now only in people's memories, or in old photographs. It was quietly busy, the multiple stores were not there, but old-established family firms and buildings full of character. We visited Last's bookshop and then went into the United Dairy and she would sit on a high chair drinking a glass of milk, telling the lady how she had loved drinking milk straight from the cow, and we would laugh and talk.

chair in Dairy

We bought a nice cake each - so hard to choose which - and took our picnic to Martin's Hill, where I'd roll down the hills getting covered in cut grass. We would walk round the beautiful Church Gardens and visit the church itself, then go to the Library Gardens and sit by the lake, watching the ducks. We always bought a crusty cottage loaf to take home and indulged in tea and cake in Wilson's before catching the train home, which finished the treat: a lovely day.

One more special day, Guy Fawkes, a very early memory, this. It was the scouts, I think, who put on a huge display of fireworks for many years, and Mum and Dad took me to it in my Tan-sad pushchair. (John was there too). Over the hill it was, on the brickfields; Millmark Road was built on it in 1931, so you see I was under four. Dad sat me up on his shoulder, so that I could see it all, so exciting and pretty, but I wanted to wee and Mum had to take me to a dark corner and hold me out, and I remember being upset and not liking it. That is by the way; on the way back, passing a long, high-walled garden high on the hill, Dad stopped and took me out of the pram and lifted me to rest on the rounded top of the solid wall. I gasped with pleasure and delight. "Look", he said "The lights of London", and there they were, thousands of them, sparkling and dancing in the clear, frosty air of that black and silent night. We hardly ever went that way at night, but when we did, I asked to see again the twinkling Lights of London, and when I was older and could see over that wall for myself, I remembered the magic of my first glimpse of them.

Holidays

We always managed to get away for a holiday, although I know that my parents had to scrape hard to save up for it. I got excited planning the holiday for days and days beforehand: all our summer clothes were washed and our white canvas shoes whitened with wet blanco and put out in the sun to dry. "This is the best part, looking forward to it", I exclaimed excitedly. "Not for me", Mother was definite. "The best part for me is when it's over, and nothing can take it away and it's mine forever and ever". We went for a week at first, then, about 1936, we had a fortnight, always Bed & Breakfast or Apartment, which meant one bedroom, use of bathroom and toilet shared with other guests, so you usually had to queue up, and breakfast in the lady's own living room. After breakfast we were not expected to come back into the house again until evening, but were usually given tea and biscuits at 9p.m. Mother made sandwiches after breakfast and we packed up for the day, including bucket and spade, woollies, costmes, towels, a ball and macs. Often our rooms were a long way from the sea, (cheaper), and as it involved a bus ride to get to the front, we tried not to forget anything. My first two holidays were spent at Lily Sawyer's at Eastbourne, but I don't remember them; various other holidays were spent at Littlehampton, Pokesdown on the edge of Bournemouth and Clacton, where I remember Mother hating the shanties at Jaywick.

I enjoyed all of it; Dad preferred the beach, so we'd spend the morning there and go walking in the afternoon to please Mum. If it was wet we would go on a bus to a place of interest inland, Mum was firm on this, so I remember the countryside then smelling warm, rich and mellow, the air heavy with damp perfume. Walking up sodden country lanes, birds chuckling and knocking splodges of water off the leaves and everything lush, green and wonderful.

So, there were mornings building intricate sandcastles with Dad, then paddling and collecting shells with Mum, our gear stacked around two deck chairs, I sat in one for a treat only!. It was always crowded, so there were plenty of people to watch; we changed in bathing huts, dark and very wet and chilly, Mother and me in one, Dad in a different row, very circumspect. My father was a good swimmer, I never was, but I could watch the sea for hours, its unceasing movement, its boundlessness, its clean stringent smell, its varying sounds - gently splashing, silently creeping, or roaring with great breakers crashing on the shore. Twice we went to the Isle of Wight, Sandown and Shanklin, that was lovely, sea, country and little towns - and a ferry, most adventurous. At considerable expense we went on a day cruise round the island, they said it was wonderful, but I was laid out all the time on a bench; I don't remember being sea-sick before then, and I'd been for lots of trips on the "Skylark". It was here that we stayed with a lady who only ever ate kippers, chocolate and strong tea; she looked so well, I thought I would like to try it sometime.

It was while we were at Clacton that Mother decided that on the first wet day we would take a bus to East Bergholt, where some of her ancestors came from, she said. There was a mad dog loose near the church, which jumped up howling terribly and bit a girl's face, blood poured out, the poor creature ran wildly off, everyone was screaming and hysterical, but Dad picked me up and ran into the church - the only time I've ever known him to do that!. We did a great deal of walking then, and my father carried me a lot, no shoving a pushchair into a car in those days.

Folkestone I remember well, I was nine, there was the bustling early morning fish market, the dearest of donkeys, they gave me a lot of pleasure, and there was "The Way of Remembrance", edged with rosemary, down which I was told, fine young soldiers had marched to embark on the ships which waited to carry them to France and so to the battlefields of the Great War. We liked to watch the Channel shipping, and to see the large ferries plying too and fro. One clear and beautiful day we climbed to the top of the Leas, "Look, you can see France", Mother cried, and slowly I perceived it there, a solid line of land across the horizon. "Is that it?", "Yes" answered my father, "What's it like there?" A sharp, fractional glance; pause. "It's better here", he said. Dad was always close; but what did he see as he stood there, gazing across that still empty ocean?. I forgot it and skipped down the twisting, wooded paths, back to the esplanade.

I should have said that we travelled to the resort by train from a London terminus, carrying trunk, bags, everything. One small incident which serves to point up the difference in the standard of living between then and now; Nell always bought us a half-pound packet of chocolate digestive biscuits for the journey, to open those was to know that the holiday had begun, we never had them otherwise. One year we found that they had been left on the scullery table; consternation, bags turned out in desperation; they were not there, I had a hard job not to cry and Mother was contrite. Next morning they arrived at our lodgings by post, Nell had troubled to pack them up and send them on; we were ridiculously pleased, our holiday was to be as good as ever! (No problems with the post then).

Once a week, whilst on holiday, we went to a variety show, there were usually two or three to choose from, often outdoor. I suppose no-one nowadays would patronise such amateur shows, we have become so slick and sophisticated, with their gaudy, tinselled, untrained girls, mediocre men and tawdry, banal sketches. Tunes were knocked out on clapped-out pianos and the choruses sung shrilly and clearly, with gusto:-

"And if I should go to heaven
As a good girl should by rights
Please don't give me wings to fly with
Give me spangles on my tights".

There were plenty of enthusiastically waving legs, enclosed from toe to thigh in brilliantly coloured tights, scattered with hundreds of twinkling sequins - and nobody else ever wore tights then; (until the 1960s ?), we would all join in the jolly choruses, but I can't remember any more. The bandstand then was a very popular centre of entertainment too, with concerts and community singing taking place every day, it was always packed and we joined in heartily with the singing.

The two years before the war our holidays were spent at Weymouth; how wonderful, we thought, to travel so far, and indeed it was special and different, and it was there that I first took an interest in the history of the place, was impressed by the beauty of its surroundings, the Swannery, Portland, Corfe, Swanage, and, yes, Mother even managed buses to Dorchester and the Hardy country - on wet days, naturally, but the weather did not diminish their impact, nor our enjoyment. There was a splendid outing from Weymouth in an old horse brake, the only time I have ever seen one; it crossed the little river Wey through a ford - water splashing up to shrieks of delight - to Upwey; it was very popular. It was at Weymouth that we several times bought a fish and chip meal for 6d., in a vast open hut arrangement - it was smashing; and it was here that we let our imaginations run riot choosing which house we would buy and deciding precisely how we'd furnish each room; we who could hardly afford the holiday at all, but it was fun to dream.

That is a general impression of my pre-war holidays, then; there were no more after 1939, which we spent with Lily Sawyer at Eastbourne, as we realised that war could be declared any minute. It is a tribute to my parents, with their differing tastes, that I enjoyed my holidays so fully, so much so that from the ages of about eight to eleven, I cried as we got back to New Cross, regretting the loss of the varied, happy days and the necessity to return to the endless streets, hard pavements and regimented rows of identical houses with neat ordered gardens, preferring the natural disorder of the countryside and the boundless sea. Not even Aunt Nell's delighted smile of welcome to the travellers, the specially laid tea (once she had embroidered a plain white table cloth with shining gold daisies), complete with fresh baked cake - and a ready ear for our adventures - could console me for the loss of that wonderful, ephemeral world; my misery was short-lived, but not forgotten.

What I would like to have got across are my memories of the bustling, colourful sea-side towns of the thirties, ebullient, bursting with visitors, vitality and life. We visitors had achieved an aim - saved hard and succeeded in "going away" - fully aware that by no means everyone could; one either went to the sea-side for days out, OR had a holiday, not both; we did not bother much about the wealthy who holidayed all the time. These towns fulfilled all our expectations, "something for everybody", with their variety of shops and their Victorian piers, where you could walk to the very end, peering through gaps in the wooden flooring at the sea, heaving and swelling immediately beneath, and stand and look back at the town itself, getting an entirely new view of it; and watch the fishermen engrossed there, absorbed and silent. Yes, it could be windy, a sandy beach was fine, but it could blow right into your eyes, hair and sandwiches, ugh; and of course it could be chilly, you just put on more woollies. Rain was worse, Mum and Dad would say, "Rain before seven, fine by eleven", but not always it wasn't, Oh no. I've often sat in a shelter eating sandwiches - along with scores of other people, but there was the pictures, slot machines, coach trips - mystery tours were very popular, even when it was wet, and gift shopping could take hours. Against that there were so many things to do and see, even with our tight purse; we walked by the English Channel, gazed contentedly at it, loved it, but never thought of crossing it.

I always took a "Last look at the sea", a ritual; our last night we'd walk along the promenade, aware of the weaving flight of the gulls, hearing their ceaseless cries as we gathered a bunch of seaweed to take home. I'd stand looking at the dark contours of the coastline, delicately outlined with chains of coloured lights against the night sky, petering out into the distance, aware of the dark lapping water around me. Next morning, I made a point of saying goodbye to the sea; just stand and look and absorb the scene, then sadly turn and walk away; it was over for another year.

Toys, Pets, Games & Books

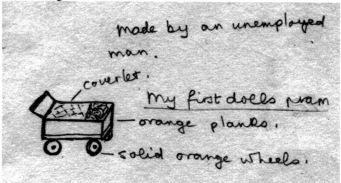

made by an unemployed man.
coverlet.
my first doll's pram
—orange planks.
—solid orange wheels.

My first doll's pram was wooden, I never played with dolls much, but enjoyed pushing a pram about, it had pretty covers and pillows and Nell also made me a rag doll called Belinda, with yellow silk plaits, also a splendid golliwog, linen buttons for the whites of his eyes, black woollen hair and a big happy scarlet smile and waistcoat. Their clothes all came off and Mum knitted them a woolly shawl, in stripes, from scraps. I had a blackboard and taught them, (I can't imagine what!), my "class" being composed of whatever was available at the time, from the old wooden dog, "Fido", to my favourite doll, Margaret, given the name I wished was mine. I faintly remember having an imaginary friend of that name, at one time, too. Mother risked giving me her own doll, Victorian, with kid body and pretty face, but it was a bad bet, I dropped her and broke her head soon after and was very sorry. We took her to the "Doll's Hospital" in the Old Kent Road and Nell paid to have a complete new head put on as we could not afford it; but I never played with her after that. Just one more member of my school, "Sunny Jim", given away free in exchange for coupons on "Force", (we never bought any prepared cereals like that, they were quite new. we had porridge made from coarse oatmeal), and given to me by a neighbour.

This odd, unsatisfactory pupil, manufactured in hard blue and white striped cotton could not sit down and resembled Punch, whom I never liked;

> *"High o'er the fence leapt Sunny Jim,*
> *"Force" was the food that raised him"*

- from large advertisements on hoardings, depicting him jumping about. Vile really; the rubbish one remembers!

Another period touch; I was given 2d. a week pocket money for years and with it bought sweets in the oil shop in Dennetts Road, a wonderful place, which smelt strongly of fire lighters, carbolic, loose vinegar and paraffin - kept in barrels, you took your own vessel and purchased by the pint - and kindling wood - faggots, which were stacked up the walls from floor to ceiling. A tiny shop, the floor covered with well-worn coconut matting, choked with bits and pieces of every description, kept by a pink cheeked, bowed old man with unframed glasses. Mars bars were new then and took all of my 2d., but my favourite sweet was chocolate kisses, chocolate containing marshmallow with hundreds and thousands sprinkled on top, one halfpenny; OR, one halfpennyworth of mustard pickle, consisting of filthy yellow, runny acetic acid sauce, dotted with bits of onion and cauliflower, tongue searing and face staining, spooned out of a huge jar into a newspaper twist, the thing was to eat it before it seeped away completely - or at least before you got home. Mother was always enraged when I spent my money on these things, telling me it was gut rot, and the marshmallow made from horses hooves - but it didn't put me off, after all, it was *My money*. She liked it no better when I changed to Tiger Nuts, telling me that they were "beastly things, fried up eastern insects", I found them very tasty, so did my friends, we all bought them.

I saved pocket money for holidays, presents and the odd purchase. I loved the Japanese sunshades you could buy in Woolworths, like the ones they stick in ices now, but then full size, wooden frames, opening and shutting, in pretty pastel colours, charmingly decorated, but so easily torn. The Japs had a large share of the cheap toy market then, and some of their products were dangerous, the metal ones had jagged edges and the celluloid ones were a fire-hazard. I had one or two such dolls, but the thing made by them that particularly enchanted me were the shells, which when dropped into a tumbler of water, slowly and magically opened to allow a spray of tiny, perfect paper flowers to grow up to the surface.

Japanese shell flowers.

I began collecting things after about seven, I suppose; matchboxes, orange papers and scent bottles - these cost nothing and were attractive and interesting. Friends, lodgers and neighbours gave me the bottles, (you can imagine the family did not indulge!). I kept them in a wooden box and the whole thing smelt wonderful; I quite regret disposing of them, but one cannot keep everything.

Scent bottle designs

Like everyone else, we played board and card games much like today, and my father had special games for me,

99

differing with my age, of course. I remember sitting on his knee for "Fly away Peter, fly away Paul" and he'd bring in a 1d. clay pipe to blow pure soap bubbles on hot sunny days and we'd watch those rainbow bubbles spin higher and higher and finally disappear above the neighbouring gardens. He liked to make a bad Brazil nut into a little candle, he was fascinated with magnets and would make needles and pins dance on a sheet of paper and cluster them thickly like bees round a honey pot; sometimes magnetise a knife, or scissors, and then they would attract - or repel - things too, and I would feel the force.

He did not have much time to spend with me, of course, working as he did from 9 a.m. to 5.30 p.m. every day and 9-1 on Saturdays, seeing his family in Kennington every other Saturday afternoon, (always giving his mother five shillings to help out), and taking me out each alternate Sunday morning. One of the nicest things he did for me was to design patterns with a compass, usually after dinner, midday Saturday when it was wet, and I would spend quite a long time carefully colouring them with crayons or coloured pencils, outlining them in black, I thought they looked like stained glass windows. (He used to get some scrap paper from the office, though nothing like the amount that is freely available today, and never anything else.) One birthday he bought me a small clockwork train set, we played with it together, he got a lot of pleasure from it, "I always wanted one", he said; I felt a small prick of compunction and tried to evince a little more enthusiasm watching the diminutive green tin engine and its solitary coach journey mindlessly round and round the little ring of rail.

We always had pets, a cat and a dog. Polly, the dog, which they had before I was born, was jealous of me, I was about seven when she died and did not really mind much. There was a series of cats; poor things, none of them lived to be more than about three, dying off in steady succession, perhaps they were weakly, I don't know, they were obviously loved and well cared for.

My father had no strong feelings about animals, they existed alongside him, but he firmly believed that *MAN* was the crowning glory of evolution and therefore far and away superior to all other animals, and definitely *NOT* made in the image of God. Mother was passionately fond of all animals, they gave her great joy, always.

There were no tinned animal foods at all, then, although proprietary dog biscuits, like "Bonios" and Spiller's "Shapes" were popular. The cats were given meat from the Cat's Meat Man, he came round pushing his homemade barrow and stuck your pennyworth - slices on a wooden skewer - under the knocker, pay at the end of the week.

He carried them in an enormous basket on his arm, day after day; cheerful, efficient, wearing a khaki overall and a cap."If you can't pay me today, love – owe me to next week", to Mum, that's how things were. He probably got the meat from the knacker,s yard – Harrison and Barber's - at Deptford, for he boiled it up himself. We also fed the cats on cod's heads (1d. each), one boiled them and picked all the flesh off - there was quite a lot, including the eyes which rolled out like marbles, the smell was obnoxious though. Lights, which formed a further variation of the feline diet, also had to be boiled. This unwieldy, springy, bloody mass was cooked in a heavy old iron saucepan, it had to be watched, as it foamed up and sprang the lid open; "Oh dear, I must hurry and get this done before your father comes in", said Mother. "He can't bear the smell of it you know". Well, it wasn't nice, but I did not realise he was so fussy. "Why ever not?", I asked. "It reminds him of the war", she said; I looked up, "However ..." She interrupted; "It's the smell, sort of sickly sweet, reminds him of burying the bodies after a battle". A shock ran through me, I never thought of that ...I went over and opened the windows as Mother opened the back door and the pure, sweet fresh air blew through the quiet room.

Cats' meat! (Spurgeon Collection)

Filling his basket from home - made barrow,

EENWICH EISURE
and Services First

Designed by Kit Gregory, Studio 4
Typeset by Blackheath Photoset
Printed by Meridian Press

Several toys I liked very much, there was the board with lots of coloured balls and you made up patterns; there was the knitting set with multicoloured wools, you just knitted and amazing patterns appeared, and Dad fitted me up with a cotton reel with four nails in the top and I made yards of "reins". One favourite was a kaleidoscope which I had for years, looking into it from time to time, shaking it gently and never being disappointed at the delightful patterns which formed, never the same but always beautiful. I feel I am doing that now, with my past - shake my memory and another different facet of the 1930s is revealed.

I have just remembered the wireless, which was born only a little before me; the first one we had (that I remember) was rather like an enclosed windmill, Dad had made it, but I recall clearly walking down to New Cross Gate to buy our first real wireless, a Murphy, it was truly a red letter day, a day of jubilation; *a Real Wireless; 1936*. After that we listened more, I cannot remember much what, *Monday Night at Eight,* Uncle Mac and *Children's Hour, In Town Tonight* were favourites. In the 30s wirelesses started to become a nuisance, thoughtless people, drunk on the latest "in thing" turned them on very loud, and in hot weather, with windows open, it could be a nightmare. Mother would go and complain.

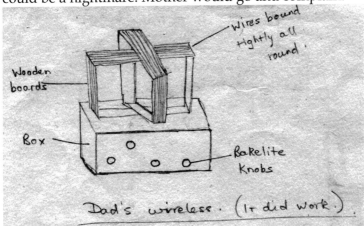

Now to books; I was not an imaginative child, and so preferred books relating to fictional people, rather than fairies, giants and so on. I was read to a lot and cannot now always remember which I read myself and which I listened to. We used the New Cross Public Library, and two of my earlier best loved books were *Milly Molly Mandy* and the *Amelia Ann* series. There was also *The World Was Young and Gay,* a delightful book which I read many times, but have not seen since and do not know the author. I became totally absorbed in them and could be much moved, for instance, the tale of *Ginger* in *Black Beauty* upset me greatly, and, when I first read it to myself, the story of the crucifixion; I was appalled and disturbed that people could behave so, and could hardly bear to finish reading it. (The Age of Innocence does not refer to sex but man's inhumanity to man.)

I never liked weird, unstable imaginings like *Peter Pan*, I felt vaguely repelled, though told I would enjoy them; (later, when I heard that Barrie was a psychological case I felt quite cheered). What else? *Water Babies,* I saw was a parable, I liked *Mrs. Bedonebyasyoudid* and *Mrs. Doasyouwouldbedoneby*, that made sense; but Grimm's Fairy Tales were just that, GRIM beyond belief, very unhealthy and threatening, a nightmare of the mind. There are some books that adults believe young children should like, but in reality they often cannot be appreciated until much later, and so they are met with at too early an age. The *Alice* books, for instance, Hans Anderson, a good, perceptive writer, but one to wring your withers - *The Red Shoes, The Snow Queen, The Shoes that were danced to pieces, The Little Match Girl,* - a social study which no young child could appreciate. My most favourite books, then, were *Little Women* and all Louisa Alcott's, and all the New England Edwardian genre tales - *Rebecca of Sunnybrook Farm, Anne of Green Gables and What Katy Did* series; also *Treasure Island.*

I have kept to before 1939 and all these would just fall into that category, although read again and again. I had no regular comic, bought one now and again, given some sometimes, and was bought *The Girl's Own Paper* from about eleven years. Nursery rhymes I've not mentioned, I knew them all of course, but more like patterns, the meaning not considered.

I feel that I should stress the different attitude to books which prevailed then. They were prized possessions, prized either for their content or the memory of the giver, for books were frequently given then as presents - as they had been for generations. So, from my earliest days I was taught to take the utmost care of them, certain ones being shown to me as a great concession. I had to wash my hands, a clean cloth was spread out on the table and the book set on it. "Turn the pages like this", Mother would say, and although it was such a rigmarole, I developed a lasting love of the things, bindings, illustrations, print and paper, the lot. Certain books from Mum's own youth were forever neatly sewn into pretty fabric covers, or else covered with brown paper whilst being read - which I hated and have never done myself. It all sounds so Victorian. I wonder if it stemmed from the influence of their nursemaid grandmother.

Other things were cherished too and only brought out occasionally; there was Mother's jewel box, together we would look at her bits and pieces, at her art school portfolio - I would gaze at its contents, very impressed; as well as sorting out Nell's needlework pieces. ("Never have anything in your house which is neither useful nor beautiful, if possible it should be both" (William Morris).

I should like to tell here of Dad's hunter - a beautiful gold fob watch that he was given for his 21st. birthday. How they had it I don't know, I have a feeling it was his grandfather's and was somehow saved from the wreck. "Show me your watch, show me", I'd say, I loved it. He would pick me up and sit me on his knee, at the table, take the watch from his waistcoat pocket and carefully prise open the front; this was a golden frame marked with Roman numerals, open in the centre, The face was then revealed, with a further set of numerals, which he explained, then held it to my ear; tick-tock, tick-tock, "Now let me see the back", I demanded; pure magic, the tiny cogwheels ticked away, and "Look, fifteen jewels", minute diamonds and rubies; and then it was shut tight and replaced. Came the day he decided to sell it; he wanted a wrist watch like his contemporaries; there was no other way, and he hoped to get a little over, too; "You go with him", Mother told me, (but I felt his indecision and regret), "You'll cheer him up". He took it to Walker's in Rye Lane and got an excellent watch in exchange, (he was still wearing it in 1980), but only a few notes over, which he handed to Mother; it was 1933.

It was my father who made me one of the best things I ever had, my doll's house. It was made with infinite care and patience and gave me enormous pleasure, it was a far better doll's house than any of my friends had - it *Worked*. The front opened in the centre, to reveal on the right, a kitchen, on the left a sitting room - with a tiny switch which lit up a brightly glowing red fire. Upstairs was a bedroom and a bathroom, each room was fully furnished, with lino on the floors, curtains to the windows and pictures on the walls. Every room had its own electric light, all the doors and windows opened, there were chimneys, a letter box and an electric bell. The outside walls were clad in red brick patterned paper, while the roof had grey slate; I was very proud of it, and continued to spring-clean it and buy extra items of furniture for it for many years, eventually passing it on to Helen.

After I started school, the games I played were enhanced by the participation of the friends made there. Skipping was popular and I delighted in the present of a purpose-made skipping rope, the smooth, wooden handles set with fine ballbearings, greatly prized, after the lengths of clothes line I had used until then, with knots for handles. There were rhymes, and I did the bumps and twists: "I'm a girl guide", etc., "Salt, Mustard", "Mrs. Simpson's lost her drawers" and so on. I became really good at "Two balls" against walls, under leg and in the air and actually progressed to "Three Balls". It was the custom to swop various little items; there was a terrible row once when I came home with a pile of old comics (for me, forbidden luxury). "Where did you get that muck?" Mother. I told her I'd swopped a little green and gold tortoise – a bracelet charm – for them. She was absolutely furious – I must get it back before Mill found out. Well, I did but remember it as a hateful episode. "If you'd had your eye-teeth about you you'd not have been so silly" – (Mother actually feared Mill's wrath. Why ?) Anyway, I'd thought the thing was *mine,* no idea of it being an "heirloom". But I was at that time careless. Mum herself had given me a tiny ring, gold set with a seed pearl ; that was silly, I was no more than 4 and loved it, yet lost it. Later Mill discovered it was missing and there was a great stink about it. Of course Mother took all the blame – and rightly. Nell gave me a girl's coral necklet – also from her Grandma Silk – that too disappeared, but as its loss never came to light, I've no memory of its going: none.

Three or four of us played together, either in our houses or when fine on a seat at the top of the road, or, "Up the park", (the lower park) lovely, no one worried that we would be molested, although we were told strictly to "Keep together", and we did. At all times it was patrolled by a Park Keeper, brown uniform with strapped leather leggings, armed with a long spike with which he stabbed up any rubbish! We always minded him. Sometimes we took a bag of broken biscuits and a bottle of lemonade and an old mac to sit on, for a picnic, or sit in the shelter there, by the grassy pool; or maybe daringly climb into the deserted band stand. By the way, if we kids saw an ambulance, the drill was, stand still, fix it with your eye till out of sight, hold your collar tight, mutter loudly and solemnly:-

"Touch yer coller,
Never swaller,
Never get the fever".

There was also the saying:- "If you drop a knife you'll see a black man". We never did. Telegraph Park offered us all endless enjoyment; after I was about eight I was allowed to take our dog Patsy there on my own, which I loved to do.

Different houses, different charms; Jackie Ryde's had a pianola, with rolls of paper punched with holes - put them in and they played unaided - the keys dancing up and down as if by magic. At my house we were fond of dressing up, I had a box which held high heeled shoes, veiled hats, old handbags, long evening dresses and other generally exotic gear donated by lodgers; we would pretend to be film stars and sing *"When I grow too old to dream", "The Isle of Capri"* and such like 30s gems. The greatest ambition of Winnie Smith and myself was to be waitresses, and Nell knocked us up little "Nippies" aprons and caps from an old sheet, and we'd lay every available table and walk round taking orders from our menus. Mum and Nell were patient, but there were always plenty of invisible customers, including a "Mrs. Green", I don't know why. Mother couldn't stand Winnie, "Always rushing off to the lavatory, silly people do, you know. So dimwitted - that's why you play with her, so you can boss her about. Hasn't a thought in her head". Winnie had a sad house, I remember an awful scene once, when her father threw his mother-in-law down the stairs, the doctor was called and I was sent home; we never went there after that. We all played mothers and fathers a lot. The way that Mother readily let me play with neighbour's children is surprising, considering that she was never keen on such. Of course, should any problems arise they'd be given extremely short shrift, but in those days, no-one was surprised or upset, for that was the norm.

School

Waller Road School was two minutes walk across the road to the right, built in 1887 for the School Board for London, and is still in use. A building typical of its time, its interior walls were painted dark brown to about three feet up, then a six inch wide green band, with cream paint to the ceiling. Hot water pipes ran round each room, which were also heated by huge coke gas-lit fires, and there was one at either end of the hall, glowing an even deep red, giving out a tremendous heat and surrounded by high iron guards. These were stoked regularly by Mr. Hales, the caretaker, with tall coke buckets kept at the ready. He lived in a dear little house at one corner of the playground, which was divided by brick walls into "Infants", "Girls" and "Boys", with toilets to match, excellent practice, though very basic toilets.

Waller Road School

110

The building had very high windows, opened with a long pole with a hook on the end, and was always light, warm and clean. The gas-lighting, lit by Mr. Hales using a shorter pole poked into a dangling loop, buzzed and sang sleepily in the grey winter afternoons. The infant's building was single storey, the junior's two, the infants had little tables and chairs and boxes, the juniors solid wooden double desks with lids where you kept your books and things; there were holes for inkwells to sit and a groove for pens and pencils; the inkwells were filled by monitors.

I expect it all comes back to me so clearly because I never mixed with any other children until then, Easter 1932. Aunt Nell made me a white Edwardian pinafore to wear, and the teacher, Miss Desborough, took me out at 12.0., the end of morning classes, to my anxiously waiting Mum and kindly explained that they were not worn anymore. It sounds antediluvian now, but I read recently that they were still worn in some parts of Kent in 1922, but I do not know when they went out. That business over, after coming to terms with the strangeness of it all, I mostly enjoyed it. One or two relatively unimportant things stick in my memory:- importantly stalking up to the teacher's desk, "look, the date is, "3.3.33". he was kind; "I'm glad you've noticed that, you'll never have to write that again, but watch out for 4.4.44 and 5.5.55", and I did. I don't remember learning to read, but figures bothered me, however, about this time - red letter day - on looking hard at our orange number cards, which had large black spots on them, like dominoes, I suddenly saw that *Various* numbers added up to ten; lots of choice!, the same kind teacher must have been relieved, for that was our task, to add up to ten; - 7+3, 5+5, 9+1 - it hit me; (I must have been thick.)

Mr. Hales tolled the bell, day after day at ten to nine. We had assembly, a hymn and prayers, and ended the day with:-

"Thank you for the world so sweet,
Thank you for the food we eat,
Thank you for the birds that sing,
Thank you, God, for everything.Amen" (sung).

Songs we sung come to mind:-

"Blossom on the hedgerows, blossom on the hills
O the happy May time, all my being thrills,
May time, May time God has given us May time
Thank him for his gift of love
Sing a song of Spring."

"It's rather dark in the earth today said one little
bulb to his brother,
But I thought I felt a sunbeam ray,
----   ----   ---   to find a way,
So they nestled close to each other.
And they struggled and toiled by day and by night
Till two little snowdrops in green and white
Rose out of the darkness into the light,
And softly kissed one another."

"Summer has come from the sunny lands
Summer is here again
Bringing the birdies to sing their song
In every wood and lane
Chirruping chirruping loud and sweet
High in the leafy tree, dear little birdies I think you
sing
Your prettiest song for me

But I should very much like to know
How did you learn to sing?

112

Who was it taught you the way to fly
And gave you each tiny wing?

We have a Father the birdie said,
Loving and kind and true,
He who has taught us the way to fly
Will think of the children too.

Thank you dear birdie for telling me
I am so glad to know,
Now when I'm asked I can always say
"A little bird told me so"   (A topical saying)

I cannot remember much else about the infant's school, mostly it seemed to flow along. I know we made a big gipsy caravan, and I was given the job of making "plates with the alphabet round the border". I cut out circles as best I could but then could not fit the wretched alphabet on to them, could only get up to M. I got into a state and the circles got all mucky with my trying, but the teacher only said that she didn't expect I would, and it didn't matter anyway - she might have said so at first, I thought. It was a silly poem that we were basing our project on:-
   "I wish I lived in a caravan,
   With a horse to drive like the pedlar man,
   Where he comes from no-body knows,
   Or where he goes to, but on he goes.
   Tea-trays, baskets, ranged in order,
   Plates with the alphabet round the border".

And as I chanted it, to myself I said,"I *Don't* wish at all that I was such a man, and I should *Hate* not to live in one certain place, my Home.

Friday afternoons were nice in the infants, we were allowed to take a toy and play half the time, the other half we were read to. We learned a lot by rote - gallons, pints, rods, poles and perches, intriguing, that one I thought.

"Four farthings one penny,
Twelve pence one shilling,
Twenty shillings one pound".

And so on, including furlongs, chains, yards, feet and inches: that is why my generation did not want to go metric, all that effort would be wasted. Mother did not realise that writing had changed and tried to get me to practise "pothooks and hangers", but I never learnt that sort of script, mine is like joined up print.

I have always been grateful we learnt our tables, they have been enormously useful, but by this decade children did not learn poetry any more, nor the Bible. We read quite a lot, and continued to be read to on Friday afternoons in the Junior School. Tales such as Kingsley's *Heroes* and sagas of the Norse Gods, Thor, Freya, the wicked Luki and Balder the beautiful were fine, but often I was disappointed; *Brer Rabbit,* and *Pilgrim's Progress* seemed never ending, and later, in the top class of the juniors Mr. Bertram Jones read us, *Jeremy* and then, as if that wasn't enough, *Jeremy at Crale* - hopelessly boring; I always managed to sit at the back and stare out of the window. He was actually a literary, sensitive and enthusiastic teacher, especially in teaching us history, which he taught through a Londoner's eyes, concentrating on the rich history of Deptford.

Nature study was stimulating too; the nature table was never empty, indeed the contributions brought along by us enthusiastic youngsters overflowed on to the window sills and considering where we lived, displayed a surprisingly varied and attractive collection, gathered lovingly from gardens and days out in the country or by the sea, carefully attended and clearly labelled.

114

Composition, on the other hand, seemed stultifying; I recall with little pleasure endeavouring to write, *The Life History of a Button* or *A Penny* - pretend you are one - who and what did you see, etc., mine usually finished up rolling down a drain with someone poking at it hoplessly with a stick; end of composition. By the way there were no school dinners provided, we all went home, but milk was issued at play-time, 1/3 pint bottles with a straw, a halfpenny each or twopence halfpenny per week, or free in case of need. While I was in the first year of juniors, someone "poohed " in an alcove, and we all had to file up the stairs to the staff room to have our behinds inspected - it was horrid. Soon after I was "done" word went round the subdued children that the culprit had been found and sent home disgraced.

The cane was used; once, in the infants on me; a list of rude words was being passed round, I never knew who wrote it, but it was stuffed with stifled giggles into my hand - *read it* - they hoarsely whispered. Unknowingly I opened it and looked, the teacher raised her head and saw me. "Come here, give it to me", she read it, "What does it say?", she asked. "Stomach, breast, belly", I answered, for that was all I'd seen. She looked at me; "I'm really sorry", she said, "But I said that the next person to interrupt the lesson will get the cane and it's you. I can't go back on my word". Taking it out of her desk drawer, "Open your hand", she said, and hit it twice. It stang and the class was silent; it was rough justice, I cried, not so much with pain as with disgrace, and above all, injustice; I believed she had made an error of judgement there, and boiled with furious indignation. However, the cane was certainly used then, I remember boys were whacked on their bums; but there was no insubordination, it was a well ordered, well disciplined school.

I remember only one horrid teacher, Mr. Evan Jones, short, fat and red faced with bold, shiny eyes. He asked me, and, I discovered, other girls, what our favourite sweets were, "Chocolate kisses", I replied, to which he responded, "I like those too, come on give me one then". Instinctively I knew what he meant; shocked, I turned away; I didn't tell Mother this, (I thought it so strange and embarrassing), but a little later, when he shouted in his typical bullying manner at me , "You are an ARSE, do you hear me - an ARSE", I felt I'd had enough of his horrible, threatening ways and went home furious and told her. Enraged, she took me back to school in the afternoon, me trembling at her wrath, not worldly wise enough to know just how badly he had behaved. She wiped the floor with him, "How DARE you call my daughter by that filthy name - do you know what an arse is?" ...Hush, hush, Madam, please, I'm sure I didn't mean..." "Hush be blowed - you didn't hush when you called her that disgusting name - just let me have one more complaint about you and I'll not let it rest here". I was afraid that he would take it out on me after that, but he never said a word, and avoided me altogether. I was about nine or ten. (How my pacifist Mother did enjoy a fight - I've met many such).

A hymn we learnt in Junior School comes back to me:-
"*Father, lead me day by day,*
Ever in thine own sweet way,
Teach me to be good and true
Show me what I ought to do.

When in danger make me brave
Make me know that Thou can'st save,
Keep me safe at Thy dear side,
Let me in Thy love abide. Amen

Songs we sang in Junior school included:-
116

Dark brown is the river
Golden is the strand
It floats along for ever
With trees on either hand.
Green leaves afloating,
Castles of the foam.
Boats of mine aboating
Where will all come home?
("Where go the boats?" by R.L. Stevenson)

Oranges are jolly things
Growing on the trees,
But on the grass their golden rings
Entirely fail to please
So when you've had your revel
With a luscious one from Seville
Don't let the folk who follow cry Alas!
Have some fellow feeling
About you orange peeling
And do gather up your litter from the grass.

The Mountain and the squirrel had a quarrel,
And the former called the latter "little prig"
Bun replied "You are doubtless Very Big"
But all sorts of things and weather
Must be taken in together to make up a year and
sphere
And I think it no disgrace
To occupy my place. etc. etc.

Song about ducks:-
Up tails all
Everyone for what he likes we like to be
Heads down, tails up, dabbling free.
High in the blue above swift whirl and call

117

We are down a dabbling, up tails all!
(Here we keep our larder, clear and cool and green).

Some poems I recall:-
> *The Wind*
> *The wind one morning sprang up from sleep,*
> *Saying, "Now for a frolic, now for a leap*
> *Now for a madcap galloping chase,*
> *I'll make a commotion in every place. etc. etc.*

> *Leaves*
> *"Come little leaves", said the wind one day,*
> *"Come o'er the meadows with me and play,*
> *Put on your dresses of red and gold*
> *For summer has gone and the days grow cold".*
> *Soon as the leaves heard the wind's loud call,*
> *Down they came fluttering, one and all,*
> *Soon fast asleep in their earthy beds*
> *The snow laid a blanket over their heads.*

And, of course,"Go down to Kew in lilac time", etc. (John Drinkwater)

Teachers were thought a lot of then, and mostly they earned people's respect, however, one other whose actions made me feel uncomfortable was Miss Wiggins, very smart, rather a fashion-plate. I had been talking to a friend; the punishment? her favourite - "Go and sit next to Joseph Collins". He poor boy, was literally ragged, solitary, snotty-nosed and unwashed, often daubed with purple for impetigo; no-one would voluntarily sit next to him, and into this vacant seat were sent the nuisances of the day. What an insensitive, mean minded woman. The School Nurse attended regularly and carefully combed each head, metal comb dipped in disinfectant, looking for nits. When, on the rare occasion she found some, how relieved I was it wasn't me!

Then there was the dentist, we had to visit the school clinic in Hanover Park, off Rye Lane. The mere thought of it filled me with dread, situated in an old house, crudely modified to contain waiting room, surgeries and offices, dark and dismal in the extreme. Sobs and screams met you as you opened the door. The waiting room had its own peculiar *horrible* smell, it was dingy, containing a few chairs in ruinous condition, bare boards, no curtains to the windows but a large old sepia print of the "Stag at Bay" hung on a wall. In here there were always two or three children, with their mothers, recovering from their ordeal - shouting feverishly and being sick from the effects of gas, bleeding and crying. The wait was long, then you were marched, alone, in to the surgery and either a great treadle drill bored mercilessly into your delicate mouth, or a large, suffocating mask was rammed over your protesting face and for a while you knew no more. Coming round was a nightmare, the nurse who'd held you down all brisk and forceful. The nightmare continued all the way home in the tram, for I was always sick again and felt like death. Fortunately I had only two or three lots of treatment; I suppose it was worth it.

There was a strict Jew in our class, Myer Zargcharkra; in winter on Fridays, as dusk fell, he would glance hopefully out at the increasing gloom, then up would go his hand, the teacher nodded, and out he trotted; lucky, but odd, we thought.

There were few notable days in the school calendar, Christmas festivities and the end of each term were celebrated, but the one that stays with me is Empire Day, 23rd. April. If possible girls wore white dresses, and one year Aunt Nell made me one with red and blue smocking

119

on it, I was enchanted and glowed with pleasure; naturally Mother disapproved, it smacked of imperialism. "Oh go on with you", said Nell,"it's just fun and games". We were lined up in the playground, the Governors attending, and sang our well practised songs and marched round waving little paper Union Jacks, 1d. each - one in each hand for those who could afford it - show offs!. We sang:-

"We are only little children,
But our part we gladly take,
We all want to do our duty
For our King and Country's sake".

This school then, was where I first made friends with other children, as mentioned earlier. I suppose we were about nine when Mavis and I became firm friends. We knew one another well before then, but about that time we started to do things together, went to one another's for tea, she and her family had lived in Queen's Road, but now lived upstairs in Gellatley Road and I was always warmly welcome there. Her father was a craftsman carpenter, her mother from Leeds, open and friendly, they were keen members of the Peckham Health Centre in St. Mary's Road and Mavis was an enthusiastic Brownie. I wanted to join too, but was strongly discouraged by both Mum and Dad, for some inscrutable political reason, which annoyed me a lot.

Nearly the end; there was a girl in our class, steeped in all matters appertaining to sex, (isn't there always?) named Mary Blair Black, Scottish. Hating her middle name, we would chant it at her, as we feared, yet were fascinated by her; like a witch. She told us she had suckled a kitten, and how babies were made (there were several ideas on this theme floating around). I was nine or ten and thought she had made it up, a dirty joke, I just could not

120

believe it was true; not long after, Mother told me all; that was it, how weird; I did not let on that Mary B.B. had already told me, in case anything was different; unfortunately, it was not. That is how we were, half a century ago.

July, 1938, our class dispersed. The Ovendens, from 155 Waller Road had moved the year before to Whitefoot Lane, Catford, newly built. I went there on my own, by tram, nervous of missing the stop, but pretty Joyce was there to meet me, with her naturally bright golden corkscrew curls (how I envied them). We met up once more, but after that I never saw her again. Another friend, Pat Sterne, moved to Brockley Rise (new estate); I was invited to the house-warming party - so *modern*, the women flash and made up, art-deco and stainless steel furnishing, and *cocktails* with cherries on sticks - very different from their dank and rather malodorous basement flat in Pepys Road. The boy opposite, Kenneth Woolfit, won a Christ's Hospital Scholarship, and came home from Horsham each holiday dressed, I thought, like a parson with yellow stockings; I looked at him with some wonder. It was said that he was immensely clever and I know he must have been; he became a bank clerk.

Here is a good place to stop; in February, 1938, I was due to sit for the scholarship examination, but got tonsillitis and had to sit it late the following September. As my teacher and the headmistress had informed Mother there was no doubt that I would go to the Central School, Walbutton Road, some well-meaning Peckham Friends suggested that I be sent to a Quaker Boarding School - money would be no problem. My distress was total, I told Mother point blank that nothing and nobody would ever induce me to accept such an offer, and if ever I was sent to such a school I would start walking straight home - I would never stay there. So final and decisive was I that this proposal was never referred to again, and it was plain that both my parents were pleased and relieved at my reaction. The Friends were motivated by kindliness, but I knew that such a life was not for me.

My uniform was ordered and then a letter arrived, I had won a scholarship to grammar school. I was proud and delighted; I remember arranging a row of hurdles - a box, the sewing machine cover and a stool and running and leaping for joy over them, right through the dining room and kitchen. Breathlessly I reeled off a list of the subjects I was about to embark upon, French, Biology, Maths and so on, to Aunt Nell, who sat busily stitching. "O my", she said, "What will you do with all that knowledge?", pause, "I don't know, but I'll have it", I answered cockily. Mr. Bertram Jones was truly pleased and wrote in my autograph album, "Do noble deeds, not dream them all day long"(Kingsley). On reading it, "I didn't know I did", I said, "Yes, you always do" was his reply.

The green Central School uniform was cancelled successfully, a great worry that, and I was interviewed at County Hall and given a place at Honor Oak School; Mavis Wadley had started there at the beginning of the academic year, in September, 1938, she helped me to settle in, but my other friends were scattered: we were not to know then, how long and how true our friendship would prove to be: "Through all the changing scenes of life". I remember my first impression of that pleasing, redbrick building, set beside Peckham Rye Park in green fields through which ran the little, tree-lined River Peck; I remember too, its attractive library and busy quadrangle.

The first day was nearly over when I was summoned by the headmistress, Miss Ashley, to her study and I was relieved to be dismissed after a few encouraging words from that august lady. There were ten minutes to go before school ended, when I could go home. It was bright and cold that January day of 1939, and as I wandered about outside, I came across an enclosed garden, full of beds of dormant roses, and walking down a narrow path discovered a large sundial, on which was inscribed:-

"This garden was planted in memory of the fallen in the Great War, 1914-1918"

> *The kiss of the sun for pardon,*
> *The song of the birds for mirth,*
> *One is nearer to God's heart in a garden*
> *Than anywhere else on earth*

I stood a moment alone in that quiet place, realising that this was a new and very different world from the comfortably confined one which I had known, but at the same time I felt that I could cope, and get enjoyment from it too; on the whole the future appeared bright and inviting.

The sun dropped, I retraced my steps, passing two prefects deep in conversation, so mature and assured, would I ever be like that?. No use wondering, the possibility was an eternity away - and who could tell what would happen in the intervening years?

Appendix 1
Electoral Roll Entries
(Seen at Lewisham Local History Library, 1990, to check that the names mentioned were correct.)

1924   Waller Road
- 131   Mr. & Mrs. Thring
- 123   Mr. & Mrs. Elias

Erlanger Road
- 54   Miss Emily Lyon
  Miss Barbara Lyon

1930   Waller Road
- 131   Helen Harriet Blundell (Juror)
  Millicent Blundell
  (though she did not live there then)
  John George Barker
  Maude Frances Barker
  Robert William O'Sullivan
  Ninian Reid
  George Wiggins

- 129   Mr. Cook
  Mrs. Cook
  Bertie Shuttleworth
  Rosina Shuttleworth

- 123   Mr. Elias
  Mrs. Elias

Erlanger Road
- 54   Emily Lyon
  Barbara Lyon

Appendix 2
Names of Waller Road School Children

Marjorie Grindley
Winnie Smith (about 141 Waller Road)
Jackie Ryde (167 Waller Road)
Joyce & Betty Ovenden (155 Waller Road)
Ellen Dearden (52 Waller Road)
Mavis Wadley
Daphne Mudge
Pat Sterne (Pepys Road)
Margery Sharpe
Albert Reynolds (Big ears)
Joseph Collins (Very poor)
Cornelius Cameron (Known as Corny)
Mary Blair Black (Smut specialist)
Pat Coombs
Rita LaTuskie
Vera Roffey
Terry Morley
Myer Zargcharkra (Orthodox Jew)
Anthea Williams (Dennets Road)
Iris Burwood (Dennets Road)
Jack ? Green
Vernon Isom

BOOK 2 - The Forties
Evacuation

I cannot think that anyone living anywhere in Europe in 1939 did not have their life radically changed by the outbreak and subsequent events of World War II. With hindsight, many things which I did, or took part in during that year, I did for the last time. Some of these events I felt no regret over, and others, being twelve, I would have put behind me in any case. Obviously there were no more *Bonfire Nights*, a faint regret?. I think Dad enjoyed them more than I did, my feet got cold and damp waiting for him to light the next firework, he always indulged in a few, Roman candles, Boy Scout Rousers and a couple of Catherine Wheels and Rockets, but the bonfire waxed hot and glowing, wonderful to stand near. It was fun helping to make the guy, and propping him on top of the carefully prepared mound of old wood and sticks, but always, as I watched his misshapen body collapse into the fiery furnace and saw his mask-face topple forward, a flicker of horror ran through me; he looked so life-like. Long ago this was done to real people, now, I believed, we were not so cruel.

I have already said that henceforth Christmases and holidays were totally different, and Easter,1939 was to be the last time Dad and I set out early to buy Hot Cross Buns, really hot and fresh from the bakers, which we had done ever since I could remember, one for each of us, we ate them straight away, dripping with melting butter, *delicious*, light, spicey and full of fruit. Easter morning Mum always picked flowers from the garden - whatever there was, flowering currant, one or two daffodils and wallflowers, to put fresh on the breakfast table (this was the only time), and we had a boiled egg each, on which I drew faces. Usually I was given two or three Easter Eggs; I liked best those decorated with sprays of coloured sugar flowers, then Nell gave me a small one, its pretty designed silver-paper concealing its crazy-paving patterned chocolate. I might get one from one of the lodgers, once at least I was given a cardboard one, pale blue with pink flowers, lace edging and a cluster of tiny, fluffy golden chicks inside. Mother and I always went to Meeting on Easter Sunday, irrespective of whether it was her *turn* to take me out or not, and we would return home gladdened by joyful ministry of the Resurrection. Easter Monday was unfailingly the same too; we went to Blackheath Fair, crowded, noisy, wonderful mechanical music, all rumbustious gusto. I rode on donkeys, won a coconut, rolled pennies - but never, ever went on any sort of roundabout after my one horrendous go years back, when after an eternity, the machine ground slowly to a halt, and I staggered away, giddy, faint and was violently sick.

I remember my last visit to my Grandparents in Kennington, a sweltering day in August, but cool in their semi-basement, always so neat and spic and span. They sat, upright and remote from me, poor, long-suffering Grandma and older, eighty-year-old Grandad, with his observant, pale blue eyes and bristling grey moustache. I helped Lily make the tea in the scullery, she was always so friendly and bright, and we laughed at her father's cut-throat razor hanging menacingly by its old leather strap from a hook beside the shallow stone sink. She took me upstairs, out on to a parapet and showed me a large lead tank - the house was Georgian - it was decorated and inscribed "1793". Banging the table rhythmically with his stained yellow knife handle, Grandad sang out in his uneven, determined voice - against a chorus of, "Oh shut up Dad, they don't want to hear that - we're talking about Girlie, she might have to be evacuated" - his ancient ditty:

"Every night I smoke my hookah
Eat my dulwah every day,
Night time comes make plenty Pujah
Sing BRITANNIA RULES THE WAVES!.

Grandad Barker, born 1855, had served as a drummer in the Royal Fusiliers in India from 1871-8. *The best years of my life,* he'd say. I was never to see Grandad again, or visit the house in Delverton Road; he died just one year later, and soon after, the house, with many others in the area, was demolished by a bomb.

War first became a reality to me during the Munich crisis of September,1938, the Germans had invaded Austria earlier in the year (March,1938), now they had annexed part of Czechoslovakia and we were all fitted with gas-masks; wearing one was hateful, and even now any rubber smell, such as that of a hot-water bottle, puts me in mind of *them*. It became obvious during the summer term of 1939 that evacuation was to take place as soon as war was declared, it was felt to be inevitable. We were issued with lists of essential clothing to take with us - goodbye to Aunt Nell's straight flannelette nighties, feather stitching round the neck, linen buttons and all - I was taken to Jones and Higgens and bought two pairs of interlock cream pyjamas, one edged with pink the other with turquoise. Liberty bodices, and skirts made to button on to a bodice were now a thing of the past, but I was well supplied with new ribbed knitted vests for the coming winter; cotton ones were worn year round, next to the skin, to absorb sweat.

I have heard that in some cases evacuation proved a disaster, and on the surface, I suppose, mine was just that. With hindsight I realise that the total experience, lasting barely nine months, taught me a great deal, which otherwise might have taken years. I learned to survive alone, not physically, of course, but independent of my family. War had always been in the background of my life, and now, at twelve-and- a-half it was to affect me personally.

ALL SMILES: But for some the journey would be a nightmare

We were told to report at Honor Oak School on Thursday 1st. September at 8 a.m., with our Mothers. Mavis Wadley and I were in the same class and kept together, not knowing what in the least to expect; everyone was tense, the Mothers crying, us girls all scrubbed clean, neat in our winter school uniforms, and wearing large name labels. Our basic belongings were carried in small canvas knapsacks, some of us carried little attache cases marked clearly with identity number as well as name; we had packets of sandwiches, and of course, the hateful gasmasks - slung on our shoulders in natty cases. We were led in crocodile formation about three miles to Honor Oak Station, where we were put on a train to Redhill, Surrey. No-one knew our destination until we arrived, in case spies found out, and I was none the wiser then, having never heard of the place.

After being given mugs of cocoa and buns at a reception centre, run by the W.V.S., we were given a card to fill in to tell our parents where we were. Then each was presented with a large block of Cadbury's Milk Chocolate, and Mavis and I were sent to a pleasant billet with a Mr. and Mrs. Rainger at a house in "The Frenches", a row of small, dark red brick cottages set beside a large pond. A quiet backwater of a busy town; the little lake rippled in the breeze and round its boggy, squelchy rim, horse-chestnuts bobbed, ancient, black and bloated; we would reach into the mud, pick them out and jump on them - bursting they emitted a most vile stench. An enormous yew tree dipped its feathery branches in the water's lapping edge, most of its berries eaten by birds, but others fell, like the chestnuts, into stagnant recesses of the pond, bubbling in the dark corners with foul gases.

We were comparatively happy, it was better than we feared; the Raingers were well intentioned and kept a well ordered home; being so young we could not appreciate the full impact of our being there, how we had disturbed their tranquil lives. (We were quiet and well-behaved, but what a job they had taken on!.) I recall so clearly us all sitting solemnly round the living room table that Sunday morning, listening to Neville Chamberlain's speech on the radio, telling us, and the world, that we were now at war. There followed panic at the subsequent wail of the air-raid siren rising and falling, never to be forgotten sound, when everyone rushed into a communal shelter, wondering what on earth would happen. Nothing did, it was a solitary instance.

We settled down to a routine at Reigate County Grammar School, sharing with the indigenous pupils, alternating mornings one week, afternoons the next. A mistake had been made, we from Honor Oak should have been billeted at Reigate, but St. Dunstan's boys had been sent there, they therefore had to journey daily to Redhill where the boy's school was, while we made our way to Reigate, by bus.

Mavis and I shared a bedroom, and after we were presumed asleep, would creep daringly along a dark passsage to an empty room used as an apple store - filled with rows of freshly picked, deliciously scented apples, set out on tables and boxes. We'd grab some and tip-toe back along the creaking boards, hearts racing, stifling our giggles, triumphant and gay. We crunched through several, carefully wrapping up the cores in a hanky, to be thrown away in the street next morning, and dropped happily to sleep.

Bent on adventure, we purchased a copy of a frightful rag entitled, *Red Star*, a magazine published on newsprint and illustrated with crude line drawings. It was advertised with a *free lipstick;* I think it was 2d. and we paid half each. It contained stories such as neither of us had come across before, one I remember was, *Seven Secret Nights*, the tale of a girl whose sister went off with another fella, but whose brother-in-law was sent home from battle blinded; as she had always been in love with him, she hadn't the heart to tell him her sister had run off, and as he could not see, she pretended to be her. It was a serial, we bought two, then circumstances changed, so we never knew what happened in the end; daring for us, then, but I suppose very milk and water stuff to modern twelve year olds!. Slushy rubbish, but no anatomical details.

There was one particular thing we hated; the nearest way to the bus stop was past a large army camp filled with Canadian soldiers. The filth these slobs called out to us I will not repeat; fortunately we did not then fully understand what these remarks meant, but the manner and attitude of these pigs so upset us, that, feeling under threat, we took to walking to our destination by a much longer route, circumnavigating the camp.

Our parents took it in turns to visit us at weekends, they explained where dull and featureless Redhill was, took us out to lunch and tea; but it was so contrived, there was nowhere to just be yourself. For a treat they took us to the pictures; I don't think I saw one film I liked, (or was it the circumstance?), "Wizard of Oz", a Laurel & Hardy, and "Shipyard Sally" with Gracie Fields come to mind.

This comparatively blissful existence was short-lived; one day, about the middle of October, Mavis and I arrived home, and there was Mr. Rainger crying dreadfully. "She's pulled up all my lovely asters", he gulped. It was awful - I'd never seen a man cry before, and it seemed such a silly thing to cry over, better be angry; after all the flowers set along the front wall had been gorgeous, but now they were fading fast. We muttered something and went up to our room, upset and embarrassed. Three or four days later, the billeting officer came to us at school and told us that she would take us to new billets that same afternoon as Mr.Rainger had been taken to hospital with pneumonia and was not expected to live.

It was a blow; Mavis and I were separated and sent to nearby houses on a council estate. Mavis's hosts were fine, but mine were bad. The man of the house was away in the army, stationed at Chichester, "Chi", as they called it, and mother and daughter were tarts who entertained Canadians from the nearby camp. They got quite a lot of money and presents, it was a new world to me. I was totally disoriented and did not know how to deal with the situation. They thought me peculiar, said I could do well - I ought to enjoy life, they said. I went up to my room to do homework in the evening, there was no heat, Mrs. Perry and Pat always "entertained" in the evening in the only room containing a fire. I pushed a table across my door, afraid of someone bursting in, but slept all right once in bed. Pat was about fifteen, looked twenty, heavily made-up; every Saturday she went to Woolworths to pinch things, displayed some of her loot and matter-of-factly invited me to join in the fun; I was out of my depth, but hoped to cope. I thought this was nothing compared with actual involvement in fighting, there were things of universal importance going on; later, I realised that I would have caused less nuisance had I involved others with my problem in the first place, and had I been a year or so older would have acted differently.

I had reached puberty while at Mrs. Rainger's and although, having a sensible Mother, I was prepared for it, it is always something of an ordeal at first. However, I dealt with that capably, but towards the middle of November began to feel low, but never told anyone. When my parents came down, about November 18th., a Sunday, I was coughing and they imagined that I had a bad cold, Mother thought I looked "washed out", and insisted she put me to bed and we all thought I would be better by morning. But it dragged on, my legs felt like lead, I couldn't breath properly, but I couldn't stay in that house, I had to get to school. I hid my unwellness, believing it would pass, Mavis got worried, I developed painful red swellings on my arms and shins. It went on for over a week, and finally unable to breath without coughing and in a raging fever I collapsed at my desk. Every thing now is blurred; I remember concerned girls, a teacher full of consternation, a big armchair by a gas fire in the headmistress's room, then being carried on a stretcher in an ambulance, covered with a red blanket, then... nothing.

Hospital

I know Mother and Dad came to visit me regularly, but it is hard to remember; what comes to mind? The first night, noticing a hot stiff blanket; "it's electric" they said; I had never heard of such a thing. I had no pillows and lay quite flat; a cage was put over my legs to keep the pressure of blankets off the intensely tender swellings. Being fed with a feeder; the nurses were remarkably skilful and patient at pouring fluid down my throat; it took a long time. Automatically my hand came up to control the "feeder", I much preferred it, and the nurses didn't mind, but sometimes Sister took on the job herself and would gently but firmly restrain me; "Just keep your arms quite still", she'd say, "I'll not pour too quickly, just relax". I can see her face now; small fine features, clear, serious, happy hazel eyes; so quiet and positive, decisive and responsible, the ward ran on oiled wheels; Sister Meredith.

The first thing I recall clearly is Christmas, they decorated my bedhead, so that looking up I could see the pretty baubles, and gave me, to my disgust, a doll, with beautifully knitted clothes, but of course I was too old for such. And then a lovely memory; it was dark and outside, the Salvation Army band started to play carols; one of the nurses came and told me about it, "A pity you can't sit up and see them", she said, "But in a little while you'll get a nice surprise". I closed my eyes, the carolling went on and on, coming nearer and nearer, I looked and saw a lantern being held towards me, throwing its warm, golden light over my bed. A group of nurses, their cloaks worn bright red inside out, joined by several students and doctors were walking the wards carol singing; accompanied by a

135

musical instrument or two, they had paused and gathered round my bed. That is the first thing I remember clearly and can see, and it still has power to lift my spirits.

Once I was allowed a pillow and to use my arms, things improved greatly, I could feed myself and eat proper food - no more runny white of egg being spooned willy-nilly into my mouth!. About the first egg I fed myself with; it was placed neatly on my bed table with bread and butter, but as I took the spoon to crack it, noticed, *Mrs. Wenham,* pencilled on the shell. I called Nurse back. "This isn't mine", I said, eggs were gifts. "No dear", she explained, "We gave it to you for a treat, Mrs. Wenham died in the night". "But she sat and talked to me only yesterday"; she realised my shock; "It was sudden, yes, but when you've been here as long as I have, you learn to take it in your stride dear, and you know it's the best way too". I didn't want that egg any more; I wished they'd rubbed the name off; but it was kindly meant; I forced it down. Some food, like tapioca pudding made with water, I contrived to keep in a bag in my locker (now I could use it), until Mum came, and she obligingly took it away.

Memories of that time are confused, but it could not have been long before I was allowed two pillows for part of the day, and then I could read, using a device for holding books attached to the bed table. I slept better, not waking in the night to see the night nurse on her rounds, or lie watching her as she sat at the table, working by a dimmed lamp, near to my bed. For after about two months, I was moved away from the seriously ill, down to the "Sun Parlour", a sort of apse at the far end of the ward, light and airy with long windows all round, partitioned off from the rest of the ward by permanent glass screens. It was a women's surgical ward, I was too old for the children's ward, and it wasn't considered necessary to change me to the medical department - there had been no room in there when I was admitted.

Interest awoke to the life going on around me, in the other patients, it became totally absorbing. For certain periods of time, other young people were in the sun parlour; I have vivid memories of Doreen Smith, we were good friends. At fourteen, only a year older than me, she was a servant in a big house in Horley, and in stepping back had fallen on to a paraffin heater, which had burst into flames. She had third degree burns on her back and buttocks and was brought in in agony; as I write I hear her screams and sedated moans and cries; continuing for some days and nights. We were moved up into the sun parlour about the same time, our beds next to one another; poor girl, I thought. Painted all over with purple, her entire trunk protected by a long cage, her feet kept warm with a bottle, she could only lie on her stomach ever. To use the bedpan she had to stand up, a screen was always drawn round, of course, but sometimes there was a gap - I turned away - it seemed just awful, all movement gave intense pain, and the twice daily dressings were a nightmare. As if that wasn't enough, more than once the burns turned septic, the smell was sickening, and she was transferred to the isolation ward. She went away before me, being sent to another hospital, possibly for skin grafting. We wrote once or twice, but lost touch, we had little in common really.

Another inmate of the sun parlour was Jewel Taylor, a tap dancing girl from a circus, about the same age as Doreen, but sophisticated and sharp, recovering from a bout of double pneumonia. Very perky she became, sitting in a chair between our beds, yarning away, prinking in a little mirror at her frizzed, dyed hair, twiddling away at her earrings. Towards the end of her stay she would tie her dressing gown tight and cockily display a few of her "routines", concentrating solemnly on the banal words and syncopated rhythms. She livened us all up - a creature from a different world. We sang together:

Whistle while you work
Snowhite made a shirt
Hitler wore it
Chamberlain tore it
Whistle while you work

If I remember rightly, this room held five or six beds, patients continually came and went, but I remained by the glass screen, through which, once I was allowed to sit up with the aid of the support frame, I could view most of the outer ward. For a long time, in the bed on the further side of the screen, was a lady with an internal complaint. This involved her swallowing a long length of rubber tubing, and after having got it right down, pulling it back up again before each meal. I couldn't take my eyes off it, for although she was sheltered by a screen, I found that by sitting unobtrusively at a certain angle, I could observe the process clearly from behind, without her being aware of me.

Just two others I would like to mention; Miss Nita Moon, who in her thirties, had had the same number of operations for cancer, she told me, as years. She impressed me greatly, for the thought of one operation frightened me, but more than thirty!. It was beyond imagining; and she was so un-self-pitying, so cheerful and outgoing, above all interested in so many things. Rarely speaking of herself, she would come and sit with me, would talk of nature and geology, lend me well illustrated books which caught my imagination, on

138

fossils, wildflowers, British birds and creatures, and the formation of our land, mountains, rivers, rocks and hills.

Lastly Trudi the same age as me, dark, pale, Jewish Austrian. Living in England only a few months, she had little English and was in any case disinclined to say much.

Naturally, I had heard of the persecution of the Jews by the nazis, now it was to be made manifest. She could get up and walk about, but would sit on her bed for long periods of time, staring into space; the nurses were kind and worried about her. Trudi had been put on a train by desperate relatives in an attempt to save her, after her parents had been rounded up and taken away by the gestapo. They were successful, but her youthful zest and joy in life had gone, and she subsequently developed diabetes; Sister made an inspired effort to involve her in things. One day she explained to Trudi that they were short staffed, would she help? could she brush and comb Doreen's and my hair?. She did, dully and half-heartedly at first, and then haltingly telling me of her pity for Doreen's plight. And so, during the ensuing weeks, she gained in confidence, several of the women asked her if she would be so kind as to do their hair?. It certainly helped a little; gradually incidents in her life of suffering came out, there were floods of tears and, fortunately, anger, but I was aware that unspeakable occurrences lay beneath her words, too painful to utter or be remembered. Her English improved enormously as well as her condition, and finally she went away with the loving, practical Jewish woman who had sometimes visited her. We exchanged a postcard or two, then I heard no more, but the cruel demoralising, agonizing experiences imparted to me by that girl in the spring of 1940, haunted me for a very long time, opened up to me

139

the insoluble problems of good and evil, and coloured my attitude to the German nation for the rest of my life.

It seemed my life was otherwise cocooned from events in the outer world, by the day to day busyness and the emotional life of the ward itself, its cures, its not infrequent deaths, its proudly upheld discipline and strict routine. We were awakened by the clanging and crashing entry of the bedpan trolley at 5.30 a.m., then washed, although once well enough, a bowl of warm water was placed on the locker and I washed my own hands and face, but blanket baths were given practically every afternoon. We were drinking cups of tea by six o'clock - no hanging about - but I never adjusted to waking at that ungodly hour; lights were out at eight p.m. I should mention that of course the blackout had to be rigidly observed, the many high window frames had been fitted with battens down either side, into which the existing roller blinds neatly fitted, in addition the lighting was kept very dim.

The staff changed over at 7 a.m., and the day nurses gave us our breakfast; then followed the taking of temperatures, changing of dressings, distribution of medicines and the charting of bowel movements, when, if we admitted to being "not regular", plentiful doses of liquid paraffin were meted out. Injections were given, beds stripped and remade, women wheeled out to the operating theatre, others brought back in, vomiting painfully for hours into the patiently held "receivers". New patients were admitted, sometimes dramatically, while the first bustle of the day being over, the ward-maids entered in their blue overalls, to begin their daily routine of mopping, dusting and polishing every surface, nook and cranny. The paper man did his round about this time every day, and three times a week a woman came round with a trolley loaded with toiletries, sweets and other goodies - doing quite a good trade. Lying on my back those first few weeks I was totally unaware of the continuous hubbub of life going on around me, but once sitting up, I realised how little time there was to relax, a little quiet after twelve o'clock dinner and that was about all.

Towards the end of my stay, along with other able patients, I was shown how to make dressings of various shapes and sizes from gauze and cottonwool, in order to build up a stock for the emergency which loomed ahead. Our instructress was a "Fanny" nurse, First Aid Nursing Yeomanry. Some of the "real" nurses made fun of her, especially one with a quick temper and sarcastic turn of phrase, partly because of her aristocratic manner and refined speech, a little perhaps, because of her distinctive uniform. Whatever the reason, I felt quite angry on her behalf, for in spite of her outward austere reserve, she really was shy, was keen on the work, and tried hard to fit in.

A pair of earphones was available, but the reception was so bad, that I rarely bothered. There was an old wind-up gramophone on a table at our end of the ward - away from those more seriously ill, and now and again one of the patients would put on a few records, the hardworking nurses were always too busy; the stock of records available was minimal, and those few were rough and worn, spilling out their distorted sounds jerkily as the spring went down, and gathering speed as it was rewound. Favourites were, Tauber singing "Call, call, Vienna mine", "Any Umbrellas", "I'm gonna hang out the washing on the Siegfried line" and "She'll be coming round the mountain", and there were Bing Crosby,

Arthur Askey and George Formby; but it is particularly the first four that conjure up visions of that ward for me.

I cannot remember how frequently, but at least once a week Matron visited each ward, deliberately unexpectedly, but the nurses always seemed to find out a little beforehand. Immediately word went round, a rush of intense activity - "Matron's coming, quick" - bedpans were hurried out to the sluice, however desperate you were you had to wait until the visit was over, and even if she was delayed you had to "hang on". Bedclothes were tweaked into place precisely and tucked in as tight as a strait-jacket. "Don't move a muscle!", we were told, and we didn't. Flowers, which were tended by the probationers daily, were re-inspected, as was each locker and the temperature charts hanging at the foot of each bed. We just lay there, waiting - anyone who was up was rapidly shoved back into bed - and a hush fell upon all. Finally the ward doors opened, nurses stood to attention, Matron was ushered in by Sister; a tiny, erect figure, I recall, dressed completely in navy blue and black; long black veil falling gracefully in folds behind her, followed by a retinue, obviously in certain hierarchy, of doctors, surgeons, and so on. Majestically this Empress of a little empire walked steadily down the ward, pausing to speak to each patient in turn and remark on them as she thought fit. It was impressive, everyone appreciated it, it was an occasion, fit, right and proper. When it was over we breathed a sigh of relief, the ward sprang to life once more, and nobody would have wished any of it otherwise.

I mentioned Matron's dress; the nurses' uniforms were a source of continual interest, their differing caps denoting status and qualification as did their various badges and belts, the elaborate buckles composed of symbols and emblems of their original hospitals and cities, some quite expensive. Being in a surgical ward, the Doctor usually came only to see me, others were attended by a Mr.! As I recovered, and remembered things more clearly, he saw me less often, but he was kind, sincere and never patronising to me. I wasn't at all keen on it, but for the first couple of months I was a subject of interest to students. He would punctiliously ask if he could use me as a classic example of pericarditis and erithema nodosum; I don't know what would have happened if I had refused. I did as was expected and agreed, not minding much, just a little. Keeping the covers up to my waist, with great decorum, nurse undid the tapes at the back of the short, dull pink shirt I wore and removed it, sitting beside me all the time, while solemn-faced students were invited to listen to my heart-beat. With professional detachment, the doctor drew a line on my chest to show that the heart beat *beyond the nipple line*. The swellings on my shins were an added attraction. I began, as I have said, to feel a lot better in the New Year, and one day as they were all taking turns at listening to my heart pumping away, I suddenly asked, *Can I hear it too?. I would like to hear my own heart beating, I never have.* Surprised but indulgent, *Certainly*, he answered, and placed the stethoscope into my ears. I was amazed, it was so loud, like the roaring of an engine and the rushing of the sea combined. That was the last time the students accompanied him on his visit to me.

Who else did I see? Visiting hours were rigidly adhered to; apart from those on the danger list, they were Sundays and Wednesdays only, from 2-4pm. My parents never missed a Sunday, catching a train from New Cross, eating their sandwiches in the comfortless Visitors" Centre, set up in a church hall for the use of evacuees and their parents, where cups of tea were available. Enjoying the full two hours with me, replenishing supplies of fruit, a little money and something to read, they would turn to wave cheerfully at the ward doors as they left, and I never cried or was upset at their going, but reassured and satisfied by their company. Just once they were late, it was a long and bitter winter, with heavy snow, a landslip had blocked Merstham tunnel and they had to travel the rest of the way by bus. In any case they always had to take the bus out to Earlswood Common.

Then Aunt Nell came every two or three weeks on a Wednesday, often bringing a nice cake of special soap or talcum powder, "Something to make you smell nice", she'd say. Mill accompanied her once, and presented me with two old books, one of Dickens, the other Mrs. Henry Wood; I remember thinking, "She never gets it right", - she'd not changed her attitude from the weekly pre-war visits, when her motto was, " I don't believe in bringing you anything, you ought to love me for myself alone". A tall order, I thought, but that was her unwavering philosophy. Sweets I didn't need, she said; no, but it was nice to show others your gifts, to share your little delicacies, flowers and magazines as they did with me. Nell, Mother and Dad knew this, why not Mill?. She was not hard-up. On one visit, shortly before my discharge, Mother told me that my dear darling dog Patsy had run away and presumably been gathered up with other strays and put to sleep, a war-time contingency. I was greatly upset, I loved her very much, I would send her little notes; a collie, she had been sent to us on a train from Macclesfield by the Sheldons, discovered on an outlying farm. She arrived an ill-treated bag of bones; but I loved her, took her out on my own to the park, and set the waves in her lovely brown coat with hair-grips.

144

Rarely, someone else came, one of the mistresses visited three or four times, with some work! I appreciated their bothering, but school work proved impossible, and they were so overburdened themselves they could not really help me. On one occasion my form mistress brought Mavis with her, but I was not well enough to appreciate it, and soon after, Mavis was taken home to London by her parents. A vicar arrived once, early on, and leaning over me muttered stilted phrases of hope, and promised to send, "a kind lady to read to me". She came soon after; she appeared to me extremely odd, loudly intoning several long, inscrutable psalms, ending in a booming, "O Selah!" I went to sleep, she poked me awake, "Shall I come again? Would you like to hear some more?" she asked. "No thank you", I said, and went back to sleep. A Quaker called two or three times, but I felt it was her *duty*. I had attended Reigate Meeting, and the second time the Sweetmans took Mavis and me back to lunch, but I cannot say that I enjoyed it much, they were naturally reticent, hard to come near.

Nell wrote to me every week, and I received letters from other people as the months went by. On my thirteenth birthday, not a visiting day, a lot of the nurses signed a card to give to me, as did my fellow patients in the sun-lounge, to put with those that came by post; I remember thinking that it was the oddest birthday I had spent so far; strange that I seemed to have no worries, not about myself, my family nor the world in general, certainly not about my school work. However, I missed privacy, and missed it sorely; amid the general noise and commotion, hustle and bustle, I thought wistfully of the everyday quiet of my home, and the solitude I could find there. As I settled to sleep each night, I held in mind my family, pictured what they were doing, and said a simple prayer; words sprang unbidden, "My help cometh from the Lord, who made Heaven and earth", which flowed comfortingly on to the end of the psalm, one of the few learned by heart at Waller Road school, and which, at Mother's behest, I had repeated to her many times. It must have helped for I slept soundly and at peace.

Soon after my birthday I was got up and sat in a chair, it was quite shocking, I couldn't walk - I'd never considered that. Looking down at my legs I saw that they were just skin-covered bones which would not function. After a while my pulse was taken and found to be faulty, it still had a "thrill" (tachycardia), they said. I would have to spend more time in bed. I was disappointed and depressed, above all I wanted to go to the toilet, use the bathroom myself - five months of bedpans and blanket baths was more than enough, and I did so want to get dressed, put on something nice and normal. Before getting me back to bed, Sister helped me into a wheelchair and took me to a window; all that time I had only seen the sky, distantly through windows, sky in all its moods, certainly, and plenty of it - but now - how stunning it was to look out at the dark green shapes of trees and bushes, to see again stretches of green, green grass. The continuous heavy rain of the past few days was over and gone, the dark clouds had lifted; there in the foreground two dogs chased wildly; and in the distance, in the pure sunlight, were people, and signs of a distant Easter Fair, while straight and slim, rising heavenward to the right of this enchanting scene rose the spire of St. John's church. That was the moment that, inside myself, I rebelled; I wanted to get out there, to walk on that newly washed grass, to feel the warm sun and the sharp blustering air, to be free.

Three weeks later, circumstances beyond my control - or that of the doctors, made it imperative for me to be just that. The Maginot Line that we had so surely and carelessly assumed to be impregnable, had been outflanked, our troops were rapidly retreating towards Dunkirk. As many beds as possible were needed for the returning wounded, as I was receiving no treatment, out I must go, quick. My parents were informed and asked to provide transport, none being available. It was May 20th. Mother arrived at my bed with a case of clothes and helped me to dress, nurses got me into a wheelchair and took me down in the lift, and there were Dad and Uncle Tom to help me into his car. I sat sideways in the back, with my legs on Mum's lap, covered with a blanket, and burst into tears, that started Mother off and we both had a good howl. It was the tension, you see; I was so overjoyed at going home, but the reason was tragic, we were well aware of how desperately things had gone wrong and didn't know what would happen next - though we could guess; and Mother had no idea of how soon I should be really well again.

I have dwelt on my hospital experience partly because things are so different now-a-days, partly because of its effect on me; I have sometimes wondered why I only look back on it with some pride and affection, never regret or resentment. I call to mind the many people with whom I came in contact, observing a probationer nurse crying and being led firmly away from her first experience of death; the gentle sorrowing of relatives of departed old folk and the bitter distress of a husband whose young wife had died of whiteleg. Amazingly little complaining, plenty of joy and good humour, as well as acceptance and anxiety, and clearly called to mind, the light-hearted, excited chatter of young nurses telling me about their boy-friends and the lives they led outside the hospital walls; all the basic, eternal ingredients of humanity were there, living and evolving under my very eyes.

Summer 1940

For me personally it was a lovely summer, hot, sunny and full of promise; for the outside world it was dark indeed. Not surprisingly I was made a fuss of, Dr.Govan, who had helped to bring me into the world, called every week, and suggested I spend as much time as possible in the garden in a deckchair Dad had bought which had a canopy, arms and leg-rest; it was considered an indulgence and cost 8/6d. Mother would cover it with an old blanket, and I, nothing loath, acceded delightedly to the doctor's suggestion and was soon able to walk out there, with help.

A neighbour lent Mum a Bathchair! I laugh now to think of it, but at the time revelled in the attention I attracted; Mother was game; twice she pushed me all along Evelina Rd., to the Co-op at Nunhead Green. We went that way not only because it was flat, but because of the old associations it had for her; she showed me her old schoolhouse, and took me into Ellis Thompson's shop opposite the Co-op.

This uncompromising Quaker, a vegetarian, who never wore shoes because made of *leather*, cobbled himself up bandage-like bundles and stomped around in those; I saw he had not changed his ways one tittle. We also went in that direction because all her life she was a fanatical Co-oper- they all were, but she was the worst, so she never bought anything from Thompson's shop, except maybe a packet of custard powder. I'd never liked that walk, so the second time urged her to go on to to Peckham Rye, to Austin's, which she valiantly did, and I scrambled out of my "conveyance", poked about, and I came across a pair of sparkling, dazzling ornaments. "What are they, they're so beautiful", I exclaimed, tentatively putting out a finger to touch one. "They're Lustres" Mum explained. "Horrid things: Mother had a pair – bright pink danglers, so hard to wash and keep clean. She was very proud of them but when she died we rapidly got rid of them". Subject closed; that was that. How sad, I thought, what a pity; I would love a Lustre. However we did buy a book for 1d. – "Comic Verse" by Tom Hood. Old woodcuts.

"A cannon ball blew off his legs
So he laid down his arms"

Hilarious stuff when you are 12.

We enjoyed that outing, but she was knackered by the time we got back, and glad of the dinner Nell had ready. "I'm not doing that again", she told me, "Or it'll be me that's the invalid". I wanted to be taken up to my much loved park, so a few days later Nell and Mum together, rather reluctantly yet with great good humour pushed me up there. It was a beautiful day and I got a lot of pleasure from it, but coming back, down that short, steep hill proved rather too much even for them, and the Bathchair was returned to its owner.

At last Mother got really fed up with the sight of me lying around being waited on; apart from my legs I really looked the picture of health - and it was her opinion that my legs would atrophy altogether if I never used them. "All this molly-coddling won't do you any good at all". "Go to the lavatory", she'd say, "You can't just slink in and out of bed using the pot forever". The doctor seemed to agree, couldn't think that it would do me any harm, and after six weeks or so, apart from long rests, I was going about the house normally, and felt fine.

Dad was not only worried about the war situation, but was preoccupied with his work at the Salt Company; Mr.

Seddon, the founder's grandson had got through his entire inheritance and the company was in jeopardy. It was saved by being bought up by Bumstead's, Dad's job was secured, although he never, for any reason, stayed away from work for fear of being replaced, he also felt it imperative to keep his communist opinions to himself, but then he always had. His work increased greatly during the war years, as, in addition to salt, the company sold oil, which was rationed, entailing much extra work. Every morning, all his working life, on leaving home he'd say, "Teeth, keys, fags, matches, handkerchief, money and watch". I chanted it with him and teased him about it. "Better than forgetting", he'd say, and repeat the story of how "Old Cotton" had arrived at work with no teeth. About this time he enrolled as a part-time Air-Raid Warden, and went on courses one evening a week at Waller Road School; but all was quiet in London, nothing happened.

For sometime now my life was spent almost exclusively among adults, I did not notice this, after all I had been reared amongst them, but Mother thought it would be nice if I could spend some time with girls of my own age. She asked around, but not one of my old school friends was living in the area any more; "How about Anthea Williams?", I suggested. "Well, she got rheumatic fever", Mum replied. "Oh, good, we could talk about it, is she home yet?" I asked. "No", answered Mother, looking down; "She died". Until that moment I had never understood what a serious illness I had had; for the first time the full implication of it hit me. Unbidden the unanswerable question arose in my mind - why Anthea - not me? That is why I remember her name.

I would have liked some school work then, but any teachers there may have been in the area were far too busy to approach. Mum got me books from the New Cross Library, I actually read some Dickens, and every day she would get me to read to her - poetry mostly, which I preferred, sometimes the Bible, while she continued with the household chores. Her choice of poetry was broad and various and I became acquainted with most of the Oxford Book of English Poetry, but was not confined to it by any means. The Bible was another matter; I could not relate to it, and could find little merit in some the most spellbinding stories. They were all foreign; even Jesus; "I wish he was an Englishman," I said, "Then I might understand him better ", Mother was not amused. She found an old French text book which we enjoyed working at together, and I drew, knitted and did some embroidery - traycloths and cushion covers were currently popular.

However, what I was doing, how I progressed at that time was of account only to myself and immediate family. Events on the Continent were so momentous that even I hardly heeded how I spent my days. For very soon after returning home I picked up the newspaper from the front doormat to see in banner headlines, "PARIS FALLS" (14th. June, 1940). I remember it so well, my stomach turned over. So many cities had fallen to the Nazi juggernaut - but if PARIS had fallen - then could London? It sounds ridiculous, but a surge of conviction swept through me; it must never, we shall not let it. I now know that this vital wave of assurance and determination swept through the whole nation; we were a united people with a common mission in life. I lived among ordinary, unpretentious people, by nature restrained, we did not speak easily of what we felt in our hearts, but we knew that everything we valued and held most dear was at stake; the collapse of Europe before the all-powerful living evil of the Nazi Wehrmacht must stop *here*.

The fall of Paris was followed by the retreat to Dunkirk; I cannot remember it without a thrill running down my spine. Reports of it abound, and I cannot go into it here, but we listened to the wireless all day long, moved with wonder and pride at those who sailed across the Channel in an attempt, often in vain, to save their compatriots. Those seamen who survived the continuous aerial attacks, dive bombing and machine gunning from the merciless Luftwaffe, went back again and again, and succeeded in rescuing thousands who waited helpless on the beaches, wading in the shallows and straggling, waiting their turn to board ship, in the fields and lanes, while the German army drove them on before their tanks and guns.

Everyone was aware of what would happen next; the Germans always used saturation bombing to break down the will of a nation in order that capitulation to their domination would be swift and easy. The Channel Islands were already occupied, and I remember a sea battle near Norway, involving the Scharnhorst and the Gneisenau.

All the main London buildings were by now sandbagged, public brick air raid shelters stood at the roadsides, there was a large one on the corner of Waller Rd., and Queens Rd., beneath the wall where the First World War shrine had hung. We had an Anderson shelter dug at the bottom of the garden, enormous water tanks sprang up everywhere and Top Telegraph Park was set up as a barrage balloon base, manned by the Air Force. Everybody perfected their blackout, our windows were latticed with wide strips of gummed paper to prevent flying glass splinters, and air raid wardens, firemen, all the emergency services were as prepared as could be. Leaflets were issued telling us what to do if the Germans landed, there was a list of rules, I can recall only; "to hide food and bicycles". Dad had a bike - where to hide it? in the coal cellar, under the bed? We decided to cope with it all when it happened, that was all we could do.

A school inspector came round, would I care to be evacuated again? Would I hell! I was here, here I was going to stay - if I died, that was it, so had and would, a lot of other people - and if my family was killed and I wasn't?? No; I would stay here.

The Battle of Britain began that July, mainly fought over Kent. Here, in London, it was relatively quiet, or so it seemed for a while. The days were beautiful, hot and sunny. Then the air raids began, building up in strength during the month of August; day or night the sirens would go and we'd pick up our ready packed bag of necessities - flask of tea, biscuits, first aid kit and torch. Emergency supplies, such as tins of food and candles were already in there. Warmly dressed, folded blankets on arms, we descended the four or five wooden steps into the shelter, listening to the uneven throb of the heavy German bombers growing louder and louder, hearing the screech of bombs, the thud and the earth juddering at their impact; the inevitable explosion. "If you hear it, you're alright", people said.

Towards the end of that month Grandad Barker suddenly died; I hadn't seen him for a year and he was eighty -five; guiltily I told Mother that I couldn't cry - I was all for doing the Right Thing, and girls in books always cried when their Grandparents died. All my unsentimental Mother said, however, was, "I shouldn't think so, either, neither can I; anyway you hardly knew him," and smiled rather grimly.

As everyone knows, the air raids of August were but a trial run before the real business began on the afternoon of September 7th., like a breeze experienced before a hurricane. We were stuck down in the shelter for I don't know how many hours, the noise all around us was intense and unceasing, the ground shook and trembled, the ack-ack guns went off non-stop, Dad peered out once or twice but ducked back in again - the air was full of shrapnel. At long last the noise of the engines receded into the distance, the all clear sounded; relieved the nightmare was over for a while, fearful of what we should see, we emerged from our burrow; and see clearly we could, for where black night should have prevailed, (there being no street lamps), trees, plants and garden path were starkly illuminated. Everyone was out talking, it was obvious that there was no damage in the immediate vicinity - it was the docks, they said. I remember hanging out of the back top-floor window, staring downhill toward the river, charred particles floated past my face in the red night sky, and the air was filled with smoke and the terrible smell of burning; it was unforgettable, appalling, lurid, like a scene glowing from hell.

That night was repeated for about six weeks until the Battle of Britain was fought and won, but the Blitz continued well into 1942. After a while I found it possible to sleep quite well, wrapped in a blanket on one of the bunks; I had two pillows, but found I slept better with one of them over my head, it kept the noise out; it is marvellous what you can get used to. I seem to remember the all clear sounding at about four o'clock, stretching, climbing slowly out of the bunk; the others had gone before me, more wakeful, to make tea and get to bed. It would be cool and dark, save for the last searchlights sweeping the sky, and quiet, save for the movement of fire engines or ambulances, and the lonely rapid footsteps of someone trotting home; the garden smelt fresh and green as ever, yet pervaded with an air of unreality.

It was all right going to the shelter in September, but the weather grew cold, wet and foggy; I never saw that a shelter was much safer than a house, if a bomb landed on it, you'd be dead either way. The rest of the family began to feel the same, and we got a Morrison shelter put in the basement; Mum and I slept on a properly made up bed in it, Dad on a camp bed, Nell on the long deckchair, ("they always said I could sleep on a clothes line," she told us), and Mr.Reid, still with us, on a dilapidated old chaise-long. We had quite jolly times down there, in the comparative space and warmth. Dad made wooden shutters, which he thumb-screwed on to the outside of the small basement windows and door glass every evening, so we could have a good light too.

I read a lot of poetry then, by a table lamp. Mr. Reid asked Mother in sepulchral tones, "What is she reading?" "Poetry", answered Mother; he shook his head in melancholy fashion, "Oh dear, oh dear", he muttered; I think he considered it a bad sign, and was convulsed with giggles; silly old fool, I thought.

We were told to use a pillow or cushion to protect our heads generally; on one occasion when a bomb fell near, Mum being out of the Morrison, and hearing it's close, screaming descent, grabbed what she thought was a pillow to put over her head, but it was a sheet, and with her forceful wrench it split and her head shot through - her dazed and bewildered look had us all in fits of laughter.

One night a week, wearing his tin hat, Dad reported for Warden's duty at Waller Rd.,School, and helped as he could at various incidents; I think the most he did was to shovel up incendiary bombs with a long handled shovel and pail of sand, they frequently dropped in batches, called Molotov Cocktail Baskets. My father was always very quiet about it, knowing that the full-time Wardens, firemen and police had a far harder, more harrowing job. Dr.Govan had long since given up seeing me, being heavily involved with the hundreds of serious casualties.

Dad never stayed away from work, nobody did, whatever the conditions, but once when a horrific dog-fight was going on over head, machine guns blazing, the tram he was on ground to a halt by a church, and the driver told them all to shelter inside. When they went in, however, they found the roof had been blown out, so they just stood round the walls until it was over, then continued the journey. But there were many such stories told, guts and humour abounded:- this is from a daily paper, referring to our bombing of Germany;

"Herr von Stinkentrouser und Herr von Schmellingpanz; "Vot vos dot?" "Dot vos ein bompf" "Und dot und dot?" "Dot vos udder bompfs" "Heil Hitler" "Heil Hitler". Lots more in that vein, the serial ran for a long time; what rubbish to remember! But memory is not necessarily selective.

We were saved from final annihilation by the Battle of Britain; many times we witnessed a screaming dogfight, although most of them took place over Kent and the Channel. It was wonderful, heroic ... never have so many etc., but the raids continued relentlessly, especially during the night. I read recently that London was heavily bombed for seventy -six nights in succession. The Battle of Britain ended toward the end of October, the raids did not stop then, but danger of imminent invasion receded.

By the end of 1940, 13,600 people had been killed in London.

It must have been sometime during September, that George Edwards asked if his niece, Doreen Browne, could have the two top rooms, kitchen and back, left empty by the Leonards. Doreen's parents lived in Devon, but she worked and lived in one of the Edwards' shops, which had been bombed; and so for a short time, she came to live upstairs. A belligerent Quaker pacifist of nineteen she was, who said she'd most like to marry a German, (paradoxically she soon after married a Canadian soldier from the backwoods, who made her life a very hell.) "If I found a German fallen from a plane lying in the garden - I would bring him a cup of tea", she proclaimed "Oh would you", said Mother, "Well I'd hit him on the head and tie him up tight with a clothes line first." Doreen was shocked; an argument ensued, for though Mother's pacifism was part and parcel of her religious convictions, she was saved from the impracticality of idealism by a streak of commonsense which saw into the heart of things. She was to attend several Tribunals for Conscientious Objectors, but did not flinch at voicing her heartfelt thanks for those men who daily risked their lives manning our fighters and who succeeded in breaking the worst force of the mighty luftwaffe, at the cost of so many of their young lives.

One morning in mid-October, early, about seven o'clock, a man knocked on our front door; I heard voices and wondered. Presently Mum came into the room, "Uncle Tom's had a heart attack and died", she said. It was a total shock; Mill had come to tea as she continued to do every Tuesday, in spite of two adjacent houses receiving a direct hit the previous night, and on returning to her house in East Dulwich Grove, had found him dead on the floor, half in and half out of the toilet. Presumably she had gone frantic and screaming had rushed next door to the Burges'. They had taken control, they couldn't let us know, as a raid started soon after, and of course, neither we nor anyone we knew had a phone; it was Mr. Burge who had cycled over with the news. Nell went straight over there, eventually bringing Mill back with her; she was devastated.

The raids continued by night, and Nell and Mill made the daily trek to Dulwich, arranging the funeral and clearing things up generally. It was the first funeral I ever attended and it was not uplifting. I was truly sorry for Mill, she was distraught and desolated; "We were going to retire to Yalding", she said; (years later John and I drove her there.) I tried to talk to her; "I've never seen your wedding photos," I remarked hopefully; but it didn't help; "We did not consider them necessary", was her brief reply, and I supposed it was because they were so old at the time. The three sisters held whispered discussions, which ceased abruptly when I went into the room; I tried to hear what was being said, hidden behind the door, but couldn't make it out, it was all very strange. There was some mystery, I knew; I asked Mother, point blank. "Well", she answered ponderously, "Uncle Tom made his will before he married Mill, he always meant to change it, but never did, so everything goes to his two sons by his first wife. Only Mill is going to contest it through a solicitor, but for heaven's sake don't mention it, it upsets her so."

So that was it, I thought I understood. But they didn't mind upsetting one another, there were some bitter and acrimonious scenes; on one occasion Mill asked where something of her father's was - that began a flaming row; Nell, as always, tried to damp down the flames, but

Mother flared, "*It was you who left home*, it was our right to do as we liked with the old family things - you left them - *you* had no say in the matter, then or *now*." the atmosphere sizzled; I felt quite sorry for Mill, she looked whipped, however she did have this annoying obsession with possessions; but after all, I ruminated, she left home *to get married*, Mum put it a funny way; after all, hadn't Mother also left home to get married ? I saw she never had; instead, my Father, as far as was possible, had been absorbed into theirs. Mill, physically had returned to the fold; but she had never been in *my* fold - just Mum, Dad, Auntie and me; it was not, and never was to be, easy for Mill to become once again part of the family unit she had left twelve years earlier. But she was determined; and remained so for the next thirty years.

Mill's probate dragged on, finalised in mid-January 1941; Mill was to receive the contents of the house, the sons the house itself. She had to accept it but it made her bitter; she and Nell went to her old home frequently, sorting out and packing. About this time, with great import, she accosted me saying, "I am going to give you something in memory of Uncle Tom." Gosh, I thought, full of anticipation, whatever will it be? It was a book about Kashmir; surprise and disappointment mingled, I had never seen this volume before ... Kashmir ... Good Heavens! how could that remind me of Tom? I am pleased now to remember that I managed to accept it politely, but it was an effort. A little after, however, I discovered his Mother's broken teapot thrown out into the dustbin. I clawed about among the ashes, picked out the bits and washed them. "You don't want that rubbish," Mill exclaimed, "If you do you'll have to ask your Mother, what a funny child you are." Mum shrugged her shoulders, not minding whether I kept them or not. I glued the pieces together as best I could; I was used to seeing it on a shelf in Uncle's study, it was something I warmed to and could cherish.

Meanwhile Mother grew extremely unwell owing to the menopause; there was little one could do about it fifty years ago; grin (or not), and bear it. "I just don't feel up to much", was all she'd say. She grew weak, and never having much colour, presented an empty wax-like appearance; depressed she would sit around not doing anything, totally unlike herself; I busied myself making a fuss of her. At this time too, Ruby Pritchard next door was dying of cancer; a woman in her early forties, with an animated, friendly disposition and quite beautiful face. She had consulted Dr. Allinson, the well-known dietician, and was trying to live on grapes, although he had honestly told her that there was little hope. It was my habit to pop in at lunch time to see if she wanted anything - we did a lot for her, as her twenty-two year old daughter Gladys, couldn't find the time, preferring to spend it with the R.A.F. up Telegraph Hill, quite normal, I know. I clearly call to mind the day I went in to find her crying with distress, I did what I could, but had to fetch Mum. Next day she made a "Phantom Recovery", she believed herself cured, sat up sprightly in bed, talked gaily of the future. I thought it was a miracle, but Nell warned me, "It won't last, you know, I've seen this happen more than once; she'll be dead within three days." And she was; suddenly collapsed and died, like that.

Early in February Doreen Browne left, and all Mill's belongings were brought over - how they managed to get all that large furniture and numerous boxes into those three rooms I do not know; it was like a depository.

I must admit these were stressful times, but never dull, one might call them invigorating. I was still not supposed to exert myself in any way, as this would expose me to

160

another attack of Rheumatic Fever, which would be serious. I became aware of feeling cooped-up, however, though never at a loss for things to do indoors, for Mother didn't even like me walking down to the Gate, for fear of an air-raid, and certainly incidents were occurring all round us. A land-mine fell on St. Mary's church, demolishing it and the nearby houses, including the Blundell sister's old family house, 1, Ansdell Rd., and the blast was such that it blew Dad's shutters right off our basement windows - although half a mile away.

Up to that time, half a dozen dray horses were kept by the council in stables at the bottom of Kitto Rd., for reinforcing the horse and carts going both up and coming down the steep incline of Telegraph Hill - one, sometimes two, extra animals were put in harness and they wore special shoes. Many times as a little child I had been walked home that way, for I loved to see those great beasts looking out over their stable doors, fidgeting their harnesses and restlessly stamping their feet. One night an incendiary bomb fell on the wooden stables, and securely bolted in as these creatures were, the heroic efforts of the local people to save them, were of no avail, and the firemen arrived too late, being engaged in rescuing people. This incident upset me as much as anything, it was horrible, I never walked that way again, for those charred and desolate ruins were haunted by visions of the terrified beasts, and echoed with their dying screams. Fanciful? No, that is how it is imprinted on my memory, and many were those who wept at the fate of the poor horses, whose eyes were stoically dry at the news of the deaths of our fellow men.

It was a typical Monday morning, the basement boiler had been alight for a couple of hours, soapy steam billowing from it in clouds; the siren went. Mother put down the copper stick, "I won't lift it out for a minute", she said; I had sat down on the chaise-long; Nell was rubbing up some fat and flour in a bowl, Mill came slowly down from upstairs, carrying a pile of papers; Dad and Mr. Reid had gone to work. There was a short, fractional shriek of a bomb, the whole house rocked, was lifted up. I thought it would come down on us - there was no time to move, though we fell to the ground, as told. The explosion was deafening, our ears popped and sang and our hearts beat; the lid jumped right off the copper, and boiling water sprayed high into the air; the trap door was flung open - the fire shot across the floor, smoke, glowing flame and all. Miraculously the house righted itself; we were shaken, but that was nothing, for outside was the rumble of falling masonry, debris was flying about, the air was filled with clouds of pulverised plaster and cement, making it difficult to breath, our hair and clothes full of it. Mill screamed, Mum grabbed the copper stick and Nell the long handled shovel which we were advised to keep ready for incendiaries, I tugged the front door open and the fire ball was thrown out. At first we couldn't see across the road for dust, there were shouts, people running, but no screams or cries; then we realised that the houses across there were still collapsing. Ambulances, fire appliances, emergency services of all sorts rushed to the spot, but it was useless, the twelve people in those four houses were dead.

When all was calm and silent, I went out into the front garden on my own; the air was very cold and damp, filled with the unforgetable smell of ruined plaster. Where the four houses opposite to us had stood, rescue workers toiled among unrecognisable heaps of rubble, broken staircases and shattered items of once loved furniture, among jagged planks of wood stuck up at crazy angles, among heaps of bricks and madly gushing water pipes. Our front garden was full of debris, but as I turned to go back indoors, something caught my attention; I stooped to pick it up - it was a wedding photograph, of the young couple who had come to live in the end house a few years previously, I can see it still. Beautiful she was, in her long white veil bound low on the forehead, bright and smiling at her happy young husband. Damaged now and almost unrecognisable, I reverently dropped it into the dustbin. I thought - if that bomb had been dropped one second later, one fraction in space further on, *we* would have been killed instead.

Soon after, Italian prisoners of war were set to work on clearing the site. Friendly, relaxed, full of song, but *foreign*. "Hello Blondie", they called out cheerfully. "I'm not blonde", I thought, and looked away. By a strange coincidence, a day or two after that, Mavis called to see me. Her Mother was visiting old neighbours in Gellatly Rd., we had kept up an erratic correspondence and knew that they had gone to live in Bromley; it sounded wonderful. She wished we could come and live next door, the house was to let, and they suffered no air raids, she told us, and when her Mother arrived she reinforced the suggestion. It never once occurred to me that we would, but we did!. My Father was shocked and appalled at what he found when he got home that night, in spite of us being safe and sound, for all the front windows were out, the back ones splintered, the front walls cracked, window frames dislodged, chimneys off and the upstairs front door would not open. Men had come and covered all the front windows with black tarred paper and stuck opaque, oiled netting over the splintered ones. The rest would have to take its turn with the many other damaged premises in the borough.

To Bromley

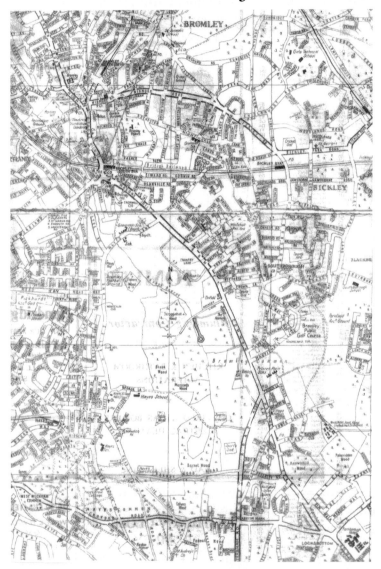

Bromley cir.1950

We moved to 4, (now 30), Copthorne Avenue on 9th. April; for me it was momentous, for the others an enriching, revivifying experience. Mother was to say later, "It's funny, the war was on and it shouldn't have been, but that was one of the happiest times of my life. The house was small,1935, said to be "Jerry built", our landlord had bought 4 for £1000. We were cramped, in spite of having left a lot of furniture at Waller, but for us it held almost a holiday atmosphere, and our personal differences were overcome by the stimulation of new surroundings, as well by our mutual reaction against the unflagging efforts of our common enemy to beat us into submission. For precisely a week after our moving in, the worst air raid Bromley was to experience occurred (confirmed, by a newspaper cutting) - a 1,000 lb bomb crashed down on Jackson Rd., literally one minute from our house, and ninety homes, ten shops, a pub, the bus garage with sixty buses were wiped out. The head girl of Bromley Grammar School was killed while fire-watching at the old parish church, which received a direct hit, and Bromley town suffered severe and widespread damage. To put it mildly, it was disappointing, though hardly surprising. The raids on London lessened in severity, for the main force of the German war machine now turned its might against Russia. We were given pause, but the Blitz did not end until a year later.

We lived there only two and a half years, but I think I may say that I loved every moment. My tiny bedroom held little more than my bed, but its window looked out onto an uneven hilly green, round which the road had been built. The side roads leading away from it were unmade, and from their edges sprang fronds of tender green cow parsley, nettles and dog mercury. From here, one day we walked into Sparrow Wood, lovely untouched woodland, and continuing along a wide path, bordered by unkempt hedges bristling with scarlet hips against a sharp blue sky, we re-entered the woods, and there deep within, we lit upon the deserted small-pox hospital, as hidden in dense coppice as the enchanted castle of any Sleeping Beauty. We were within only ten minutes walk of Scrub's farm, Lower Gravel Road, too, where one summer there was a glut of runner beans sold at 2d. a pound, delicious.

Copthorne Avenue, 1941

That first spring was a revelation to me; I could walk up to the end of this short road to where it tailed out in to a muddy footpath, and turn right into a hilly, uncultivated field bounded on either side by deep woods. It was simple, too, to climb through a hole in our back fence, the only barrier between us and Knowle Wood, and here there was peace, stillness and space, springing with the bright young green of April. The woodland edges were dotted with primroses and violets, starred with stitchwort, while the woods themselves glowed white with wind flowers, later to be bathed with the indigo of bluebells. It was a little paradise; Mavis and I would walk into the woods together, seeing stagnant pools of frogs

166

spawn, gathering bunches of wildflowers, treading gently on the mossy turf, jumping the tiny, clear- running streams, untouched and beautiful, disturbing the birds who bathed in the shallow waters and drank on the pebbly edges. It is hard to believe, but the nightingale then sang so loud there at night, it was a positive nuisance, (but it is a long time now since by destroying their habitat we usurped the nightingales), and once Aunt Nell said of the cuckoo, "If that damn bird doesn't shut-up I'll go and strangle it", so loud, so omnipresent was it, for weeks on end. I call to mind the time Mavis and I went primrosing and how we jumped back at finding a grass snake neatly coiled round a clump, hidden beneath its luxuriant leaves, but more frightened than we, it rapidly slipped surreptitiously into the undergrowth. An example of how comparatively rural Bromley Common was then is a note in a book of Mum's:- "One Spring, during W.W.2, the windows of Trinity Church were blown out, and the following Summer 2 swallows built their nest in one of the upper broken windows. Of course when the window was replaced we saw the birds no longer" (Winged Builders; by Nancy Price, p.37). Mavis and I remember walking down to see them.

Summer, Autumn, even Winter - I never liked the cold, hated snowballing - were enjoyable here. We walked regularly across the field, through another wood and on to an exclusive road of houses to Locksbottom. There was never anyone much about, and as for those houses, I'd never seen anything like them!. Opulent mock-Tudor, set in lush landscaped gardens, they held echoes of a golden past, of orderliness, harmony, they represented an ideal. In my innocence I believed the folk fortunate enough to inhabit this demi-paradise *must*, by reason of living there, be good and happy people; a common illusion. One day

167

in the school holidays, Mavis and I decided that one of them was empty, we reconnoitred several times, then greatly daring, with many a furtive, backward glance, we darted into the front garden and picked an enormous bunch of daffodils. Oh, the thrill of it!. Triumphant, dividing our spoils we gave half each to our Mothers, the scent, the luscious dripping sap, the bright freshness of them - and - *free!*. We concocted some yarn that they had been growing, "Outside a boundary", but they seemed not to believe us, "They must belong to *somebody*", they said, arranging them in vases. We decided we had best not do it again, but it was enormous fun - and you would never have known there was a war on.

In autumn, the hazels hung low with nuts to be gathered for eating, rose hips collected to make jelly - full of vitamin C, they said; enormous blackberries were there for the picking, and we'd go with basins, across the cobwebby fields sparkling with heavy dew in the early morning light. I have never, before or since, seen the sky alive with glittering stars so large and clear as they were those frosty winter nights; there were no artificial lights whatsoever to diminish their brilliance. I recall that many times the open field was bathed in moonlight, and I was free to walk alone, -unobserved, had time to stare at the black, bare branches of trees, silhouetted against the moon, while owls called into the silent darkness in the pure cold air.

It was not only my age which lent a peculiar magic to that time, but the stark contrast between life at that moment in time on Bromley Common, and life as we had experienced it for the previous two years: my life in say October, 1939 was totally different from that of October, 1940 and that of October,1941 different from either: but the deep, basic difference was this, whereas before we were confronted by the powers of darkness, evil and death, here we were in contact with the renewing forces of life and hope. A blessing indeed. *Behold, I have set before you life and death, blessing and cursing, (good and evil), therefore choose life.*

Mother and I both improved in health rapidly, indeed Mother went so far as having her hair cut for the first time and permed!. By the second summer she and I would sometimes take the 47 bus, and picnic at Farnborough; it was the idea then to take salad in a jam jar. Once, walking beside a High Elms boundary, we came to a place where the fence was down, and wandered in softly, through a wood, to a sudden opening. Secret and dark it was, tranquil and intensely private; there in this sequestered spot stood a number of Lubbock gravestones; a haunting memory - I have never seen them since. Frequently on Sundays, Mother and I would walk to Meeting at Hayes through the peace of Barnet Wood Road, there was no traffic whatsoever. Mother remembered it thus:-

> *Sunday, May 18th, 1941* "Meeting was held in a small wooden building, in a large garden, flowery curtains at the windows, birds singing loudly in the trees, sunlight pouring in (so different from Peckham). We walked home through Barnet Wood Road, partly skirting Hayes Common and all the way beautiful with hedges, fields and woods".

However I will add a word or two of my own; a friendly and lively group met regularly in this idyllic spot, a summer house in Dr. Barrington's leafy garden. Diverse in age and opinions, but mainly united in things considered vital, as the *Friend* had printed on its cover:- *In essentials Unity, In non-essentials Liberty, In All Things, Charity.*

Among them were several older Friends from Peckham, now moved into the area, a varying array of conscientious objectors, and Theodore Harris. This awful old man of about 70, lived in Lower Gravel Road with his housekeeper of about the same age, dowdy and worn and said to be his concubine. I could not understand it, but even worse, he was such a rabid pacifist that he would not register for a ration book, nor allow his "housekeeper" to get one, but relied on Friends to supply them both with food!. I found this totally unacceptable and vowed he'd never have any of *my* rations. Once or twice Mother took him something, but it caused a great family row and she gave up. "Let him live on grass, there's plenty of it about", shouted Dad. "Tell him that from me; why does he think that he's different from anyone else? Bloody cheek". One or two Friends admired him, "Strong in belief, like a martyr", they would gush approvingly. Perhaps he was. Not my type of Quaker at all.

Another Friend remembered from those far off days was Effie Nash, a good friend of my Mother's, a charming woman, whose dress I admired enormously. One day she wore a loose, full, reversible coat in oatmeal with French navy revers - it could be worn inside out, of course. I told her how much I liked it, how attractive she always appeared, with her harmonious, well-chosen accessories; "well", she replied gently, "I think of the people who have to look at me, and try to make it as agreeable for them as possible." Ho, I thought, what a wonderful philosophy - especially if you have the money to carry it out; it was an aspect of religious truth that I had not come across before; you couldn't lose, could you? You pleased yourself and presumably everyone else as well; no wonder her manner was so serene and beatific. There was, however, much more to Effie than this; her outward appearance *was* most pleasing, but the exterior would not have been half as engaging had not her inner self shone through - I was aware of that, too; the combination was impressive. Enough of Bromley Quakers, though it was here that Nell started to attend Meeting, while Mill sometimes went to the little Baptist chapel in Cherry Orchard Rd., where she made a friend (a woman!).

We went for long walks from the house, a favourite being up Oakley Road, where we peered in at the old rustic gate of the "Glebe", hoping for a glimpse of Richmal Crompton, and so on up to Keston, to return via Gravel Road. We walked as far as Farnborough, but took the bus back, and this was all so enjoyable that not going for a holiday was not missed, it certainly was not possible. Soon after our arrival, a neighbour passed their unwanted pup over to us, and so Paddy, a mongrel terrier, became a cherished friend to us all for the next 14 years

For my fifteenth birthday, 1942, I was given a new bicycle; I had never had one before and took to it like a duck to water - it was paid for with some of the War Damage money, just received. Mavis got one too, and from then on we felt as free as birds and rode for miles, on Saturdays and holidays, whenever weather and homework permitted; we never saw one another on Sundays, for that was still retained for church going and family. All round the Bromley area we rode, to Chislehurst, free wheeling down hill from the old water tower, uphill to Downe and out along to Crofton Lane, a narrow country lane then, with ancient flourishing hedgerows, hardly a house in sight.

I shall never forget one bright sunny Sunday afternoon. Dad suggested we go for a spin, he'd always had a bike, Mum never managed it; "come on", he said, "Let's go to London"! The roads were empty, save for the odd bus or tram, or solitary car - we sped through Bromley, Lewisham, straight down the Old Kent Road, careful of tram lines, across Tower Bridge and arrived at the Tower. Mighty pleased with ourselves, we strolled about and bought an icecream, it tasted strongly of black-treacle, but however odd it went down well. The place was sandbagged and heavily guarded, but solid as always, majestic and strangely reassuring. Pausing briefly to look at our beloved Thames, we made our way back the way we had come, through the quiet, unbusy streets of London.

School

I have put these various impressions down together, as I cannot always separate them in time; however, I remember exactly my returning to school; it was traumatic; I knew it would be, but it was something I had to live through. I wanted to be like other girls, live as they lived and to achieve that was not going to be easy, after being isolated with adults for eighteen months. The Head Mistress of Bromley Grammar School, Miss Whiting, dignified, weighty, wearing as was usual an academic gown over a well-cut tweed suit interviewed me. Used to authority, to summing up situations and making right decisions rapidly and with gravity, she accepted me straightaway, depending on a medical; the doctor's opinion was that I should start school after the beginning of Summer term, 1941, by immediately attending twice a week. It was a painful business, though Mavis helped a lot; twice a week was not enough to get to know anyone else, let alone catch up on work, though I brought a lot home.

After several weeks of that, it was stepped up to three days a week which was an improvement, and towards the end of term I attended full time. Quite honestly, a lot of the time I didn't know what they were talking about, had to feel my way, as indeed I realised later they were with me; they had no idea which subjects to enter me for School Certificate, the course for which began next term, Autumn 1941, for the exam. in June 1943. I may have had to wait a year, psychologically that would have been bad, as I had managed to establish myself with a group of good friends, from whom fortunately I was not parted as it was agreed I should embark with them on the preparation of the following subjects; English, which included elocution, English literature, French, Geography, History, Domestic Science and a paper in Arithmetic. Those I coped with, other subjects I never attempted.

I must say, once I became accustomed to it, how much I enjoyed the company of my own generation. I always set off with Mavis at ten past eight, catching a bus from the garage to Holmesdale Rd., whence we walked to school. There was no shorter way, for Bromley South or Market Square was another fare stage, so Holmesdale Road it was, and there at the corner of Havelock Rd., Joan Ashby joined us, serene, contented, emitting always a simple, contagious goodness, and usually Joyce Hearne was with us too. Joyce was practical and phlegmatic, she later served as nurse on the famous, "Castle Lines". We four friends were all in different *Houses* .On entry to the school, each girl was allotted to a certain House, in which she would remain until leaving. The four Houses were named after Kentish worthies; Chaucer, Darwin, Harvey and Wolfe. We were expected to know about the lives of these men in some detail and felt a pride in the fact that they were born in our County. The House colours were blue, green, red and yellow, respectively. There was always so much to talk about and discuss we never noticed what a truly boring, long distance it was. In spring I was initiated into the chewing of tiny fresh May buds - "Don't you know, "bread and cheese?" they said; it was delicious, we champed as we walked steadily on. We talked of everything, everything, that is, except my evacuation experiences, for they were in the past and done with; they tended to exaggerate the differences between them and me, and that at all costs, I aimed to avoid. I hated to stand out in a crowd, my whole wish was to become part of it, unnoticed, accepted.

So, conversations diverse and wide ranging; "You know X and Y go up to Biggin Hill and go with airmen?" "Yes, yes, everybody knows that". "Well, X told me she uses Rendells Tablets". "No! What if they don't work - the risk-how *awful*." "Do you have to suck them or swallow them?", I wanted to know. Some of the others didn't know either, but Joan and Joyce fell about, welcoming the opportunity of displaying their superior knowledge. Hilary Duddy, from Bickley, strolled towards us, past the gas-works; frivolous, inordinately proud of her "sexy nose", "You'd be so attractive, Dolly, if you shaved your eyebrows -and" - staring, "Your eyes are the wrong colour, they should be brown". Her shoes! We exclaimed - very smart, black, yes, but with a bold, red, "V" for Victory signs on the toe, would she get away with it? she had spent her coupons on them....?

The rules concerning school uniform were rigorously applied and no-one demurred; they were simple, unpleated round necked gym-slips with white blouses up to Lower Vth, which I never wore. From then, the School Certificate years, one wore white blouse, maroon and white striped tie, navy skirt and cardigan; girls in those years wore stockings all the year round, but the younger ones put on long white socks for summer. Naturally girls of all ages wore navy locknit knickers with elastic round the legs as well as the middle. We all wore gingham dresses in summer of a fine blue and white cross check, shirt waister style; bought at Dunns Outfitters on the corner of Market Square and Widmore Rd., made up, or the fabric by the yard. We greatly preferred these dresses, at first signs of Spring we couldn't wait to leave off the skirts and cardigans. "You'll get a chill" warned Mother and Nell would chant her grandma's mantra:-

"As the days do lengthen
So the cold do strengthen".

True but I just didn't care. By 1942 hats had been abandoned because unobtainable, but the rules concerning head-gear were not relaxed, and we wore navy blue berets, with the school crest sewn on to the front; should we be seen in the street without one, by either a mistress or a prefect, punishment was meted out immediately. We were smart; our navy gaberdine raincoats were buttoned up and belted, we were reprimanded if we slummocked, if our shoes were scuffed or we appeared in any way grubby or generally sloppy; that was to be expected and we all took a pride in looking neat and business-like. My hair had been cut at fourteen, and like all the other girls, I had my first perm when about fifteen for birthday or Christmas.

Memories of these schooldays are not particularly sharp, for I was completely integrated and happy, it was so good to live orderly, planned days again, to attend a well-run school whose basic curriculum was undisturbed by the events of war. Whose pupils were not evacuated, but attending school normally, with an undiminished supply of relaxed and dedicated teachers, whose circumstances allowed them to concentrate not only on their pupils but on their subjects too. I found the work challenging, was mainly in the B+ range, but frequently achieved A for English, which, with history, I came to love.

Day began with Assembly, and hymns were chosen from "Songs of Praise", by votes taken in form rooms at the beginning of term; some of the most popular I remember well; "All glory, laud and honour", "Thou, whose Almighty word", "Praise my soul the King of Heaven", "All creatures of our God and King", "Teach me my God and King" and "Immortal, Invisible" will serve as examples. I call to mind how lightly then and with what confidence our voices rang out with,

> *"We blossom and flourish as leaves on a tree,*
> *And wither and perish, but naught changeth Thee"*

Very often this brief ceremony ended with the familiar prayer; "Teach us, good Lord, to serve Thee as Thou deservest..."

Joan was my next best friend, podgy and pallid, affectionately known as, "Pudden", she lived in a little Gas Company house, her father was an invalid and the family were very poor, but so welcoming, an old metal tea pot was kept simmering on the range all day long. Her elder sister Marjorie also went to our school and was a prefect, but she lived with an uncle and aunt up the road, who had brought her up as they had no children. Her brother Peter, a year or so older, a dim-wit, worked in the laundry; one visit sticks in my mind, while I was there an air raid warning went and we all got into their Morrison shelter, but Joan and I quickly crawled out, shaking with laughter, as Pete kept on farting loudly, each time saying, "Pardon me!", most solemn and unashamed. We felt it was healthier outside the shelter than in it.

177

Joan and I joined the choir, it was just splendid, Miss Collins was an inspiration, her enthusiasm so infectious, one of those exceptional teachers who bring out talents you never knew you possessed - we sang to the music of Schubert, Mozart, Warlock, Arne, and so many more, and merely hearing a chord or a few notes will bring those melodies flooding back to me. "St. Patrick's Breastplate", the whole of Tennyson's "The Lady of Shallot", and the first singing of "Messiah" - I looked down to see many of the parents dabbing tears from their eyes; glorious, heavenly, to remain with you for ever.

At the other end of the scale was Games with Miss Wilson - my bete noir. It was all right during my first year, I was not allowed to do any, after that, I was and I regularly hid in the cloakroom behind a row of coats with a kindred spirit, but it did not always work out, and games of hockey, rounders and cricket, even netball, I remember with intense dislike. The grounds, however were large and pleasant; and brick-built shelters had been erected in them, air raid drill took place every week, including putting on gas- masks. These shelters were locked and out of bounds, but one day our group found a door open, and nosing around in the pitch dark, discovered several large, old tins of Ovaltine. The contents had solidified and for many days we spent our lunch hours hacking away, with anything we could lay our hands on, breaking off lumps of the stuff, eating it greedily, like sweets; delicious, and we were never found out!

Quite often a group of us would go home via Nightingale Lane and Stockwell Slip, and enter the Market Square by Tutts, and if there was some fish we always queued for it. Once I managed to get a fine pair of kippers, but because they had to be wrapped in newspaper, by the time I got

178

home the oil had soaked through to my English text book. Although it was covered in brown paper, as were all our books, the cover was badly marked, luckily the teacher was understanding, accepted my explanation and passed it off lightly. I mention this trivial incident as books were precious, no-one could tell when more would become available, and we had to fit two lines of tiny writing into the lines of our ruled exercise books to save paper.

Which brings me to Domestic Science; for needlework we resorted to alterations - a considerable degree of skill required here. I made a really smart blouse from an unworn, blue and white striped shirt of Uncle Tom's, and set it off with tiny red buttons down the front. Mavis loathed sewing; having slogged away at an apron, unpicking the hated hem untold times, and still not getting it right, she furiously rammed the offending article behind a radiator; we never knew if it was discovered. Cookery lessons were crippled by rationing, but we got by remarkably well. We all took school dinner; the menu was the best that circumstances would permit; we had a rota for serving, and one for pouring water, and I will add here, that there was no problem with discipline in the school whatsoever. However, we spun our knives round on the polished wooden tables and wished for a husband, mine was always for a museum curator! The only main course I really disliked was, "Patriotic Stew" - greasy water, with bits of potato and gristle floating in it; I much preferred the sweets.

The school had adopted, "H.M.S. Broke" and sent comforts to the sailors, scarves and socks were knitted - you should have seen them! We were not the skilled knitters our Mother's had been. Adml. Evans came to talk to us; we sang, what else?, "For those on peril on the sea", and the orchestra ground out, "Land of hope and Glory". It was supposed to be a memorable occasion, but to most of us it was a farce, pointless, a relic from the past.

During my three years at Bromley Grammar School, I did voluntary work; vegetables were grown on a large area of the playing fields, some girls stayed after school and *Dug For Victory*, but I preferred working at a War-time Nursery held in Elmfield Rd., We went in pairs, I went with Joan, and helped for about two hours, from four o'clock until six. She literally doted on these mites, knew how to handle them, having had plenty of practice with neighbour's offspring, but it was unexplored territory to me, and I gained a lot of practical knowledge which came in useful in later years. The babies were left there while their Mothers did war work of all kinds, and I remember the youngest we had was six weeks old, I had never seen one so small. I also put in a number of hours at the British Restaurant at Sundridge?, mostly Saturday mornings, with Mavis. British Restaurants were started in 1940, eventually there were over 2,000 in England, set up in Church Halls, empty shops, etc.. The meals were cheap, 10 pence to 1\2d., the full meal. I shall never forget the horrible smell - and appearance - of their Fish Soup; cod's heads were thrown into a great iron boiler of simmering water, and when it was ordered, you turned on a tap and let out a steaming plateful of it. I have never eaten fish soup from that day to this, although I believe it to be - even in that uncomplicated form - most nourishing. We were not allowed to do more than four hours per week, but occasionally I helped out at an Old People's Home at Chislehurst; I recall the first time getting out of the 227 bus, the blackout was complete, it was pitch dark, I had no idea where I was, or which way to turn, and several bewildering minutes were to pass before I discovered my way, and entered another, different world.

180

These particularly tranquil and fulfilling days came to an end in July 1943, when, the School Certificate examination over, all my friends left school. I was the only one recommended to stay on, dependant on my passing well enough; I failed only Domestic Science, for lumpy custard and cutting out a pattern for a pair of *drawers* with two left legs. Towards the end of the Summer Term I had gone with half a dozen others to St.Thomas's Hospital, hoping eventually to enroll as a nurse; we were shown Florence Nightingale's statue, various wards, theatres, lecture rooms and nurses quarters, which were delightful, I thought, a room of your own, with beautiful views across the Thames to the Houses of Parliament. However, I failed the medical on the spot and, very disappointed, had to rethink. I was upset, for contrary to most people's expectations, I looked back on my life in hospital for months afterwards with affection, and it had left me with a deep seated desire to join the nursing profession. Over the years many girls went from our school to this hospital, but during our last year we were encouraged to consider various options - we were taken to Boroughs Welcome in Beckenham, where I was sickened by the sight of a dog strapped helplessly down on a board, its guts wide open and raw. It made no sound, its eyes gazed at us, helpless, full of tears. I have never forgotten. In the ensuing summer holidays several of us worked for two or three weeks at Morphy Richards new factory at St. Mary Cray, manpower being desperately short.

It was Aunt Nell who came to the rescue, she showed me an article in a magazine describing Librarianship as a career, it caught my imagination, and I spoke to the careers mistress about it. She encouraged me to pursue this course, but consulting the material she had on the subject, told me that I needed another language. It was decided, after my results came out, and I became entitled to two more years education, that I stay on in the sixth form for one year, along with a mere eight brilliant pupils who had planned it that way, taking two or three German lessons every day, by joining various forms. The times were out of sympathy with the study of that particular language and I felt no inclination to come to grips with it. Latin was preferred, but it was considered too difficult to achieve the required standard in one year. We used, "Deutches Leben" with its hideous black letter printing, and I was taught not only by Miss Dakin, who oversaw my progress, but by a Frau Lachmann, a Bavarian; "I am ze laughing Munn", she explained. I remember sitting there thinking, "How can she stand there, admitting to being German; how *awful*"; and was truly embarrassed for her. It was depressing, I failed the exam. in June 1944, and although encouraged to return to school and resit it in December, I preferred to leave. I missed my friends more than I can say, on the whole the year seemed a wasted one. However, I continued some French with Miss Mack, and the Head Mistress took us into a depth study of the Book of Job, but I was young and callow and out of sympathy with it; preferring her new text book entitled, "Clear Thinking", relating to ethics. English progressed from strength to strength, as my imagination was caught by the WW1 poet, Wilfred Owen and I completed a really good project on him. I played truant twice, feeling defiant and enormously exhilarated; I walked alone around Farnborough and Downe, having told Mother I needed sandwiches for that day for school. By this time we were back at Waller Road, so it was an extra treat; the first time there was light, glistening snow on the hills, frost in the still air; the second time it was spring, warm sunny and enchanting; both times I returned home elated, for I loved to be either alone or with friends, not to be virtually alone amid an intimate group.

These, then were the end of my schooldays; on the last morning the deputy head invited me to her room to say goodbye. To my complete surprise she told me that had they realised my potential, I should have been streamed differently, but they had no way of knowing; a great pity, but it was too late to do anything about it now. It mattered to me very much that she had taken the trouble to tell me; I treasured her words, they warmed and reassured me, and continued to do so as time went by. I look back now on the mingled experiences of my school years at Bromley with pleasure and gratitude. "Now thank we all our God", we sang as ever, at the end of term. "Nun danket alle Gott", I echoed.

We were allowed to remain children longer then, I was still a child at fourteen, and expected, within reason, to behave like one. I was still called, "Girlie"; Mother would say, "For goodness sake use your gumption, Girlie"; and when I was cocky Nell would remark annoyingly, "I suppose you know all about it, like the little dog that went to church." Annoying because true. We are all bound by the conventions of our time, I was no different from my contemporaries in considering myself not "grown up" until the age of about seventeen; we were expected to be - and we presumed one another to be - chaste and celebate. The war enabled me, and many of my peers, to emerge from my "teens", a word not yet coined, with far less rebellion than may otherwise have been the case. We were taken out of our petty selves, all differences were overcome, there was neither old nor young, rich or poor, learned or unlearned, male nor female who was not imbued with the spirit of total loyalty and dedication to our native values and our own dear island. No-one who lived then will ever forget it, nor see its like again, nor those who did not experience it will ever fully understand. This all pervading spirit was paramount and united us all. So caught up was I in this, the very air we breathed was infused with it, that in carrying on with everyday life, *I did not notice growing up.* This miracle, this mystery went on; not for a day, not for a week, but for years - until the war was over and we were at peace again.

Back to Waller and Life in General

In October 1943 we returned to live in Waller Rd., there was no reason not to as the house was fully repaired, Mum, Dad, Nell and Mill found the proximity forced upon them by living in such confined quarters at Copthorne constricting and disagreeable, especially as Waller was lying idle, ready and waiting. My father's fares would be much less; my parents were still paying Nell and Mill for the house, and saving what was possible for old age, every one did then, who could. I argued a lot, couldn't Waller be sold? No this is too small anyway, and we can't afford a larger house in Bromley; they looked at one or two to see; Mother was sad too. "Why must we all be together?" I asked; all three sisters agreed they always had been; like Siamese triplets, I thought. Nell wanted to buy a house on Sheppey, there was one going for £200, near to a friend of hers; Mill was fraught with anger - to do with splitting money up; so poor Nell's dream was never realised, a little house of her own. Back to New Cross we went, away from the hedgerows and verdant underwood; Nell and Mill were supposed to have the upstairs flat, and admittedly they went to their sitting room before Dad got home, but would they use that dear little kitchen? Not once; it had to be communal; shopping costs were carefully noted down and religiously worked out by Mill to the last farthing. Obviously, this was the best way of living, taking rationing into account, and the cheapest way, too; it must be remembered that neither Nell nor Mill were entitled to any Old Age Pension; Nell was sixty in 1938, Mill in 1940.

There were now no lodgers to supplement income, but both aunts were in great demand for their needlework skills, they had more than enough work and had to refuse it. People wanted garments altered, turned, and remnants made up - always cheaply, of course. Nell did work for various local people, including altering an old coat of Mrs. Wadley's for Mavis to start work in, two pretty dresses from her mother's that Mavis still remembers with pleasure. She made her a skirt from a bedcover too, "Oh, look, its just like a Goray", Mavis crooned, delighted. Very clever indeed she was, lost none of her old craft, got quite a kick out of it. Nell also worked for the Jennings, a well-off Quaker family in Keston Park, and after we returned to London, used to go and stay for two or three days - as she did with the Edwards; she thoroughly enjoyed it, always one for a change of company, and was greatly appreciated. She turned her hand to anything, care for an invalid, help with the spring cleaning, run the house if it was needed - I wish she was around sometimes to help me!, but there, I have so much automatic assistance they never had - or could ever envisage.

Meanwhile, Mill had been recommended to a family at Shortlands, the Huffners, and went to them sewing, one day a week until she was about seventy, when I think one could claim Social Security. Mr. Huffner was an Armenian carpet merchant, very wealthy, but trade was bad. They kept a "daily" and Mrs.H. did elaborate cooking; tragically, their daughter in the Wrens was killed in 1944, at the age of twenty-one.

Of course, we had come to see to the house in Waller Rd., regularly, I had been several times myself and found I had quite an affection for it, but not the neighbourhood, not any more, not after two years in Bromley Common. However, my links with that area were far from broken, I remembered what a treat it had been to be taken to Bromley by Mother when I was little, now I went by

186

myself. As I said, I continued at school, travelling from Nunhead to Bromley South with a season ticket; and so, usually on a Saturday, I went there as well, frequently meeting Mavis, but other friends too and we would walk round the shops. When I started work, I sometimes went to Bromley on a Sunday.

Bromley evinced a very different aspect from today, for one thing a narrow line of green still separated it from Downham, certainly a very thin line indeed, but it existed; and it was quiet, with comparatively little traffic, there were many fewer people about, and so you could meet friends casually and pause for a gossip. The shops, all closed of course on a Sunday, had character, were attractive, Skilton's porticoed establishment dominated the Market Square, and there was Isards for hardware, Attwoods the haberdashers, Medhursts, Dunn's, Ayling's, Maunders and Last's bookshop, dark, inviting, where you could readily pick up a bargain. There was Harrison Gibson's first class furniture store, where in 1941 Mill had sold her Queen Anne dining room suite and Mum and I had later seen it set out tastefully in the window for five times as much; we never told her. You could sit upstairs in Wilson's cafe and look across at the old Methodist church; the last, faint echoes of Bromley's Market-town past still lingered. Above all it was not choked with traffic, it was an entity to be enjoyed and appreciated, not an impersonal row of multiple stores, identical with any other town in the country, with herds of worried shoppers scurrying along beside a trunk road full of unceasing traffic, noise and fumes.

I would go back to Mavis's house, and we'd play records as we had when I lived next door, Bing Crosby, Vera Lynne, Joe Loss and so on, and naturally, just talk. It was cosy, in 1939 her parents had bought a three piece suite, and although we had just got rid of the two black american cloth, buttoned Victorian chairs, our home still looked old fashioned; also her parents were affectionate, *together*; I want a home like that, I thought. At the same time, in my heart, never disloyal to Nell; but I think she would have understood; for I feel that her own parents had conformed to that prototype too.

What else did we do? Occasionally we'd look through our autograph albums, all of us girls at school kept one, and I wish I still had mine, as Mavis has. We all treasured them and pressed our family and friends to make a contribution on the softly-muted coloured pages.

Somebody always wrote:- **UPSIDE DOWN**
Upon this page you look
Upon this page you frown
And think of the girl who spoilt your book
By writing upside down.

That precluded anyone else from from writing it and they had to think again. Paintings were much sought after, Mum, I remember, painted me an idyllic sunrise over pine-clad mountains, Nell, a posy of shaded purple pansies and Mr. Wadley, Mavis's father did me a fine pen and ink sketch of Clarke Gable - he was adept at that sort of thing. Of course all entries were clearly signed and dated. Nell wrote in Mavis's album one of her favourite dictes and sayings:-
A wise old owl lived in an oak,
The more he saw the less he spoke.
The less he spoke the more he heard,
Why don't you be like that wise old bird?.

She'd said it often enough to me and Mavis seems to like it - now. In my album, Dad wrote, typically:-
2 Y's U R

2 Y's U B
I C U R
2 Y's 4 ME

Such were popular then. I think of Mill's contribution, now I understand it, then I did not and felt it most unsuited to my album:-

God gave his children memory
That in life's garden there might be
June roses in December.
(Rev. Studdart Kennedy who was the Woodbine Willy *of World War I).*
(From Mavis's album; signed M.B.H.1941)

Ironically, that neatly encapsulates the essence of these memoirs.

Four of us, for some years played tennis at Wendover Road, my only sport, and for a treat would take the bus to Hayes or Keston. I remember so clearly one summer day in 1944, suddenly becoming aware of the reverberation of guns going off, through the ground I stood on, it vibrated, deeply, regularly; across the Channel I was told; "My God, how near it is", I thought. Realization washed over me in that quiet, familiar spot.

Mavis and I often stayed the night in one another's houses; the neighbourhood of Copthorne Avenue retained its enchantment despite the scattered bomb craters which were now to be found in the surrounding countryside albeit rapidly clothed in green. Many a time we would wander out into the fields and woods, where the unkempt hedges tangled with briar and rampant brambles, where the underwood, a riot of grasses, lay thickly carpeted with age-old rotting leaves. Here martins still dabbled in shallow, muddy pools, and larks spun high, singing their unceasing song in the ethereal summer skies.

189

Several of us would go to the pictures together, Mavis and I remembering how several times we had **run** from Honor Oak School to the *Tower Cinema* in Rye Lane to get in before 4p.m. (school ended at 3.30p.m.). It was an awful rush, but we thus got in for 4d.- gasping for breath. Now things were different and there were many excellent films, "In which we Serve", "One of our aircraft is missing", "Clive of India", "Lady Hamilton", "Gone with the wind" and lovely Deanna Durbin come to mind; at the Gaumont, Odeon or Astor in Bromley, the ABC at Beckenham. Occasionally we went to the Lewisham Hippodrome for a musical comedy or ballet. The sweet ration was 2oz. a week, so when we went to the pictures we took a bag of chopped carrot to chew instead - there were continuous gluts of them, it was said that pilots ate them to help them to see in the dark - so we ate as many as we could.

On a different level, Mum and Dad took me to the opera; my Father, almost completely unappreciative of the arts, was always keen on this most complex one. Mother and I enjoyed them, but he - he was transported; any opera would do, Verdi, Bizet, Mozart, Wagner - he was happy, wrapped in wonder. He had started going to them early, at the Old Vic, never tired of them; I saw several, loved the music and the occasion, but often found the stories morbid and the action just plain grotesque. However, the highlight came, my birthday, was it 1946 or 7?; "The Magic Flute" at Covent Garden; magic indeed.

Poor Dad! His love of Russia never faltered and the fact that Britain and the U.S.S.R. were now allies gave rise to bouts of total euphoria. As I had been taken on Labour Day marches many years before, I allowed myself to be dragged along to the annual *Daily Worker* rallies at the Stoll Theatre, always, to my amazement, packed to capacity. On a stage draped with the motto, "From each according to his ability, to each according to his need", and blazoned with gigantic hammer and sickle flaunted on blood red banners, great choirs and bands played stirring Russian music.

Folk songs, patriotic rabble rousers and so on - mind you, it was highly professional but so motivated, so "not for art's sake", but Russia's. We were handed the words and supposed to join in as others did, lustily, "Fatherland of mine so vast and spacious", "Steppe land, my Steppe land" etc., The audience so remarkably generous, the collection all notes! "Well", said Mother, "It pleases him so much, and it doesn't hurt us." I got out of going as soon as I could though!.

Aunt Mill planned three outings; Donald Woolfit was doing Shakespeare - would I go with her? - she'd pay. I was very ungracious- (quite a pig), Mother spoke to me and in the end I agreed to go, and, am glad to say that I enjoyed my first experience of Shakespeare on the stage. I'd only done him in class, reading round for "O" Level; this real live performance was a totally different matter and a whole new world of delight opened up to me.

The war years are renowned for their, "Make do and mend" style of living, but this was nothing new; my family were well inured to that, that was how they were all reared, how they survived the depression, so no bleating from them about shortages - and no false pretence that those years were particularly bad either, no, that was how things had always been. They had to use their ingenuity and sharpen up their wits a bit, but that just added to the spice of life, kept them on their toes.

I speak not only for myself and my family, but for millions like us; we never had bought anything we did not *need*. My diet was basic, real stuff; tinned food was rare and pricey, never was I showered with goodies, such as sweets, shop cakes nor crisps - just invented. Foods from tropical regions were comparatively cheap, cocoa, rice, and "Five for six bananas", shouted the costers, meaning, five for 6d. Even so they were dealt out sparingly, this was pre-war, of course, during it these commodities were not much dearer, but scarce, bananas totally unobtainable for about five years. There was a fiddley "Points System", included in the ration book, you were allotted so many and used them as you pleased on what was available, in addition to basic rations. For the vast majority rationing was a great leveller, and I remember wishing that it could continue into the future. We were not divided into the "haves" and "have nots", it was share and share alike, except for the favoured few, and I never came into contact with any of those.

Vegetables were all home-grown, Cornwall supplying most of the new potatoes now that the Channel Islands were occupied, and to supplement the now intensive farming, allotments sprang up in every conceivable unused corner of land, areas of parks were dug up and put into production, we all, "Dug for Victory". My parents worked very hard in Waller Road garden, Dad always good at general maintenance, was now roped in to do the digging, he manfully wielded a spade, but never really enjoyed gardening, and he was to like it still less, when hearing that human dung and urine were excellent fertilisers, Mother collected what she could from whom she could, (it was difficult to make people co-operate), and grew, among other things, huge hearty lettuce and enormous runner beans on the proceeds. This continued for a number of years, special utensils being kept for the purpose; I need not add that her compost heaps were a work of art, but there was no more horse dung now, horses were a thing of the past. Mum put flower pots over dandelions to blanche them, and used the white leaves as chicory, exceedingly bitter, and I should add that she always paid herself, cheaply, for her produce, and saved the money thus collected to buy, "something special". Droughts occurred more than once during the war years, and it was illegal either to water the garden or to have more than five inches of water in the bath, so Dad painted a "Plimsoll" line in it, and fixed a hose to the out pipe so that she could water her plants. The water was *siphoned* out of the bath, I watched him go red in the face, eyes popping, as he sucked the air out of the pipe before the water would run.

That food was in short supply made us inventive, crumble toppings were thought up, National bread crumbs were dried in a slowly cooling oven, after it had been used - never waste fuel- and eaten as cereal, very tasty, too. Mum once tried to make a trifle from stale buns, for years she made orange peel into an inferior sort of candied peel, chopped up finely in a jam jar. We used dried eggs, horrible omelettes, like pale yellow leather and once or twice tried to eat whale meat - ugh - red meat tasting strongly of fish; and snoek. By the way, kitchen scraps were kept in a bucket for the Pig Swill Man.

Mum said, eyeing the materials on the table before her, "Anyone can be a good cook if they've got the ingredients, but they'd be a damn marvel to make a meal out of this." But, like most women then she was resourceful, she managed. It brought out the best in people, they evinced a sense of duty, were generous, calm, and they proved to themselves they had the wherewithal to cope. My reactions were obviously more light hearted than Mother's, coping was her responsibility, I only helped, was on the periphery.

Was Christmas any different? In essence it was the same; I became aware of the perennial hush that accompanies the shortest days, and for me nothing ever dimmed the joy of English, and Anglicized, carols. We hung our well-used decorations as before, but the chain of silver bells had lost their gleam, were tarnished and shabby; the little tree which once I thought so pretty, now resembled a tatty, bent old bottle brush, and the coloured lights had mostly lost their paint. We had stored items of grocery up for this special Day; I once queued up and got one orange - no more were greengrocer's shops gay with piles of these vivid fruits and tangerines wrapped in jewelled silver paper to enliven the festive season. Under the circumstances Christmas could not be other than muted, and on the whole fell rather flat. Had it lost its charm? For me, as already written, it never had much. We gave nice, small presents wrapped in bits of brown paper, listened to seasonal programmes on the wireless, and made sure of a blazing fire, and still took pleasure in paper games. We not only sang carols round the piano, but old "favourites" as well.

To tell the truth, by my mid-teens I was fed up with them, things like, "Polly-wolly Doodle", Excelsior" and "Oft in the stilly night", especially the last with its, "I feel like one who treads alone some banquet hall deserted.… the eyes that shone, now dim and gone, and all but me departed," and so on; gave me the creeps. We would have readings, I appreciated those, but we were a motley, yet enclosed crew, Mill never getting out of her "Scrooge" rut, Mother desperate to keep us on the right track and balance any conviviality would read a solemn passage from, "*The Friend*", Nell trying to get out of it and make some tea, though oft-times submitting, would choose a bit from Pickwick. Dad pressing us to a glass of sherry, singing, "Christmas Day in the Workhouse", and then in

194

response to my continued nagging, "the Miner's Dream of Home"; I loved that, he could never understand why, not keen on it himself; I screwed myself up to imagine leaving England forever, and found it unbearable.

Our Christmas dinner in those years was usually a rabbit, which we purchased from some Quakers at Keston, the Hopkins. To digress a moment, impressed on my memory is the fact that, after long deliberation, it was felt necessary to "elder" Hollis Hopkins, a retired Engineer who had spent all his working life in Egypt, for using Meeting for Worship as a political platform for his radical beliefs, speaking for at least twenty minutes every Sunday; the situation must have been dealt with very sensitively, because although not a member, he continued to attend Meeting regularly until his death years later. The Hopkins had a household whose setting and cultivated way of life typified many Bromley Friends of that era; they presented an engaging picture to the world, and I was ensnared; "that's it," I thought, "that's what I like"! To return to the rabbits, they were delicious, ready skinned, we were lucky to get them and they kept one for us regularly. With the skins they made pugs, i.e. gloves without separate fingers, Mum and I both had pairs, quite luxurious; and fetching the rabbit from Keston made a pleasant outing for mother and me, and we brought home bunches of greenery, holly and ivy.

I have said that I continued to spend a lot of time in Bromley, but Mum went often too, to shop and attend the Women's International League of Peace and Freedom, held at the home of the Bradley's, "The Glen", Farnborough Park. She also visited friends in Copthorne Ave., in particular Mrs. Hawkins, who, until rationing ended in 1954, eagerly exchanged her cheese ration for a quarter of tea, that was our reward for drinking tea like dishwater, and most useful it was; from these outings to Bromley, Mum often returned home with a bagful of nettles to boil up as greens. My Father was by now right off meat, except sausage, ham and tripe, and Mother was vegetarian for ethical reasons, so they both had vegetarian ration books. Nell and Mill, who liked nothing better than a good roast or thick stew, and I, ordinary books. Between us we managed well enough.

We did a lot of shopping down at the Gate, but were registered at the Co-op at Nunhead Green, that puritanical, teetotal, profits-for-the-workers, institution, "Each for all, All for Each", they claimed. I wonder what ardent co-opers of old would make of an advert seen today suggesting that if you have visitors, breakfast should start with Bucks Fizz, champagne now available in all stores!. I never learnt the names of joints, as it was all, "carcass meat" or offal, bread was all "National", neither brown nor white, just khaki, margarine was called that, the alternative was plain and simple "Cooking fat". I believe that the butter ration was 2oz. per person per week and the cheese ration the same. Chicken was rare, a treat for special occasions, they weren't bred by the thousand in batteries then. Eggs were scarce, as was everything, but I have read that this was a blessing in disguise, keeping us fit and healthy. Natural foods still followed the pattern of the seasons, so in spring when a glut of eggs made them cheap, they were preserved in a pail of isinglass; runner beans were salted in large preserving jars, and apples peeled, cored and dried on lines in the sun; other fruits in their season, bottled; Graham Farish, a local Bromley man, invented a special lid and clasp to fit ordinary jam jars, most successful and thus secured himself a fortune.

One needed to be both imaginative and industrious to deal with the clothing situation, Mum was useless, but Mill shone; Dad's collars, cuffs and trouser turn-ups had always been "turned", of course, but now elbows of our knitted garments were finely re-knitted in, you would never have known; she unpicked a suit of Tom's and made a skirt and simple jacket for me, incredible. She also "turned" one of her excellent Harris tweed coats, that is, unpicked it all and remade it, inside out - it looked good - I've never known anything like it. Nell was outstanding, as I have said, there was nothing she couldn't turn her hand to; we did insertions, darned, mended, and turned sheets sides- to- middle. One could buy parachute silk, good heavy stuff in odd lengths, and rice or bean bags in which these commodities were delivered to the shops, coarse, unbleached cotton, printed all over in indelible black ink with description of contents; these were snapped up, just wash them and sew on four tapes, and there you were, a pillow case for sixpence and no coupons, they lasted for years.

I think it was in the last year of the war, when Stanley Hills, a Quaker chemist, brought Mother some white powder in a jam pot. "Here you are", he said, "Try this on your washing, you'll all be using it in a year or so, it's synthetic soap, we've almost perfected it." "Aren't you clever", she replied sarcastically, "It'll be synthetic everything before we've finished". That was the first time I saw detergent, as it came to be called.

Entering into the spirit of the times, among other things, I once decorated some plain drinking glasses with festoons of flowers with old oil paints, quite a success; another day I made three nice flower pot holders from old wax gramophone records; Mother paused to admire my handiwork, saying ironically, "I just hope you never marry a rich man." I looked at her blankly, uncomprehending. "Well your talent for making something from nothing would be completely wasted, wouldn't it?" I thought that one over.

War had become a way of life; we never threw anything away - we never had, and we weren't likely to start now; it might "come in handy", and often, it did.

Holidays, Flying Bombs and Rockets, and my first job

During the Easter holiday period, 1944, when we were settled back at New Cross, but before I left school, I went with Nell to stay with Lily Sawyer and her Mother for five or six days. It was the first time I had been there since our last holiday of 1939, and Eastbourne had vastly changed (so had I). It had suffered greatly from both raids and bombardment, and Lily and her 91 year old Ma now lived in a small terraced house near the Redoubt. There were no visitors, many of the shops were boarded up, the entire coastline was a restricted area, no one had access to it, the boats had all vanished, and where once bathing huts and kiosks had stood along the promenade, ran great roll upon roll, many lines deep, of barbed wire, completely blocking off the pier. Beyond that, where the land met the sea, was a triple row of "Dragon's teeth". large four sided concrete blocks set closely and alternately along the coast as far as the eye could reach. I suppose really, it presented a desolate and uninviting appearance, and their house had few amenities, but I got a lot from that visit. Old Mrs.Sawyer was crabby and malicious, with narrow crafty eyes, thin silver hair done up in a tight little knot on top of her head and one single tooth. She was tiny, bent and withered, draped from head to toe in black, she made pointed, sly remarks, but she impinged on me but little. Nell and Lily were the best of pals, Lily was affectionate, gay, with a sharpness which gave a zest to life; she was one of those rare people who live totally in the present - and find it good.

Thereafter I stayed with them once or twice a year, until I married; the pattern for these visits hardly varied; sometimes Nell and I went by bus to Lewes,

Crowborough or Seaford, or the three of us might go a shorter distance to Alfreston, Pevensey or just Old Town, but the marvel to me was, I could go out and explore on *my own*, for hours at a time, even at night. The abnormal darkness incurred by the blackout enhanced the beauty of the sunsets, and no lesser lights detracted from the magic of the moon casting its silver path across the restless sea, bathing the scene in its pale and subtle light. These days were simple yet wonderful; Lily always had stale bread to spare for the gulls, and as I stood alone in the midst of those greedy, aggressive creatures, I knew that to stand on the shore, the open sea before me, held for me the same spell that it had always done. And then I felt so well, it seemed I trod on air; once I walked to the top of Beachy Head in an impenetrable white sea mist, fog horn blowing, surprised Jackdaws skimming my head, everything was dreaming; a blessed realisation swept over me, "What bliss", I thought, "Nobody knows where I am!". I had experienced this same heady thought when playing truant, but this was better, unimpaired by guilt. By the time I reached the road above Meads once again, my hair was saturated and my coat running with water, but back at the house, my elderly companions simply agreed that it was a great adventure, I boiled a kettle, washed my hair and was soon warm, fed and watered; I've rarely known such freedom.

It was in June 1944 that I took the German O level examination; three years since the blitz, and life had returned to a form of normality. The bomb sites were desolate gaps, some vast, but the rubble had been cleared, wild flowers had taken over, devastated London foamed rosily with self-sown rosebay willow herb; nature is so generous and forgiving.

On that particular morning I climbed the steps up to the platform at Nunhead Station as usual, at that time in the morning it was deserted, I didn't have to get to school until 11.0 o'clock. I was early, so walked to the end, and stood in warm sunshine, my mind running through the complicated, unreasonable rules of German grammar, when suddenly I became aware of something abnormal, and glancing up saw a small plane, apparently diving directly at me. Immediately I knew what it was, - a flying bomb, or doodle-bug as we called them, - the first ones had been sent over only a few days before, exactly a week after "D" Day. I felt very vulnerable, Nunhead station is high and exposed, I could only watch in horror; in less than a soundless minute it had buried itself in a row of houses lying immediately below, I saw the impact, there was an almighty explosion, screams, people running, crying out, as clouds of dust and debris flew high into the air. Dear God, I thought, what can I do?. I was answered by the arrival of the train; "Crofton Park, Catford.... Shortlands, Bromley South", the guard - there was no porter - called out, as if nothing had occurred. That appeared to be the answer, carry on regardless; no one knew anything about it at Bromley, everyone going about their business as usual, but Mum had heard it and had dashed up there to find out what had happened.

These weapons were universally hated, there was no warning, they dropped anywhere, any time. Our troops had landed in Normandy, and although in no doubt that the going would be tough, hard and slow, expectations ran high and there was a feeling of exhilaration abroad; and so, to be suddenly showered with these things was galling in the extreme and considerably lowered our spirits for a while.

Nightingale Lane, Bickley – June 1944

I remember so clearly another sunny day, just after I had
started work, of which more anon. I had walked home to
dinner as always and was at the table eating the usual
thick vegetable soup, knobs of cheese floating in it,
scattered with dried mint- "To expel the wind"; windows
and doors were wide open to the hot sun, geraniums
bright on the window sill. Facing the window, I looked
up into the clear blue sky, and my eyes fastened on to
another V1, silent, silver, menacing, "Oh", I gasped, "It's
coming, coming straight at us!" ineffectually pointing.
Only Mum and Nell were there, they jumped up as it
exploded, immediately at the back of us in Erlanger Rd.,
Nell's face ran with blood as flying glass splinters
embedded themselves in it. "I'm alright, alright", she
insisted, "Well, you don't look it", said Mother, dabbing at
her with strips of old sheet, kept handy for just such
emergency, delicately removing tiny splinters of glass. I
made a good strong pot of tea and left them to it; back to
work.

I had finally left school towards the end of July; before starting work I spent a week at Poole, with friends of my parents, Lizzie and John Bryant. They had retired there in 1938 after their father died, he had been one of the builders of the Haberdasher's Estate, Lizzie and Mum had gone to St. Mary's church and evening classes together at Waller Rd. School; now their Mother was dead too, and they frequently asked whether any of us would care to stay with them for a rest and a change? My parents decided that such a holiday would do me good, and I vaguely thought it might be pleasant, was attracted by the idea of doing something quite different. I went from Paddington, thrilled to be travelling about on my own, and I enjoyed my stay enormously. The house was solid 1930s, on a hill high overlooking the harbour, and I remember my bedroom; wallpaper being unobtainable, they had newly distempered the walls beige, and effectively stippled them with soft blue flecks. The view from the window was glorious, the harbour busy with boats of all kinds, while Catalina flying boats rode majestically on the rippling waters; Brownsea Island lay in mid- distance with the hills of Purbeck on the horizon. La, as she now preferred to be called, took me by bus to Bournemouth and Wimbourne, and by train to Wareham, which seemed to me the model of what a small country town should be, with its attractive High Street, beautiful old churches and quay side washed by the Frome; it has never lost its appeal to me. I wandered about Poole on my own, the old harbour was a hive of industry, and it was a privilege to watch the great flying boats land and take off from that enclosed stretch of water.

John Bryant had had polio as a boy and was crippled, he rarely went out, but had a deep interest in music, owning the first hi-fi equipment I had ever seen, two large, separate loud speakers. Everything was played terribly

203

loudly, but I remember my first hearing of Bruch's violin concerto, found it absolutely ravishing. On their mantelpiece stood a magnificent art-deco vase, swirls of red, gold and purple, which I admired. "Isn't it lovely?" said Lizzy, "Mother's in there - we had to get the best for *her*!". Totally non-plussed, I thought she'd gone mad, or I hadn't heard right; seeing my blank expression, she hastily added, "It's her ashes, you know". No, I didn't know; how morbid, I thought, and moved away.

It proved a good week, and next year, my parents vowed, they would go there too, if invited.

My first job, which lasted two weeks, was at the Library of the University of London; the Librarian was Miss Quinn, a Quaker, and I was invited to work there a month to see whether I liked it; I did not. I found it stuffy and exclusive, the air so rarefied that I could hardly breath and I was relieved to be told during that time, that there was a vacancy for me with Deptford Public Libraries, I had already had an interview. I started work at New Cross Library, New Cross Gate, 3rd. September 1944, exactly five years after the outbreak of war; I was happy there; under war-time conditions it was a challenge, I liked the borrowers, and I earned my first real wages, 37/6 per week, paid out in a semi-transparent envelope. I got an old cigar box of Uncle Tom's, and divided it with cardboard into sections:- Holidays, Birthdays, Christmas, Clothes, etc., and, giving mother £1 a week, divided up the rest accordingly, regularly putting in an allotted sum, 2/6d. 5/- whatever. I was well organised and born to thrift, but now and again had a binge - early next spring Kingston's was stacked with great bunches of mimosa, I'd always loved it, now I could buy a 6d bunch each week if I wanted - and the same with cherries, so juicy and sweet; the notion that it *was in my power* to buy as many as I wanted went to my head like wine.(a tram-conductor earned £2-10-0d. per week in 1946)

There were three of us at New Cross Library, Miss Hayward, Branch Librarian, an agreeable woman of forty, engaged to a small, hairy lorry driver, whose deformed hand, thumb and two fingers joined with a great nail, kept him out of the forces, in a reserved occupation. *Forty*, I thought, engaged, how *old*, how could she? and to that horrible man? Ugh! We were allowed a ten minute coffee break, no more, two of us went up together and often she would burst into paroxysms of tears, agonising whether to wed him or no; young and brutal, I advised her not to bother. I couldn't hope to understand, but perhaps the "good cry" helped to ease her stress. The other assistant, Brenda and I were entitled to National Cocoa, as were all employees under eighteen, a seven pound tin of it was kept in the staff room, a stark affair indeed by today's standards - an ancient armchair with its stuffing dropping out, two rickety wooden chairs, an old table, an older cupboard, decrepit gas fire dumped in the original fire-place, gas ring and sink; no frills. The National beverage was an acceptable mixture of cocoa, dried milk and sugar, you poured on boiling water and Bob's your Uncle, a tasty, nourishing drink; we paid a little for this.

But quiet, reliable, hardworking Brenda was entitled to much more than this; two months younger than me, but starting work a year earlier, and paid less as she had passed no exams, she found herself pregnant, and greatly to my surprise and relief was thrilled by the prospect of becoming a Mum. (My God, I thought, rather you than me.) She was superb; Ian, a naval rating of eighteen got compassionate leave, they got married, and back to his ship he went. Normally she would have continued to live with her parents, but being the eldest of five, (unusual then), living in a little house in Deptford, she jumped at the offer of a tiny flat in Pepys Rd., and lots of people, including borrowers, gave her things; Miss Hayward, (note the formality), and I both covered for her towards the end of her pregnancy when she got tired; her dark, regular features became white and drawn, but she continued to work until about a month before baby was due, she needed the money. I learnt a lot from Brenda.

We were still under attack from flying bombs, and they continued to be directed against London until well into September, but the full force of their destructive powers had by then been overcome by brilliant manoeuvering on the part of our fighters, who intercepted them by hooking up their wings and throwing them to the ground; incredibly dangerous. The allied forces were making headway in France, but to the North on the Dutch coast, the Nazis had just completed gigantic concrete rocket launchers, pointing straight at London, and on 8th. September the first one fell, it caused havoc. For the V11s, like the flying bombs, there could be no warning, these horrendous weapons crashed down haphazardly at any time of day or night, but, as in the Blitz, we carried on with our lives as normally as possible. Went to bed, to work, went out and about, cooked, dusted, swept and gardened; we knew in our hearts that this would not last, it was a last desperate, vicious attack from a now slowly disintegrating enemy; all we had to do was hold on, and hope and strength were given to us to do just that.

New Cross Library had a glass roof, which completely blew in one morning when a V1 fell nearby; the caretaker came, we closed up, and all spent the day, dressed in our blue overalls, clearing up heaps of shattered glass.

Perhaps two months later, one Saturday lunch hour (November, 25th.1944), I was on duty alone, not unusual, Central were too short staffed to send a relief, when a rocket landed on Woolworth's at New Cross. 160 people were killed and many more were terribly injured; the explosion was deafening, and the tarpaulin which now covered the roof was torn right off. Borrowers came in shaken, with rumours of what had occurred; my two colleagues returned from lunch and I walked up the hill to mine; my folk were so glad to see me, they didn't yet know precisely where the rocket had fallen; there were dark and terrible days that winter. Altogether 447 V2s were fired at London, killing 2,700 people and injuring three times as many.

We worked broken shifts; every third Saturday was off, the next worked until 5.0pm., the following until 9.0pm. Saturday was our busiest day, and from 5.0 until 8.0, with only two of us there, we stood at the counter working fast, non-stop queues forming at either counter; after eight o'clock the rush subsided, we made a cup of tea and started clearing up - piles of returned books, queries, requests - we never once sat down.

Before leaving 1944, with its strong blend of starting work, flying bombs, rockets and holidays, there is another item I should like to mention briefly. A village I stayed in many times, from about 1937 until I got married, and then John and I visited together. "Uncle" George Wiggins had retired to Buck's Green, Rudgwick, in Sussex, in the early 30s; a friend of the family, when they had all been members of the Ethical Society together, he had been a lodger of ours, but left before I was born; he and his wife were separated, but had come together again on retirement. After her death George managed very well on his own, with Rex, a large Sussex spaniel for

207

company; Mum and Dad visited occasionally, Dad wondering why, "*old George* had buried himself down there". Nell went to stay for a day or two once a year to do a bit of mending and cleaning, and I went with her.

I always looked forward to going and packed a small case happily; we travelled by train from Rye Lane to Horsham, had coffee and a look round, then caught the two hourly Cranleigh bus from the Carfax.

The bungalow was a basic retirement property constructed of asbestos boards, with asbestos tile roof. There was no electricity, no street lamps, we used a hand-pumped "Aladdin" pressure lamp which had a gas mantle and was filled with paraffin, which shed an excellent light, and was supplemented with lovely old oil lamps. There was no sanitation, down the garden, a chaotic riot of flourishing plants, stood a little shed containing a strong wooden frame supporting a bucket, into which one did what was necessary and there being no flush, simply sprinkled on some disinfectant. George emptied it every morning into the sump at the end of his plot, which was cleared out by the Council once a month. There was no water supply either, but a well in the garden, from which a pipe had been fitted to a further pump at the sink - no taps- one pulled this pump back and forth and hazy looking water jetted out spasmodically from a faucet.

Of course there was no milkman, every morning I'd go next door with a jug and get what was ordered from the cowman and his wife who lived there. I've not forgotten them either, not because they were kind and friendly and took me up to the milking, but chiefly because I thought Isaiah Lillywhite was Mrs L.'s son, not her husband - he was thirty years her junior - and I was flummoxed, not having come across that combination before!

Sometimes I would walk round by the "Cricketer's" pub, with Rex straining at the leash, fearful lest he escape to indulge his obsession in rolling in fresh cow muck; powerful and full of glutinous sediment, at least once every time I was there this animal had to be shut outside, his long coat, every inch of it plastered, as George put it with, "Cow's crap". A further walk took one to the church, there was nowhere else much to go, apparently a great lack of footpaths. Nell kept busy, though once we took the bus as far as Guildford. Every evening we played cribbage, he was a dab hand at it, and if my attention wandered, old George would snap out sharply, "Wake up England"! He could be blunt and sardonic when he chose.

I think really the charm of "The Bat's Wing" lay in its being so primitive, so entirely different; the name I found inscrutable. George Wiggins had once worked for Young's of Bromley, who made carriages; he gave me a miniature set, and owned a fine large scale model which he kept in a glass case in the living room. The visits were not exciting, but it was real country; farming, although intensive, had not then become the mechanised industry it is today. There were lots of workers in the fields, the whole area was pretty if unspectacular, unspoilt and completely rural.

Always now, when I smell the pungent green of a soft spring shower, or catch the scent of privet flowers, I see once again that lush, unmanageable Sussex garden, a riot of cabbages, wallflowers, roses and forgotten sections of ancient untamed hedgerows full of nestlings and birdsong.

I cannot think now what pleased me so much about those brief excursions, but please me they did, very much.

The End of World War II

One thing stands out clearly in my memory of early 1945, conscription for women ended; it had caused me much concern; I could readily understand and accept the Quaker testimony of pacifism as an ideal, but found that it was in danger of becoming a dogma. In the circumstances under which we were living I was not convinced. A large percentage of Friends were, (and are), radicals by temperament, I was not; I saw myself no different from my fellows, I aligned myself with them. I saw evil as an amoeba, a growing living thing, forcing itself into any path open to its power. Some things, I thought, are more important than life itself, and I was by no means the only person with pacifist leanings to arrive at that conclusion. I had intimations that one should fight for love of something, and that that was of a different order from fighting based on hatred.

However, I was still only seventeen, and had considered as carefully as possible what to do when called up; the forces were out, my first choice was the Friends Ambulance Unit, but still I hankered after nursing, I would apply again, and thought it highly likely that I would be accepted, I seemed quite well, and the need was desperate. I will admit, too, that I fancied myself in a nurses uniform, the flattering white cap, full skirt and trim belt, really fetching, but I knew too that I should like the life and do well at it. As an alternative the Women's Land Army beckoned, I loved the country and animals; but had an inner misgiving - if I wasn't strong enough to be a nurse, could I cope with work on the land in all weathers, all hours - and how would a townie like me manage with pigs - and bulls? But still, working in the country held its charms, and again, the uniform most certainly did! I pictured myself in jodhpurs, shirt, neat, dark green pullover and round felt hat tied with a cord; pretty good, I thought - not considering how I'd look at the end of a twelve hour stint in bad weather.

When conscription was ended, a little before my eighteenth birthday, I felt that I had been let off the hook, was relieved and grateful to be able to continue working uninterrupted at the Library; the thoughts I'd had on the question of pacifism never left me, they changed and altered over the years like everything else.

Now for an ordinary, everyday story, which, however humdrum, left a deep impression on me. I was sitting at the old living room table writing letters, and Mum was stoking the fire, when Nell poked her head round the door;- "If there's a ring, I'll go, it'll be Mary (a school friend's elder sister) coming to have her skirt altered." We noticed her come and go, and carried on with what we were doing. I shan't forget Aunt's face; she came in silently, shutting the door behind her; something about her made us look up; slowly she said, "She's going to have a baby. She's at least two months gone". I gasped, "She can't be; anyway how do *you* know? It's too early". Nell looked at me tellingly, "My dear, when you've fitted as many women as I have, you're in no doubt". Mum and Nell exchanged glances. "Let's leave it, shall we; there's nothing we can do anyway, but let's hope and pray this time you're wrong", said Mother.

Only a week or so after that I met this friend at Charing Cross; thoughts of Mary eddied in my mind, but nothing would have made me mention her. We walked across Trafalgar Square, busy in the bright, cold sunlight, and she bent to look at the droplets falling into one of the fountains. Staring at the water, "Mary's going to have a baby", she said, turning to me with shocked, pained eyes. The earth moved beneath my feet, paused a second, then

211

went on its old, a-moral way; only rarely have I experienced that; I called on something inside myself to give me the right thing to say as she talked. Pretty, lively Mary, in the Land Army, had been seduced by a Canadian soldier, at the Crooked Billet; she did not want to marry him, she was going to stay with an Aunt in Lancashire, then go to a Church of England Home to have the baby. "But it's Mother", said my friend, "She is devastated, the humiliation, it's all a nightmare, and it will never, never end, she'll never stop crying".

Mother went to see the girl's mother and found it was so; she was ill with weeping and remained so for a long time. However, once the baby was put into her arms, she gathered herself up, accepted the bitter pill and within a few months Mary was fully accepted back into the community and went to work again. And the baby? Her grandmother cared for her for the next five years, when Mary got married. "She's lucky to find someone who'll have her", folk said.

This run-of-the-mill tale is set out in detail to show how things were in 1945, and to let you know what a marked influence it had on me; the moral was not lost, I grasped it and vowed to learn by it and did. I was not the only one by far; a little healthy fear of the consequences taught many of us, as it had taught women from time immemorial, to toe the line. For the results of casual sex were too terrible to contemplate, spreading ripples of pain, anger and degradation through family, friends and neighbours, however compassionate, warmhearted and loving they may be. That is how it was; perhaps it was unjust that it should be so, but at the same time we acknowledged the reason for this discipline; society was far gentler then than even fifty years before - and the

Canadian did have to pay an allowance until his daughter was sixteen.

The years rolled on; I enjoyed my work and attended evening classes at Catford studying for the Library Association Examinations. I experienced a general sense of well-being and confidence; I wore scarlet, wooden soled sandals and an oatmeal jigger; I achieved an excellent "page boy" hair style, running the front hair through with a comb dipped in peroxide of hydrogen, kept in the house as a disinfectant. "How fair your hair goes in the summer", remarked my unsuspicious Ma. I fully agreed. My hair was quite long, sometimes I wore it in a snood, I liked those, had several different colours. In winter I wore a "swagger" coat and had a "halo" hat; Mother always impressed upon me the unimportance of outward appearance - apart from keeping myself neat and clean; but I found this unacceptable and felt sure that many a Quaker in her spotless dove gray, demure, pristine white collar and fetching bonnet was as aware of the subtle attraction of her garb as many a painted lady was of her ostentatious silks and furbelows. Nor did it follow that one woman was "better" than another.

From 1945-48, I had a series of boy friends, met through work or Young Friends at Peckham. Occasionally I wrote to my old Sunday School teacher, since 1939 in the FAU, and for several years a POW in Stalag ... Vague romantic thoughts floated through my mind concerning this individual, however, on his repatriation it immediately became apparent that he was in reality a complete stranger, and nothing could have killed off my dreams more surely than his informing me that his aim in life was to join a commune called the "Bruderhof". Needless to say, aims diametrically opposed to mine! Why did I continue to attend Meeting? Hard to answer. Habit?

213

partly; partly also to do with the existence of a group of young Friends of like age, who could discuss subjects of mutual interest and be companionable together. Several of us actually enjoyed Monthly Meeting, it was a good occasion in those days, and it was usual for the women to take their knitting, I certainly did - it was an added subject of conversation!. To be honest, it did not take me long to discover that these potential Quakers were not *per se* more interesting, more spiritual, responsible, thoughtful or sincere than the people I knew who were not connected with the Society. I had somehow expected them to be, and they were not.

Previously I have mentioned the enviable life-style of some Quakers; I was materialistic and immature, the way they lived contrasted so sharply with my own background that I was dazzled. That is in truth only a shadow of the reality; there was something indefinable about many of these "weighty" Friends which appealed to me at a deep level; they evinced a "goodness" in all its diversity, a wholesomeness; they were aware of, and paid attention to, the spiritual side of life. I find myself remembering not any one friend in particular, for a Meeting for Worship is like a cake, and its members are the ingredients. Its composition will vary, it may be rich and fruity or plain and simple; it should not be allowed to become stale, there may be a dash too much zest, or an overloading with treacle, a souring with too much acid vinegar, whereas a dash of ginger, a hint of spice and a good pinch of salt-which-has-not-lost-its-savour are as essential as the basic ingredients which give it body and cohesion. Any of these items are of small account on their own, but fused in the *Light of the Holy Spirit,* the attributes of each blend, and are transformed into spiritual nourishment for all who partake.

The attitude of these Friends to religion affected everything they did, there was a richness and sincerity, a strength of character and faith without which their comfortable homes, their tasteful clothes would have been but vulgar shells and vapid accoutrements. I should add that denomination has never been a strong point with me; I was not a Quaker by convincement, but by tradition; I believe I would have found people evincing similar characteristics in any church or chapel, or indeed outside them altogether, for I have since done so.

From about 1948-53 I rarely went to Meeting or to a church service at all; life seemed just brimming over, bubbling full to overflowing, mostly with peaks of happiness, but naturally a few pits of desolation too. Apart from evening classes, I went to plays, to the pictures and to London, one older admirer took me more than once to the New Theatre (now the Albery), most vividly I remember Laurence Olivier's Oedipus, and, I think, School For Scandal; but I got fed up with him (not Olivier). Lyons Corner Houses were a favourite rendezvous, "Always gallivanting off somewhere", Mother would snap with ill-concealed annoyance. "Upon my word", she exclaimed more than once, "You've got a mad streak in you, like Aunt Harriet, hasn't she Nell?" Nell agreed that I took after her Aunt, not particularly to look at, just in manner. However, I also stayed in sometimes to do my hair, darn my stockings and so on; by the way, John gave me my first nylons in 1948, sent over from the US by his sister. "You don't do enough in the home", growled Mum. "Well, there are three of you, you don't need me as well", was my answer. Nell would say, "Enjoy yourself while you can - you'll learn fast enough when you have to". Which I did. Remarks like, "You're never at home, where are you gadding off to now?, you're getting to be a proper little flibberty gibbet", were constantly on my Mother's lips, but I was becoming aware of the merciless bonds of love which had so constricted the lives of these three sisters. For in very truth, where many children are painfully deprived of this commodity, I was in danger of being inundated, and determined to be "free"; not easy to achieve while yet responding with continuing affection on my part, but this I set out to do.

Healthwise I was fine, apart from several severe bouts of tonsillitis experienced between the ages of about fifteen and twenty, which were a worry as caused by the same streptococcus which caused Rheumatic Fever. Imprinted on my memory is the first time I was prescribed the new cure-all, the anti-biotic, M & B tablets; I was given to believe that after the first one, I should jump out of bed cured, instead, I thought I would die. I went stone cold, was violently sick could hear my heart beating like a drum but couldn't breath, awful; I preferred tonsillitis; Mum put them down the toilet.

I well remember the great build up of excitement as VE Day approached; we were given two days holiday, and a tense joyousness enveloped all; the war was over, there was enormous relief and thanksgiving, the Lights of London shone once more, and the nation celebrated with gusto. Huge bonfires, prepared during the week previous, blazed on many of the desolate bomb sites, such as that in Erlanger road, and there was plenty of torn and broken wood to be had from the previous months of rocket disasters. There is something primitive and cleansing in a great communal bonfire; it does things to you; people from the whole neighbourhood were drawn to them as by a magnet, stood in desultory conversation in the heat of the flames, thinking of the past, wondering about the future, revelling in the knowledge that now, at this moment in time, they could relax and be glad.

The excitement was a tangible thing, everyone was outside, bunting and flags were dug out and appeared in profusion - those who hadn't any, like us, put fairy lights round the front windows, and street parties for children were arranged overnight, there was one in Waller Road; it was incredible and wonderful. But was it all delirious jollity? No; beneath it all lay a strata of grief, for the millions who had perished during the last six years of war, for the millions more mutilated, for the broken lives, broken homes and for those still fighting, or held prisoner in the Far East. In spite of all that, we had need collectively to rejoice, to dance, sing and make merry.

On the afternoon of VE Day itself, Ann from the Library came to tea and we all sat in the front room playing "Oujah", one tap for "Yes", two for "No". We put one finger each on the tumbler and it moved mysteriously round the alphabet, spelling out words, we were all a little mad and frightened ourselves silly; I have never played it before or since. Ann and I were going up to Trafalgar Square with two other Library girls, and started to get ready, and feeling light-hearted and frivolous, I actually put on some powder and lipstick; Mill dared to reproach me and I was livid:- "You'd have been the first to use it if it had been available in your day", I said. (I didn't know how right I was!)."With your papier poudre and tonka beans - you went as far as you dared.". Funny what sticks in the mind. She looked up as though I'd hit her, but said no more, (nor did she ever), as Ann came in, and eager to be off, we set out. Not infrequently after I've been cuttingly rude I've felt a pang of remorse, but not this time - I felt damn glad; interfering, sanctimonious busybody.

In the West End any trace of underlying grief was obliterated, it was unbelievable, unforgettable a surging mass of exultant people, vibrant with excitement and gladness, all caught up in the intoxication of that unique moment. In Trafalgar Square all so amazingly good humoured; all ages, sorts and conditions of men (and women). We four girls - all under twenty - were safe, confident, exuberant; there was no fear or threat, only frothy delight, plus a vague air of unreality which hung over it all. Reluctantly, as it grew late, we left the heady delights of the noisy, singing city, and went home by loaded tram, everyone singing - lights full on - after midnight; but no-one minded, everyone else was up too, except the Aunts, the radio on, the kettle boiling and a snack ready.

After the brief, crazy exuberance of VE Day, things rapidly returned to normal, by that I mean we quickly shed any gaiety, took stock of our various private situations and got on with living. I certainly do not mean that life went back to being as it was in 1939; not for a single person; and for millions life had been cruelly extinguished altogether. It was soon after VE Day that the first news concerning concentration camps began to seep through. None of us will ever forget it, the impact of those first pictures, the early reports of what were found to be extermination camps were seared into our consciousness forever. There had been propaganda against the Germans, naturally, but no-one, not even their bitterest enemy had envisaged *such* evil; total, unimaginable, remorseless abounding and refined. Words are futile; but I remember, deep inside, feeling that my decision not to be a pacifist was justified. It was forty years later that we stayed with an elderly Quaker couple who had retired to Weymouth; Dr. Barrington served in the RAMC and was one of the first men to enter Belsen in

218

April 1945. That night, for the first time ever, he talked about it and showed us his own notes and photographs; I thought, hell must be like that; death, unmitigated suffering, cruelty and madness. That night he walked for long periods in his sleep, talking of what he found there; and that was why he never came to Meeting, a birthright Friend, he could not reconcile God and Belsen.

BELSEN

The discovery and findings of these camps were made public during the next few months. I was given two thick packets of photographs to open in the Reference Library, not knowing what they contained. It took a strong stomach and a stronger soul to pause and assimilate the facts; one felt numb, frozen in disbelief. Stunned, we had thought ourselves inured to horrors; until then we as a nation had not fully understood the degree of barbarism we had so narrowly escaped. Ten million people, mainly Jews, but also Christians, gypsies and socialists, men, women and children had been exterminated. I had to force myself to remember that nothing is black and white, that there were good, kind and brave Germans too.

219

Perhaps until then, even having lived through that war, and filled with knowledge of war from my earliest years, I believed vaguely in the perfectibility of man; as an abstruse, distant ideal. If I did, then after Summer 1945, I did no longer, and subsequent events have done nothing to alter my outlook. I was brought up among people who still believed in the hopeful Victorian maxim that once everyone was educated, well housed, had enough to eat, we would automatically all become saint-like, inhabiting a minor utopia. How wrong they were; and I had once innocently believed that burning one's fellow men alive on bonfires and such like, was a thing of the dim and distant past; how wrong I was there too. Equally, however, I was filled with awe at the resilience of the human spirit to overcome such evil; resolutely we turned to face the future.

La and John Bryant did invite us all to Poole for a week that August; they were as welcoming as previously, the scenery as beautiful and my parents enjoyed it very much. But always, when memories of this holiday return to me, I have a vision of the three of us standing by the harbour wall, looking out over the sunny waters, people relaxed and at ease, while the placards scream, "A Bomb dropped on Hiroshima". I had no notion of its implication; Mother did, she said bitterly, "Man has an infinite capacity to destroy himself, there's no end to his ingenuity - you'll see." Looking across to the distant headland, my Father disagreed, he said firmly, "You might not think that way if you were stuck out in the East being tortured to death. I think they both expressed aspects of the truth.

Afterword

Basically my life continued along the lines already described, until John and I married at Peckham Meeting House, according to Quaker tradition, in 1949. The conditions of the early days of peace were little different from those of war, rationing continued until 1954, and there were severe fuel shortages and power cuts, felt most keenly during the long and severe winter of 1947. Excitement ran high at the election of a Labour Government, we were full of wild euphoria, as a local government employee, I acted as polling clerk. I remember too, the programme of Nationalization, the Partitioning of India, the frightful slaughter which followed, and the agonizing time of the Berlin Crisis.

1946 was the last time I went on holiday with my parents, and then unwillingly, to Torquay. We stayed at a nicer guest House than ever before, (Dad was earning more money), we discovered Devon, they loved it and I grudgingly accepted it. In 1947 Mavis and I went to Ireland, and in 1948 to Scotland, although by then John and I were engaged, but I had promised her and it was a good fortnight.

I should mention that towards the end of 1946 I was transferred from New Cross Library (no longer in use,1991), where I had settled into a comfortable routine - after Brenda left in 1945 I was second in command - to Deptford Central Library, opposite Pynes, Lewisham Way. There was a staff of about twelve there and it took me some time to adjust. The move was arranged in order to further my career, but I resented it at the time, could not foresee that it would later prove a blessing. I cycled to work, about ten minutes, so still went home to dinner, as did the others; Brockley Cross had trams then and I had a bad fall from my bike getting the wheels stuck in the tram lines, folk from the fish shop picked me up, gave me tea and a wash, and I pushed the bike on to work.

I was given a thorough grounding in all aspects of Library work, and soon became accustomed to working there and appreciated the move. I never liked the Chief Assistant, Miss de Montmorency, who was in charge of us girls, though I didn't dislike her as much as some who were told in no uncertain terms to, "Wash off that make-up before you go on the counter", or to comb their hair, or scrub their hands. Then we had to wear stockings, not cover our legs with dark cream which many of us liked to do in hot weather, it was comfortable and saved coupons and money. Our time-keeping was strict, we never, for instance, went to the dentist in working hours, but on our afternoon off.

I was delighted when, being in charge of inter-library loans, which was centralised, I was given a small partitioned-off workroom of my own, and brought a big bold red geranium to brighten up the window sill. By then I was fully integrated and enjoying the company of the rest of the staff, joining Goldsmith's Choir with one of them, to Toynbee Hall for drama with another. We travelled there from New Cross Station, via Surrey Docks and Wapping to Whitechapel in rickerty old trains, through a spooky tunnel under the Thames. Exhilarating, free to come and go as we wished, no thought of harassment or fear. A Music Appreciation Group was started, held weekly and Mavis would often join me in this. She travelled from her work at Shell in the City to Mum's, where she remembers a warm welcome, lots of talk and grilled kippers. However, I refused to go for a free "holiday" at the newly founded Common Cold Centre on Salisbury Plain to which several others resorted!. Never allowed the use of a radio in the workroom, it was decided that the wedding of Liz and Philip was different, and a year later we listened for hours, too, while we worked, to the hyped up event of the birth of Prince Charles! By this time the Chief Librarian, Mr. Rengert, having returned to civilian life, had taken up his post again and a number of other senior assistants had been de-mobbed too, from Wrens, A.T.S. and Land Army: a changing stimulating time. John joined the staff in the Spring of 1947, from Camberwell, having spent nearly 6 years in the R.A.F. We ran excellent Christmas parties there, with ballroom dancing, doing the Lambeth Walk, the hokey-cokey and snaking the Conga all round the building. In the light of today's informal manners, it is funny to realise that I remember my colleagues, even the females, by their surnames - on the roster we were:- Cole, Gibbons, Green, Barker, Rooke, Downer, Carter, Williams, et al. For my twenty-first birthday they gave me a lovely vase, brim full of fresh young daffodils and narcissus - nothing could have pleased me more.

We kept in touch with Hilda Rooke, Joan Downer and Pat Williams for several years, certainly until after our move to Sunray Avenue, Bromley Common, but Mossy remained our friend until she died in 1981. Florence Moss had secured the post of Library secretary in 1943 during a period of great dearth of labour, and somehow, poor lonely soul, she attached herself to us. One of natures mis-fits, awkward and insecure, given to sudden unpredictable outbursts of aggression typical of the truly inhibited and shy, she lived alone in squalor, her home a dark, mouldering basement, with uneven, rotting floors and the most meagre of aids to civilised living. Frequently harking back to the days of her childhood, of her father, a cooper at a molasses warehouse in Surrey

Docks, her Mother, her clever sister and brother, and "Spot", their much loved dog. Her voice warmed as she recalled the happy, simple life they led, and when she spoke of her Mother's sudden death, I assumed it to have been quite recent, in fact, years were to pass before I was startled into realising that it had occurred *the year I was born:* 35 years ago. Had time stood still for her since then?. Her parents and brother dead, deserted by her sister, I perceived with cold certainty that she mattered to no-one. Unloved, except by her two flea-bound cats, who really cared if she lived or died? Who mourn her passing more than a day?

Mavis & me, 1950

Mavis and I decided to celebrate our "coming of age" jointly, and organised a party at Peckham Meeting House, for which Mum made a delicious marble cake. John remembers this party too. He had joined the staff in

April 1947, as Chief Cataloguer, but we were both interested in someone else then, and we first went out together when he invited me to the New Year's Ball at the Town Hall in 1948. After that we spent much time together of course, both enjoying museums and art galleries in London, and delightful trips into the adjacent countryside, but in retrospect we both agree that one of our favourite outings was to eat at one of the many little cafes which sprang up in the area, for a meal of real ham, homemade chips, brown sauce and tea, often followed by a visit to the cinema. These eateries were issued with a special catering ration after the war.

I will mention that I passed parts of my LA exams, but discontinued them on marriage. This fitted in with the social set-up of the time, and although to his credit the Chief Librarian strongly advised me to finish them - reminding me that I might be widowed or divorced any time - yet this advice went right against the grain of a twenty two year old on the eve of her wedding. Also it was inopportune for in any case I had to resign, it was against the rules for a married couple to work in the same department; it seemed to me totally unfair and illogical, it would have meant a great deal to me had I been able to stay on, but that was it. Later I regretted not qualifying, but that was in the future, and when older still found that it no longer mattered. The work of running a home and bringing up a family was then still considered an important, full-time job, and more complex than it sounds, for it also involved maintaining good relations and frequent contacts with close relatives, including caring for the sick and elderly. In compensation this allowed a certain freedom of thought and movement which brought its own fulfilment.

That brings me briefly to the setting up of the National Health Service and the emergence of the Welfare State, but readers will know all about that. We became engaged one warm, moonlit evening in the Inner Temple Gardens, July, 1948, most romantic and fitting. How vividly I recall displaying my ring to everyone next day, amid showers of congratulations; engaged! a full and public committal. We started preparations for the wedding in twelve month's time, and so, just a decade after involuntarily leaving home for evacuation, I left it to get married in 1949. The mystery is, how completely my new life obliterated all that had gone before, it was as though it had never been, I seemed hardly the same person. The present was all engrossing, all consuming.

"If I have freedom in my love,
And in my soul am free,
Angels alone that soar above
Know no such liberty"

(With apologies to Lovelace), but that was how I felt at the time; but what is liberty? Some people, viewing the way my life unfolded would consider I had precious little; maybe it's an attitude of mind.

Our Wedding, July 1949

Forty years later the present is awash with the past, and life blends into an homogeneous whole. In "Little Gidding" Eliot says that, "History is a pattern of timeless moments"; which sums it all up nicely.

BOOK 3 - The Fifties

The 5O's: A Mixture of Facts and Impressions

"There is a history in all men's lives... ·
Warwick (Henry IV, PT.2. Act III, Scene I LINE 80)

Foreword

I have found it hard to write about the 50's, to stand back and look at them objectively, because for me they are not gone, remote, left behind forever, but held within the present. "Time present and time past, are both perhaps present in time future, and time future contained in time past·. (T.S. Eliot Four Quartets)

I have tried to write of things as they were, without hindsight. I realise that even one generation, say 25 years ago, we were not just like we are today - and today we are surely different from how we might be in another 25 years. There are constant human characteristics, but 35-40 years ago behaviour normal then, would be thought peculiar, even wrong now, but we cannot blame anyone in retrospect for not doing then what we now consider everyone should do.

Each generation faces new challenges. The taboos still observed in the fifties have gone, the mechanisms of sex in all its details and deviations now given full exposure, whereas the consummation of sex as the ultimate expression of mutual love is given scant recognition.

Mulling this decade over in my mind, I considered Harold MacMillan's famous saying in 1957, "Most of our people have never had it so good", and have come to the

228

conclusion that, for me and mine he was right. Pondering these ten years, I have felt them to be years of gentle change contained within an ambience of a society kinder, more relaxed than today's. While there has been and always will be, a destructive element in society, there is no doubt that that element is more noticeable today. It was usual then to accept individual responsibility, on the whole to behave with restraint and self-discipline. Much is now lawless, coarse and brutal - I am thinking especially of the media.

So I look back with a certain nostalgia to the 50's, the decade before the upsurge of the permissive society, the *swinging sixties*, and the technological explosion which so violently changed society. A decade in which dignity, discretion and courtesy were still held in esteem; restraint is now seen as self-repression, and family life a strait-jacket.

Age? Hindsight? Probably both come into play here, for it is usual, if one has average luck, to look back to one's 20's and 30's as a golden age, one is at the height of one's powers, veiled future invites, challenges, everything seems possible.

The war was over, after an epic struggle we had won, and in the days of austerity which followed, this buoyed us up in a manner hard to formulate. As for John and me, we had a marriage of like minds, held similar opinions, assumptions and expectations; for a time we became complaisant, smug, but time would alter that.

Mill, Nell, Me, John & Dad, Waller Road, July 1949

Prelude

Memories, the residue of time, lie deep in the recesses of the mind. "It all seems such an unimaginable time ago" (Auden?), the floods of tears on the last morning of our honeymoon, facing reality, that now we were to return to Brockley, to the flat we had prepared with such love and enthusiasm in the preceding months. How totally irrational, but then that fortnight had been almost too perfect, and mankind is made to live in bliss a mere fragment of time only - if at all. I had experienced more than my share, but it was to be a springboard for life that lay ahead.

Forty years ago Tintagel was still a magic place, totally uncommercialised, isolated, holding a powerful and mysterious charm. Never had I journeyed so far, never felt so vibrantly fit and well, the strong air, hot sun, gigantic headlands, rocky coastline, above all the wild Atlantic capturing all in its entrancing light, held me in thrall, imprinting that time, that place, forever on my memory.

Transport was strictly limited, we were met by the hotel car at Camelford Station: visitors, even in July, were few, the hotel, an old farmhouse, was small, excellent - great bowls of enormous ripe raspberries, fresh picked from the garden, were served with lashings of local cream.

Above all, I recall the feeling of immeasurable freedom, to do what I wanted when I wanted. Of course it couldn't last, but Eve cast out from paradise could hardly have been more distressed than I. What a spoilt callow thing I was. But like Eve, I was apprehensive of what the future might hold, not knowing how things would pan out. Had I been returning to work, such fears would have been minimised, the framework of routine would have lessened the shock of change. However, as I said before, I was compelled to resign on marriage. There was nothing in the least unusual in a young married couple living in part of a relative's house, it was the norm, indeed you were lucky to find rooms in which to settle. "Squatting" was unknown, couples frequently lived in with the family.

Having transformed the ground floor front room into Gran's bedroom, we had entirely redecorated the three upstairs rooms, created kitchen, bedroom and big front sitting room. The kitchen and bedroom at the back, the front with a large bay, against whose glass the bright green leaves of a beech tree gently tapped, and which looked out on to a large and busy RACS (Co-Op) shop, and to the left Lodge's Dairy. Fresh curtains were made, we gathered up our relative's unwanted furniture and bought Mill's Heal's 1930's bedroom suite from her for £50 - which I thought a lot, and set out our Oh so practical wedding presents. We had saved carefully and bought an oak dining room suite, utility brand (government mark), which ensured its good quality. Of Jacobean style, currently in vogue, it comprised the usual table with two pull-out extenders, four chairs with American cloth upholstered seats and backs, and sideboard, solid and well-made. Forty years on it is still in use by younger members of the family. I will not forget to mention the nice green and cream kitchen cabinet a dream of mine come true. There was no hot water system so we had a little electric heater installed over the sink, and stood a row of bold red geraniums on the window sill. I was very pleased with my kitchen.

In those days it was customary to save for things, even a Pyrex dish say, or an egg whisk, and the pleasure gained from obtaining them far outweighed the joy I feel in the easy purchase of some far more expensive item today - this is a common experience.

I missed my work very much. For a time I went daily for an hour after school-time to teach a little French boy and his mother English, but I missed the companionship of the library staff, the coming and going of borrowers, the books and essentially my work. John worked split duty in that first year, coming home for an hour or two and then going back, awkward and uncongenial, but Deptford Central Library was only 15 minutes walk away. Split duties were thereafter abandoned.

Once my pregnancy was confirmed in January 1950, my life changed completely, and all change, however much one determines positively on it, entails gain and loss, pain as well as pleasure. Never in my life was I to experience such a tangle of emotions, such disorientation and frustration, such wonder and delight.

Babies

Tony was born in our bedroom. I had attended the new Relaxation Classes at the pre-natal clinic, so I knew what to expect and how to react. But it wasn't like that, labour began with sudden breaking of the waters at 11.30 pm. as I was drifting off to sleep; the midwife was called from the phone opposite and cycled round on her bike within a quarter of an hour. She administered gas and air, but as I had eaten only a short while before, I was very sick. Tony was born at 3.10 a.m. next morning, a Thursday, weighing 8lbs. 2ozs. and as I held this wet, warm, slippery being, love and wonder washed over me. John was with me all the time, indeed, from the moment they were born, as far as work allowed, John took his share of caring for our babies. Always it was he who got up in the night, burping them, walking up and down, cradling, rocking, generally comforting and getting them back to sleep.

As John's Mother found it hard to climb the stairs, Nell took on the job of Home Help, to pay for which I received a Maternity Grant of about £2-10-0d. per week for four weeks, but which of course, she would not accept. 72 years old when Tony was born, she'd be with me by 9 o'clock, having had 20 mins. walk, "Over the hill", bring me drinks, wash out buckets of nappies, all done out of gladness of heart. As Gran hung up the washing in the garden, she and Nell would have a nice old gossip, they got on fine. I was kept in bed for eight days, but a week later John and I took our new baby for the first outing in his pram, up to Hilly Fields.

I must admit that the bottom dropped out of my world when I found that I was pregnant again. Everything was changing too quickly, we had hoped to save a deposit for a house of our own, at this rate, I felt we never would. Aunt Nell was walking back with me from the Bagwash, now dumped at the end of baby's pram. "Don't be upset", she said, "You never know, this one may bring you as much joy as the one you already have".

It was decided to have baby number two at Waller Road, where Mum could look after Tony - no paternal leave in those days, and Nell could cope with me. It worked well in practice, and we stayed there four weeks. We had been settled in barely a day when Helen was born at 1pm., Sunday lunch time, just as we'd started dinner with runner beans - I had to leave them, I remember. She was born within half an hour of the onset of labour, the midwife arriving in the nick of time. She weighed 8lbs. and was very yellow for a couple of days; with shock, and, not surprisingly, I haemorrhaged - very unpleasant, and rather frightening as I could feel the warm blood flooding around me. As with the previous birth, John buried the placenta in the garden. I was kept in bed this time 17 days.

The midwife warned me against having any more babies for five years, owing to strain on the heart after rheumatic fever. After five years, I certainly didn't want to start that business all over again, and we made sure we didn't. Mother told me that they could not help like that again, the strain and the work were too much (she was 59), so that was it; I decided she'd never have to. Three years later Nell told me she first found a lump in her breast three days after Helen was born, no one would have guessed. I was close to her, but at such a time noticed nothing different in her manner whatsoever, nor for the ensuing years, until she could keep it to herself no longer.

We had to make changes in the flat, of course, Tony's cot was moved to the front room and after a few months

Helen's also, and there usually one of us would sit and sing them softly to sleep, lots of nursery rhymes, and then sit snugly together by the little coal fire in the kitchen - coals carried up and ashes down daily and firelighters still made, as during the war, of tightly rolled up newspaper. As the babies grew older we'd read them stories, there was "The Ginger-bread Man" and Alison Uttley's "Little Grey Rabbit" books were favourites, as were Beatrice Potter's tales, "Thomas the Tank Engine" and "Alice", Later, John took them on to Stevenson, "Treasure Island' and Ballantyne's "Coral Island".

Food was still rationed, and they were allocated children's ration books, but groceries generally were not in quite such short supply. Bread and flour had been rationed since 1947 (to help Europe), but there were rather more cakes about, and biscuits - custard creams for instance reappeared. I remember (why?) as we walked them home one winter's day, noticing a new thing - tins of Ravioli in a shop window. We tried it for a treat and found it very tasty, something completely new.

With two babies of under 15 months there was no time in which to regret my lost career, life was completely fulfilling, but I could sometimes be engulfed by the realisation of the overwhelming responsibility of it all. I had to come to terms with the fact that in the short space of two years I had committed myself to play not one new role, which I had anticipated, not only wife then, but mother X 2 and daughter-in-law too.

However, I was now absorbed in getting to know these two little strangers who had so ruthlessly burst into my life. How well I recall the warmth of their chubby little bodies, for a while still, their eyes locking so profoundly with mine it seemed they could perceive my very soul. It could be unnerving, but I gazed as intently back, and all seemed well. "It was (you may say) satisfactory". I was able to breast-feed both of them, Tony for five months, until Jan,'51, when I found I was pregnant again, Helen for only 3 months as my supplies ran out, which I regretted, for who can forget that concentrated, leach-like feeding? Then sated, the sudden letting-go of the nipple and that great gaping milky smile of love and recognition. I must say it is not only indescribably rewarding, a placid 20 minutes locked in love and tranquility with the little one, intimate sweet smell, tiny hands dabbling, busy mouth dribbling, moments to savour, but also the best, easiest and cheapest way of feeding a young baby.

Once Helen was born, Gran invariably took her and Tony - he at first sitting at the end of the pram, later trotting beside it - to the local shops each morning. Especially they loved going to see Fish Fred the Bomper Man, who had a stall by the "Breakspeare". Here Gran bought fish, mainly for her two cats, Toby and Sandy. Coming home, she'd sit them up to her table, "2nd breakfast" they called it and have crusty white bread, sometimes (if I wasn't around) the butter had white sugar scattered on it. We all got a lot of pleasure from this routine, not least me, who gained an hour's peace and quiet, and could get on with the chores.

Tony with Dot at 4½ months and with John at 9 months

The water-heater proved a boon, infinitely better than heating up a kettle. All the washing was done in the deep white sink, except the heavy things like sheets, towels and so on, which went to the bagwash at Brockley Cross. I forget what it cost, so much for 5lbs., reasonable and worth every penny. Very popular, you took your bagful round in the morning, and it was ready a few hours later, half dry. On fine, hot summer days I could hang it straight out in the garden, otherwise it was kept to hang out next morning or, as a last resort, dried indoors.

At first the babies also were washed in the big white china sink, but as they grew larger they were plunged into a blue oval enamelled bath. We all went to Waller Road weekly for a real bath.

When we married there were half a dozen chickens at the bottom of the garden, but soon after Helen was born, Shan came round and killed the remaining two. He had

238

prizes for his birds, and had supplied these - Gran plucked and cleaned them and they cooked up beautifully - a rare and delicious treat. The chicken house demolished, John concreted the space over and it made a useful area in which the kids could play and we sit.

I noticed the review of a book published recently (1991), entitled, "Green Parenting", advocating such things as, hanging washing out to dry, using terry nappies, preparing babies' food from an adult meal using a food processor, and constructing a playhouse from blankets draped over a clothes-horse - - - but I, and everyone like me, did all that - except the food processor- not then invented, I used a sieve, we never knew it was GREEN, just everyday living. It seems extraordinary that anyone has to be told about it, but we had not then been sucked in to the Consumer Society,

As for the clothes horse, that was always prime favourite, set up in the spacious front room, and other toys were equally simple - stacks of various sized wooden cotton reels, one with nails to make reins, jars and lids for example, happy hours making scrapbooks. But with doting grandparents Tony and Helen were far from deprived. After John made a wooden gate for the top of the stairs they were free to run about, for instance Tony had Fido, a furry brown dog on wheels, and a favourite with him was his bomper-set, various shaped pegs had to be knocked into appropriate holes with a mallet. Helen had a well-upholstered doll's push-chair and several dolls which I dressed, and John made her a doll's cradle and a Noah's Ark, and Tony a farmyard. I well remember them a year or so later ('53) playing in a tent in the garden, Helen riding a rocking horse, and Tony graduating, at 4 years, from a tiny trike to a large one with rubber wheels.

239

Our kitchen table of strong deal was fitted with two drawers, in which Tony & Helen kept their colouring and drawing paraphernalia - books, paper, plasticine, sticky paper, pencils crayons, scissors etc. Sometime in 1953 John covered the table top with a sheet of pale green formica, newly available, neatening the edges with beading. It was a terrific improvement, nothing seemed to damage it and it was cleaned in a trice. They talked away, some of their funny words spring to mind: "Nazzers" (nail scissors), "Bilbows" (elbows), "Owbryes", (eyebrows). Gems.

Everyday without fail, after lunch, as soon as they could appreciate it, we tuned in to "Listen with Mother", on the radio, 1.45 - 2.0. it became a fixed routine. "Are you sitting comfortably? Then I'll begin..." Started in 1950, it ran for years. Then, clothes on for a walk, the weather hardly mattered. First, both in the pram, then, as they grew older taking turns in the push-chair. It was one of the most enjoyable parts of the day, for there was no hurry, and there were several different routes to take, each involving at least 30 mins. walk, so never monotonous or dull. The changing seasons alone ensured variety, mellow hours of autumn, sensuously shuffling and kicking the piles of dead leaves covering the pavements as I pushed the pram homeward, sniffing the familiar acrid smoke of bonfires. Short, dark days of winter, taking hours to get them well wrapped up, turning for home as shop and street lights flashed on, gazing into uncurtained lit rooms, curious voyeur of other people's worlds.

The charged and vibrant air of Spring, mild, invigorating, filling London with sweet scents of new mown lawns, incense of flowering privet, startling the eyes with mosaics of crocuses, sweeps of daffodils and the burgeoning green of fresh young leaves. Shimmering heat of summer, the pram canopy up, cup and bottle of water not forgotten. Grateful for the shade of the great plane trees, yester-year's bark now shed, massive trunks shining cream in the somnolent heat haze. Always familiar, always new.

Obviously we often went to the shops, shopping was easy and pleasant then in Brockley, a variety of small shops existed on *The Pavement*, others nearby at Brockley Cross. Previously, I mentioned the Co-op opposite our house, a large crescent of shops, comprising grocery, baker, butcher, chemist and greengrocery - here I remember regularly buying two pennyworth of potherbs - a carrot, turnip, onion, stick of celery - you never knew what you'd get, many a bowl of delicious soup was made with two pen'orth. Here neighbours and shoppers generally would congratulate me on having two such beautiful babies - *How clever of you, a pigeon pair!.* ' Rubbish' I thought, considering it far more clever to have **No More**.

If I wanted a department store, Pyne's opposite the Central Library, Lewisham Way, lay within easy walking distance. Such an expedition proved utterly boring to Tony and Helen except for one thing; in a certain corner of this emporium stood a large golden cage, put a penny in the slot and the blackbird within would hop, flutter and trill mellifluously for about two minutes. Sometimes it seemed longer, I wanted to get back home, but one glance at those children's faces, their rapt expressions of wonder and delight, and all impatience melted away.

There was a pleasant walk through wide, quiet tree-lined roads of grand Victorian villas to Hilly Fields, but great care had to be taken to avoid the most direct route which led past St. Peter's Church, as for some unknown reason,

241

Tony at first sight of its grey stone tower, would point accusingly at the turrets and scream and howl. Awful, most disconcerting. The first time I couldn't believe it was that, so tried again two days later when he put on a repeat performance. For a year or more I avoided that road like the plague, then forgetful, turned into it. I was so cross and embarrassed, there were not many people about, but those there were must have thought I'd beaten him. Angrily I shoved the push-chair along, at great speed fled past the offending church and turned a corner, where he gave a great gulp and a sigh of relief, Helen all the while gazed at him with fixed attention, a silent, close observer. I wonder why he did it?. There was nothing out of the ordinary I could see. It was about here, in Breakspeare's Road that I met Grandpa Homewood who told me that we were standing where he had stood sixty years before to guard Parnell & Kitty O'Shea.

Where else did we go? A longer walk of 30 minutes uphill to Brenchley Gardens, lovely formal gardens of flowering cherries, fine herbacious borders, magnificent rose gardens and pergolas. We mooched about eating an apple, watching the men playing bowls, noticing the trains which ran at one side. Only ever once or twice crossing the road and climbing up Honor Oak Hill, a steep, ancient-wooded hill on the summit of which was a vast iron-railed oak, fallen into decay now (c.1953) where Queen Elizabeth had held court. By the time we reached Brenchley Gardens, I was usually too tired to attempt the hill, especially with a loaded pram.

Of course from the summer of 1951, split duties ended, John was out at work all day, and we did other things at the weekend, but I had in mind a trip to Peckham Rye Park for a change - the 184 bus went there from opposite the house. However, I jibbed at it on my own with two toddlers and a push-chair, but Nell was more than willing, "a nice jaunt" she called it, and at least twice each summer we'd have an early lunch and set off. She was older then, I don't suppose we walked far, but there were plenty of seats and plenty for fresh young eyes to see, and we always finished up at the refreshment hut before catching the bus back.

Once a week we'd go up to Telegraph Park (there were upper and lower parks) and meet Mum, she'd be sitting there in Top Park opposite the tennis courts, where but a few years before the barrage balloons had floated high in the air. She usually brought some fruit and we'd meander round, watch the old men playing bowls and have a good talk.   With reference to this, Mother was fond of recounting how, on one such occasion, while we two sat on a seat deep in conversation, Tony quietly unscrewed the push chair in which his little sister peacefully dozed. We noticed just in time that it was about to collapse, were very cross indeed, when he pointed to the nuts and bolts all carefully arranged in order along the seat edge. Immediately he set about putting them back, all in their correct places. Mother was greatly impressed. These parks were to me as pretty as ever, and I often wondered whereabouts the old telegraph signal was situated, certainly one could see a long way from there, on a clear day an uninterrupted view across the Thames and all the City as far as the Hampstead Hills.

One occasion stands out, skipping down the hill in the park, on my own with both babies in the pram, I suddenly experienced immense joy. The world is so beautiful, wonderful, I thought and I shall be able to help them find it so (Hubris). Filled with elation I flew along; that sweet and precious moment of vision lingered with me over the following weeks, to be vividly recalled 40 years on. Maybe I was a trifle dotty (I never spoke of it to anyone), for at that time the Cold War threatened doom, the Korean War was at its height (50-53), the US had become embroiled in an orgy of McCarthyism, there were the shocking spy-scandals of Burgess and McClean and the Rosenbergs, and the US and Russia were busy testing Atom and Hydrogen bombs, each desperate to excel the other in destructive power. My individual experience of wonder and delight was therefore highly irrational.

Funnily enough, I remember reading a chillingly prophetic article in the "News Chronicle" around this time, concerning trouble in French Indo-Chine, outlining the possibility of war there reaching world shattering proportions if it were not brought to a speedy halt. Disturbed yet incredulous, I looked the place up in an atlas, I'd hardly heard of it, had no idea where it was; I'll notch that up in my mind I thought, it's journalism, I didn't see it could possibly be true.

After much discussion and some argument, we bought an old car. John was always very keen, having learnt to drive in the R.A.F., and to keep up his driving had hired a car once or twice a year ever since. I was not so enthusiastic, preferring to save every penny we had in order to save up a deposit for a home of our own. We married on £390 p.a. and I never managed, quite, to keep us both, as I tried to do, on a pound a week housekeeping. Well, we got Betsy Mark I in 1952, and, I must say, she certainly earned her keep. Numbered "PO", she was an Austin Ten, with a solid aluminium body, leather upholstery, cable brakes and a starter handle in case of necessity. Occasionally John and I and the kids went out alone, but almost invariably we took a relative or relatives along with us, that's how things were in those days. As you well know, our particular family consisted of a motley array of variously minded characters, there was confrontation, stimulation, but above all, and through all ran the unifying, resilient bonds of immense, practical love.

Cars were still a comparative luxury, they were "special", certainly to the older generation who had witnessed their advent, they were very special indeed. The oldest member of the family, John's Grandad Homewood was no exception, his preference being a run to Hayes or Chislehurst Common; and in the summers of the next four years we drove to see my Grandma Barker in Whipps Cross Hospital and had tea with Grace and Lily. We were fair, short trips, e.g. to the Bromley villages, Sevenoaks area and Gravesend, and whole days out - Hastings, Eastbourne or up the Thames to Marlow, being justly allocated. What fun we had, how our parents enjoyed it all, we'd picnic and everyone was keen to contribute, they helped out with the petrol too on longer journeys and brought tasty bits and pieces. Often it was just an afternoon ride to Farnborough or Keston, on one such day Mill presented us with the methylated spirits lamp she'd had to make tea when cycling, 30 years before, and made tiny muslin tea bags to go in the kettle. I still have one, I keep a brooch in it; commercial tea bags were not produced for another (20?) years.

Holidays

Our first holiday, in 1950, was at Beltinge, a village near Herne Bay. A cottage was lent to us for a week in May. Still quiet and rural then and very pleasant, I was 7 months pregnant, but we got about easily, Canterbury, Minster, Sturry and Fordwich by bus. It was a short walk into Herne Bay, there was a little cafe we went to for milkshake or coffee, the juke box was always playing, "Put another nickel in, in the Nickelodeon, all I want is loving you and music, music, music," etc. the sound clear as a bell across the years. Once we walked to Reculver, stark, lonely and desolate then, not a caravan in sight, but the distance was rather far, the last bus had gone, and the last mile or so back was quite hard going.

In 1951, I being pregnant again, we decided on a week's holiday, again in May, having Bed, breakfast and evening meal with Mrs. Whitaker, a motherly woman with a large Victorian house, just off the front, at the rear of Broadstairs High Street. She catered especially for families with young children, it didn't matter what mess or noise they made, she could cope, would dry nappies and clothes, help in every way possible; very reasonable, central and heaps of food. The following year a Friend at Peckham Meeting lent us her "cottage", - 30's jerrybuilt at Warden, Sheppey, for a week in early summer (*Belle View, Cliff Drive, Warden,* the last house on the right towards the sea). Having the car made it possible to drive around, greatly increased our freedom of movement and enjoyment generally. We brought my parents down for the weekend (Dad was still working of course), and Gran came down by coach, we met her and she returned home with us.

Most of Sheppey was still, apart from Sheerness, green and unspoilt, we relaxed, paddled, walked, had morning coffee at Old Warden Post Office, where there were always three home-made sponges to choose from, chocolate, coffee or jam - Oh such bounty - which to choose?. When fine we sat at tables set out with white tablecloths in the garden; sat and munched; what more could anyone want? As a relative was with us we were free to go out for a while in the evening, not that there was anywhere much to go, for Leysdown was as yet untouched, but we found a quiet little pub in the middle of nowhere.

The weather at this time was violent and extreme, for as well as the severe "smog" of 1952, on the night of January 31st – February 1st 1953, occurred the worst flooding ever experienced in Britain. 307 people were drowned in the East coast floods, it was shocking and terrible, everybody wanted to help in some way, but all we could do was make up parcels of clothes and toys for the distressed survivors, who'd lost everything, homes, possessions, farmland washed away, all they'd owned and cared about lying under feet of ice, cold silt and sea water.

Helen at Gravesend in June 1953

When we stayed in the cottage at Warden again, that June, the damage done by the Great Flood four months earlier was starkly visible, for Kent had suffered badly. The Saxon Shore and coast of Sheppey had been seriously affected. At Warden whole cliffs had been washed away, there was great erosion and landslips, landmarks had disappeared and whole houses had fallen into the sea. We stayed there two weeks, the rent was very cheap, 7/6d. per week, plus electric meter, it was basic, but just what was required with toddlers of that age. They loved the sea shore, feeding the local ducks and the freedom to wander. Gran came for several days, as did Mum and Dad and Nell and Mill and it worked out remarkably well. The furniture was ramshackle, there was a large dilapidated pram to use, and the bath water was emptied via a hose pipe on to the cliff-side, causing it to erode further, before our eyes. I clearly recall an old sea captain lived on a high promontory nearby, and for a penny each you could look through the telescope in his garden,

248

watch the passing ships, the ruined coastline, and the great World War II platform forts that stood at the mouth of the Thames, built in 1940 ready to fend off the impending invasion, which after all thankfully never materialised.

1954 saw us return to Mrs. Whitaker's at Broadstairs for a week in June. The journey there took longer than usual, instead of driving over the old Medway Bridge, up Rochester High Street, through Chatham and Gillingham, we were diverted round Maidstone, moving an inch at a time the traffic was so heavy. Outside Sharp's Toffee Factory both children were sick simultaneously in my lap in the back seat, and altogether the journey took over four hours.

There, at Mrs. Whitaker's, we first met Roy and Joy, with children of similar age, who immediately invited us to share their beach hut, which we found a marvellously convenient place to keep essentials, buckets and spades, towels, sun hats, cardies, sandwiches, and so on. There was so much there to see and do - build elaborate sandcastles, watch Punch and Judy, ride a donkey, collect shells, paddle about and there were music concerts, too. We all got on so well together that we decided to return for another week in September. We took it in turns to baby-sit, made full use of the beach hut and gained an affection for Broadstairs which has never left us. Years later the four of us would reminisce on the happiness we experienced there, and of course of our war years, they had both been in the navy, he, at one time at Trincomalee.

Tony & Helen at Broadstairs, July 1954

Smog

As opposed to the open road and fresh salt sea air of the holidays of the early 50's, we Londoners had to cope with "smog", mentioned earlier. One experience of that and you never forgot it, and there were several occasions when impenetrable fog mixed with sulphur dioxide, (from the smoke and fumes of open coal fires) and other chemicals, turned into a mixture of sulphuric acid. The result was acrid, yellow-hued smog, eye-smarting and choking, reaching its deadly peak early in December, 1952. There was no daylight, no sounds, everything muffled and obscured. If you ventured out you couldn't see the kerb; houses, trees, all landmarks were gone, one walked fearfully, one step at a time, or if possible remained indoors, most people did. John had to get to work, though London was reduced to a ghost city, and like everyone else he wore a smog mask, anything, scarf or piece of cloth tied over the nose and mouth. But I stayed indoors with Tony and Helen, they were so vulnerable. Notices were issued on the radio to keep the young, sick and elderly indoors with a fire, to keep it going all night, and to drink plenty of water (oxygen). So we banked up the fire for four days and nights, sleeping together on mattresses on the floor. It was awful, seemed an eternity, you cannot imagine the relief on looking out on the morning of the 9th., to find that the air had thinned, the outline of the roof of the little factory beyond the garden was visible once more, trains were running and birds came to life in the beech tree. But over 4,000 people died from its effects; in 1956 the Clean Air Act finally became law.

It was in the autumn of 1951 that my Father was made redundant - Cerebos took over his firm. It was a bitter blow to him, he was 56 and took it badly. During the "smog" of early December, he became ill with bronchial pneumonia and took months to recover. In the further days of "smog" the following March, it was expected that he would die - he certainly looked like it - but he was to live another 30 years to enjoy the company of great-grandchildren. He continued unwell throughout 1952-1954, one attack of pneumonia following another; invariably, however, he rallied round. He would sit in the big armchair in the front room and he always thoroughly enjoyed seeing Tony and Helen (3 & 4 years). He'd bought an articulated cardboard puppet of Charlie Chaplin which he rigged up on a string tied across the room and jigged it about to a record of "The Trishtrash Polka". They all found it hilarious, great fun.

About the factory at the back, it was single storey, quiet; a gate in our back fence opened on to a track, rich in wild flowers in summer, which led to some allotments, on railway land. John had one, I helped in the evenings, in fact I was planting out leeks an hour before Tony was born - gone 10.0 at night (Oh to be young and have energy!). It was really nice down there, good loamy soil, and he grew excellent vegetables, in one year 60 Ibs. of potatoes and 78 Ibs. of tomatoes, then there were huge cabbages, beans, cauliflowers, leeks, savoys, radishes, lettuces, spinach and carrots.

In the evenings of the first year of our marriage, John finished working for, and gained the Fellowship of the Library Association. If he finished work early enough, I would walk up Upper Brockley Road to meet him in the Memorial Gardens which lined Lewisham Way. However, he started work as Chief Cataloguer at Chelsea Public Library, Manresa Road, in July, 1951 and began teaching at evening classes at Croydon that September. Soon after he was working voluntarily at the Library of the Spastics Society, based nearby in Chelsea. A year or two later during his lunch hours he catalogued the Library of Crosby Hall, headquarters of the Federation of University Women, a short way away, this time for payment.

The car therefore played a big part in our lives, for as well as the frequent outings, John used it to drive to work, taking the south circular route over Sydenham Hill, driving was mostly a pleasure then, to own a car an undiminished asset. In the Spring of 1952 Dad agreed to have a garage built at the bottom of their garden, and there John put it away each night and fetched it every morning. Mum was right against cars, and the garage, but she thoroughly enjoyed the outings, and later, much later, was to tell me that she'd had to revise her opinion of them, "For how could I get to Meeting? How could I ever come to see you if John was not kind enough to pick me up?" How complex our lives are, life had changed so much since Mother was a girl, she was forced to compromise, realising even then the damage being done to the environment - to increase dramatically - and to set that against our individual pleasure and increased facility of movement.

John's new job at Chelsea made quite a difference to our social life, I enjoyed going up to meet him, this was a new area of London to me, artistic, cosmopolitan, with the Royal Court Theatre putting on the controversial, contemporary plays by the "Angry Young Men" - John Osborne, Arnold Wesker, etc. ("Look Back in Anger", 1957).

Clothes

We approach the middle of the twentieth century, the centre of this decade, and the end of our time at Brockley. Maybe this is as good a time as any to pause a moment and take a look at the way we dressed then. Aunts had made my trousseau exactly as I'd envisaged it. For winter I always liked a good tweed coat and a matching skirt (as well as others), now I was made a soft dove grey flannel "dust-coat", this swung from the shoulders, turned down collar, buttons from neck to waist, very full at the hem and bishop sleeves, with all-round pleated skirt to match. There were dresses, blouses and four pairs of cami-knickers. I always bought my own material and to my disbelief, Aunts made these garments as pretty as you like, in fine materials of various cream and pinky patterns - deeply darted bodice, fitted waist, brief legs, lots of lace. Remarkable. It was those or french knickers then.

John's Mum, my Mum and I, we all knitted for the babies and continued to do so throughout that decade. Mum and Gran went in for holey patterns, I preferred working Fair-Isle designs. Aunts made practically all Tony and Helen's clothes until they went to school, many of these appear in photos, though not their "rompers". Matching navy blue coats, concocted from some stored fabric, with tartan collars and self buttons, then new Harris tweed coats of soft autumn browns, with brown velvet collars, all lined and plenty big to allow for growth.

Tony & Helen, 1954

Except in very hot weather, when going out, we wore hats - older people always wore them, and gloves too. Clothes were far more formal than today, as was life. Houses not being centrally heated our clothes were warmer, lots of real wool in winter, pure cotton in summer, man-made fibres had not taken hold, although nylon stockings became plentiful (tights years later), we all sported suspender belts. Stockings were lisle of fawny, neutral colour, always with a seam at the back, and I invariably bought fully-fashioned. Never black = skivvy or granny overtones. We wore galoshes, (big rubber overshoes) in wet weather, and everyone had a mackintosh - didn't just dodge about with a brolly (or gamp). (We always wore large aprons, some housewives overalls, hair tied in a square scarf for dirty jobs - fire place etc.)

Late in the '40's the Americans tested atom bombs on Bikini Atol in the Pacific, thereafter followed the fashion for "bikinis", I could never see the connection, it seemed horrid. Boleros enjoyed a certain popularity, often called BOleros.

Skirts, during the war were just below the knee (to save material) and continued so until about 1949-50 when Dior's "New Look" became the rage - goodbye austerity - and skirts dropped to about 3" above the ankles. I kept to an inch or two shorter (thought I looked a dowdy "Polly Longfrock" when any longer). "Twin-sets" were the rule, hand-knitted or bought, I always felt comfortable in them, with a row or two of pearls you were really elegant. I remember the fashion of "halo" hats, really becoming, but, as I've said, generally everyone wore a hat when going out, felt for women in winter, a nice straw in summer, both could be garnished afresh for the oncoming season by the addition of new ribbon or spray of flowers. Girls wore them too, and gloves, while usually men stuck to trilbys and boys to caps.

Men's clothes didn't alter much from when I was a girl, though the fifties spawned Teddy Boys and Spivs, with greasy hair and wide, rude ties and some wore drainpipe trousers. However, I remember that at that time men's collars were separate from their shirts, though of the same fabric and John always took his to the local laundry to be starched - about three a week, very cheap, - because I could not deliver a fine enough product! .

I remember those incredibly full nylon half-petticoats, wonderful, tier upon tier of stiff gathered nylon, so feminine. What else? I suppose handkerchiefs. No paper ones of course, so all were boiled with soap and bleach in a big old saucepan, scrubbed, YUK, rinsed --- finally ironed. When colds abounded this became a real chore, one fell back on rags kept for that purpose, and discarded. The "teens" were, I think, a product of market forces of the late 50's and were, from then on heavily market-targeted. Until then you were a child till 14 (when the vast majority left school), after that an adult, earning very low wages. So there were no "teenage" styles of clothing, as there were no "leisure" fashions, just work/school, Sunday best, old things (though clean and mended) for everyday, which obviously changed with the seasons.

Sunray Avenue

And so, by the end of 1954, the time was ripe for us to move on. We drove around many areas, weighing up the advantages and disadvantages of each, finally settling on the Bromley area. We placed a deposit on 77, Sunray Avenue on January, 23rd., and before arrangements were finalised, went to see Mrs. Beale, Headmistress of Princes Plain School, to enroll Tony for the following autumn; that done we registered for coal. We needed to borrow £250 towards the deposit, and approached Mill (the only one to have that amount available). Business-like as ever, she needed to inspect the house and its environs before committing herself. Having done that, she agreed, and we arranged to repay her £2 per week at 2 1/2%, an arrangement quite usual at that time, (the banks were then probably charging 4%).

To hear the moans and groans from our parents, you'd have thought we'd decided on the antipodes at least, if not Mars. Through the wails and suffering resignation we ruthlessly pointed out that it was vital for us to move **Now**, the accommodation once so eminently suitable had become overcrowded and inconvenient. We would see them all every week, and so we always did. If you have no knowledge or understanding of earlier generations, this must all sound unbelievably strange, but up to and until our generation it was usual for families to live within walking distance of one another. Of course, young folk did move away, but it was not easily accepted, for still people were unaccustomed to the ease which the motor car gave to intervisitation. The fact that I was an only child, whose parents loved me far more than they loved each other, and that John was as good as, must also be taken into consideration, (though none of this was our fault), and it is an indisputable fact that the grandchildren were truly breath of life to their grandparents.

Front garden in mid-May 1967

It is hard for me to write about those first months at Sunray. If any one time can be called the "Happiest Days of Your Life", those were mine. We were monarchs of all we surveyed, we did as we pleased, because what we did it pleased us to do. You may imagine the tremendous satisfaction of having our own bathroom and indoor toilet and the intense pleasure of being able to walk straight out of the kitchen into the garden. This garden was an absolute delight; as we moved in on the first of April the pear and apple trees were clouds of scented blossom, bulbs were bursting into vivid flower, fruit bushes unfolding their first bright green leaves and their fat fruit buds. A crowded network of old plum tree branches screened the elegant Edwardian house which lay at the end of our long garden, and old-fashioned roses ran riot everywhere, over fences, the old greenhouse and air-raid shelter. What a wonderful, unforgettable welcome!. This house in Sunray Avenue, was a semi-detached chalet-bungalow, with bath and toilet downstairs, steep narrow stairs led to two double bedrooms, each fitted with a small gasfire. A large airy roofspace could be entered from either room, lit by a small round window, and once the floor was boarded over it became usable, eventually to store an untold amoumt of cumber. The kitchen was well fitted up and the whole house in a state of good repair. However, John and Dad set to and did a lot of work on it, they renewed the fence, (a condition of mortgage), thoroughly repaired both garage and porch, and stripped out and made the greenhouse as new. John was given an old railway bench, (six feet long), by a friend of his Mother's who lived at Brockley Station Cottage. Painted, it made an excellent garden bench which we still have. At the top of the garden, in a remote sunny corner, John dug a sandpit, and made a lid to go on top to prevent cats peeing etc. in it.

Washday was quite modernised, what with a pulley airer suspended from the kitchen ceiling and a gas copper left in the garage by the previous owners, a most tremendous boon. I boiled the washing there every Monday, and had beechwood tongs to lift it out and drop it into a bath; it was rinsed in the sink, then put through the wringer we brought with us, also kept at one end of the garage. Being out there, it didn't matter how much water flooded the floor - the boiler was filled and emptied by pail, and proved a great asset, admired by all our friends. We covered the floors with linoleum, a large carpet in the front room, rugs and mats elsewhere; we hadn't a lot of furniture, but enough to be comfortable, and we were able to add to it without strain over the years.

During our first week at Sunray Avenue Sooty joined the family, she was just eight weeks old. Aunt Nell often stayed as companion, doing odd needlework jobs for a

Mrs. Jennings at Keston Park, a warm-hearted semi-invalid, she had kept this dear little black kitten-with-white-locket for us; we could not know that she would remain a dear companion for the next 20 years. It was at Jennings, on our regular visits to tea, that we first sat and watched T.V., where Tony and Helen first saw "Andy Pandy".

The following spring John, with Dad's aid managed after great and prolonged exertion, to knock down the blast-wall fronting the brick air-raid shelter. They then fixed a swing to the far end, knocked a hole in the stout wall for a window, then made and hung a proper door. It really looked quite nice, what with the massed branches of winter jasmine netting bright gold all over it in winter, and the untameable old "Alberic Barbier" smothering it in summer. In 1957 we "snow-cemmed" the whole house and painted the woodwork cream and pale green.

Dad always enjoyed working there, he was both dogged and skilful. Not being entitled to O.A.P. until aged 65, for the next five years following redundancy and three years of poor health, he had to register at the Employment Exchange, receive unemployment money and was required to go after any jobs available and they were few for a man of his age. However, he worked a couple of years at a Greek shipping magnate's in Lime Street, City - (where he got a lot of unusual postage stamps). Then, after a further period of unemployment, he finally found work at Sellotape, Blackwall Tunnel Avenue.

We decided not to book a holiday that summer, but in July drove my parents down to Hastings where they had hired a caravan. Tony, Helen and I stayed there for 3 nights, with John bringing us and taking us home again and staying the day, it was rather a squash, but made a change of scene and was well worth it.

Tony learnt to read that summer, and started at Princes Plain School in September without trouble, quickly becoming integrated. We always walked there, of course, allowing 15-20 minutes, that way we soon got to know our neighbours, that was how we became acquainted with Stan and Phyl Baxter (he had fought at Dunkirk) and Phil remained my very good friend until her death in 1990. Gradually we settled into a routine, one or two mothers worked out a simple rota, one taking two lots of children to school, another bringing them back, but this took time, and for Tony's first year I made 4 journeys to the school each day, down winding Magpie Hall Lane, still bordered on one side by ancient hedgerow, past the one or two shops, St. Luke's redbrick Victorian Cemetery Chapel and its Graveyard with the striking tomb of David Greig (the grocer), watched over by its gigantic black angel, wings forever proudly extended; a fearsome unexpected sight. Thus I walked morning, dinner time x 2, and again at 3.15, always taking the pushchair for Helen, as it was too tiring for her to walk there and back so many times a day.

So, in all weathers, streams of children from 5-11, and many Mums (none of us drove) could be seen and heard converging on, or emerging from, that school. In my mind's eye I see the children now, in great scorching heat, hot, red-faced and sweaty, or soaked to the skin and terrified by torrential rain and thunder, or frozen cold by bitter east wind, the tender skin on their thighs chapped and raw.

Once Helen was established there too, life gradually became easier for me, although it took a whole term for her to settle in, even though Tony was there and helped look after her, and she was already a good reader. They worked on the Janet and John readers, I remember, and her reading progressed remarkably well, I know that she read "Little Women" when she was only 7. On her third term they started to stay for dinner 2 or 3 times a week, and by the September term, 1957, it had become a regular routine.

Living in such an environment ensured privacy (a great bonus), however, one day, only a day or two after Tony had started school, weeding the front garden, Helen moping disconsolately around, missing him, Josie Maunders came by on her way to the shops with Graham. She being pregnant and Graham alone, she invited me to coffee to see how our two children got on, and we decided to try a scheme whereby each of us in turn had both children two mornings a week. It worked surprisingly well, to our mutual benefit. I remember so well galloping down the slip opposite our house to hers, and vividly it came to me, "How well I feel, how bright and light and WELL". Josie and Ray had T.V. a couple of years before us, and Tony and Helen were always welcome to go and watch it. It was not uncommon for us to take the pushchairs and walk to Petts Wood, shop and walk back. (Mrs. Selway had already lived at 20 Manor way 25 years!). We have remained friends with the Maunders ever since, in spite of Helen's efforts to stuff beads up Graham's nostrils - once she succeeded and I had a frightful job getting it out, there was a terrible shemozzle, screams and tears all round, my heart banging with dread. Ray Maunders was in the Navy in the Pacific in W.W.II and only later told us hair-raising tales of the Kamakazi raids on his ship, for folk did not talk about their war experiences at all then.

Tony and Helen were bright, normal, affectionate, lovely little children, usually cooperative, got on very well with one another, but were naturally sometimes irritating and rebellious. Rarely, they got a smack on the fat little back-of-the-shins, and two or three times when they both ganged up on me and I lost my temper, they were shut out in the garage; never singly. After they'd both hammered on the door and kicked and yelled, we all calmed down and were very sorry, but it was rapidly over and done with. Oh well, it happens to all of us.

Normally I shopped at the Parade, and used the Library there, only 5 minutes walk away, a convenient crescent of shops catering for every need, pleasant too, fronted by a grassy bank and mature beech trees. I usually went to Bromley on the 94 bus once a week, and I reckoned to save the fare money on the cheaper vegetables I bought from stalls there, and I enjoyed the outing.

In 1955, Bromley was little altered from the town I knew 15 years before, David Greig's impressive emporium still occupied one corner of the Market square. College Slip was still a rough and rural passage connecting with Walter's Yard (now occupied by Sainsbury's store). Love Lane, a quaint and rural footpath (fast becoming an anachronism) still ran, as it had from time immemorial, behind and parallel to the High Street, from Widmore Road, crossing Holwood road and coming out at the back of Bromley South Station. The main shops remained as I have described them earlier - 1940s, but that was to change. I think the first signs of impending modernisation at that time took place in the Market Square, when, in 1958, Skilton's distinctive Victorian butcher's shop was demolished, along with Isard's ironmongery next door, to make way for the town's first supermarket. Cater's was comparatively small for such a store, nothing like the vast caverns of today, but to me it was bewildering and I, along with many like me, felt overburdened with sudden surplus choice. The first time

I went in there with Tony and Helen, the girl at the checkout hid a sweet bar I was buying them under a heap of paper bags. Tony's head was on a level with the desk, watching with his sharp young eyes and quickly he shouted out, "Where's my chocolate?". Sheepishly she produced it, I don't suppose she did it again.

ended about 1973. FRY'S From 1930's?

DESPERATION PACIFICATION EXPECTATION ACCLAMATION REALIZATION

You will realise that this was the very beginning of what was to become a revolution in shopping practice. Retailers were then keen to oblige, we had not only a daily milk delivery (no fridges), but the Co-op baker called every weekday, he had a horse and cart, carrying his wares to the door in a huge wicker basket, not only various breads, but a wide assortment of cakes and buns. The local Co-op delivered our groceries from Chatterton Road. Co-op Members had a number, mine was 225582 - and a dividend accrued over a half year. The local family greengrocer delivered my weekly order and the butcher called twice weekly, each time bringing, among other items, Sooty's bunch of lights.

Our current shopping hours legislation was last drawn up in 1950, and as few people as possible worked on Sunday. It was above all a family/ church day; after moving to Bromley we all attended Meeting regularly, ate a full Sunday dinner (1.0 pm) together, which had been prepared the evening before. We rarely saw relations then, though sometimes had visitors; we relaxed, walked, drove a little way and/or played games. So Sunday

265

remained, as when I was a girl, different, slow-paced and quiet. We experienced each other's company, fell back on our own resources, enjoying the quietude, the peace and togetherness.

To help pay off our debt to Aunt Mill, we decided to take a lodger in the downstairs single bedroom. Again, nothing unusual in this, several neighbours had one, including Phyl & Stan, and after all, I was quite used to them. We were advised to advertise for a "Christian tenant", and this brought Mr. Clarke, a pleasant, quiet, serious young man, who, when he wasn't at the Baptist Church, spent his time at evening classes. He came in in the evening, ate his meal and went out, never late in, no radio on, out all day Sundays and in only to lunch on Saturdays; it could not have been better. We got on well, he liked my cooking - and my washing - and would liked to have stayed on, but after 18 months Mill's debt was paid and the bedroom was needed for Tony. This was late 1957.

I always got great satisfaction from working in the garden, and took care of the front, which like so many others, was edged by a low, double grey stone wall, smothered in varying shades of aubretia, a picture in Spring. We were at Sunray 17 years, and in the first months removed an old privet hedge (we had seen enough of those in London), and put in massed irises - an excellent position by the dry wall. After a few years I tired of them, though wonderful, they were only in bloom for 3-4 weeks in the year. I dug them up and put in shrubs, all of which I had grown from cuttings or seed, and these proved most satisfactory and was admired by the neighbours.

At the back the herbaceous border came to look really good, and I also worked with John growing vegetables and saw to the fruit bushes - black and red currants, red and rare white raspberries and gooseberries. Most years the yield of blackcurrants was around 12lbs. Gran, Mum and Aunts all helped harvest, I made pounds of jam, was able to share that and the fruit too, they were thrilled to bits. We had scores of pounds of eating and cooking apples and pears and succulent Czar plums from over the back. Obviously this was before freezers, and we had no fridge as yet - nor did anyone we knew, so it was all bottling and drying. We made wine and kept a ginger beer plant for several years, also I used to make a delicious elderflower drink. Most mothers did all this, there was a great community spirit; never deride the outer suburbs as bourgeois to me, life at Sunray was rich, full and wonderful. I had flowers to pick at all seasons, from earliest snowdrops till autumn when there were copper beech leaves, various seedheads and corn – all for the gathering. And there among the dead damp leaves sprang up the spires of iris stylosa in mid-winter (January).

I recall with gentle nostalgia the view to the left of our front bay window, looking towards the "Links", lined along Magpie Hall Lane by a succession of ancient elms. Walking by these, (in Spring "the lowest boughs and the brushwood sheaf round the elm tree bole are in tiny leaf") one took a footpath past a coppice, in whose bosky depths stood a fine Victorian house, in which lived two elderly spinsters. Recluses, they were rarely seen, but maintaining their garden as a bird sanctuary, would here and there festoon certain trees with peanuts, bird-cake etc., there were nesting boxes too, it was a delight to all who passed by, a place to cherish, we thought. So, within 2 minutes walk from our house we were into the Recreation Ground itself, originally part of the now much reduced golf course, and separated from it by an undulating line of copper beeches, enclosed at the far end by the still untouched Sparrow Wood.

During the first 3 or 4 years of our time there it was crossed by a tree-lined, clear running stream, the Blackbrook, picturesque and charming. Several times I'd take the children on a picnic over there, sitting on the bumpy roots of the old trees, watching as they jumped daringly from bank to bank, splashed in the water, made dams; if you sat silent and still birds came to drink, a place of great contentment.

Sometimes, on an enticing, warm summer afternoon I'd bring Tony and Helen home that way from School, past a farm where the brook widened, and often at the weekends we'd all cross the playing fields and walk through the woods, so entering again that country in which I had loved to wander during the war. As the children grew older we walked further, it was so good to walk straight out of the door into green fields into fresh and scented air past ploughed fields where the skylarks sang, past great muddy puddles where the martins still paddled and dabbled as in my youth; it was marvellous.

Between April and June, 1958 and 9 we all rose early on several occasions in days of hot sunny weather and were out soon after seven, making our way to Sparrow Wood for a before breakfast walk. It springs to mind clearly how fresh and pristine everything was, how pleasing the soft, muted colours, flecked by bright sun and deep shade. No one else was about, in the stillness birdsong filled the air, the cuckoo called endlessly, loudly. We picked wild- flowers, lady's smock, stitchwort, etc., etc., too many to mention, identifying them at home as we put them in water. Those were special visits.

Sometimes I would imagine how this area looked before I was born - none of the houses I've lived in, except Waller Rd., were built before then. How much England , indeed the world, has changed in my lifetime. Later, maybe 10 years? Dutch elm disease killed off all of the elms, the bird-loving old ladies died, their plot purchased by the Council who uprooted all the trees, razed the house to the ground and on that bare ravaged site erected a building of brutal 60's style as a day centre for mentally ill folk. By then the lovely trees along the Blackbrook had also been cleared, the stream put in a drainpipe and the area grassed over; unlovely, bleak and characterless, By a miracle, Sparrow Wood has been saved, for that we are thankful indeed.

Did I ever get fed up with domestic economy and kids?. Yes, of course, and the answer to that was a stimulating discussion with Phyllis Arglet next door, a passionate animal-lover, who inveigled unwary tomcats into her home, then took them to be neutered. A well-read woman, too, we discussed writers and literature generally. I read when I could, but found it far from easy. I got hooked on Ngaio Marsh, Margery Allingham, Hammond Innes and Patricia Wentworth, also on historical novels - Jean Plaidy, Georgette Heyer and Victoria Holt. The Winthrop Woman and Vows of the Peacock I loved, and avidly escaped into books on ancient Greece and Greek mythology.

Phyllis and her husband Ted, court reporter on the Sunday Express, introduced us to the Orpington Field Club, we took part in many a Fungus Foray, walked in cowslip meadows and joined night expeditions to see badgers. We travelled to Westerham to listen to nightjars, a dozen of us in heavy rain, exhorted to silence, as, single file, umbrellas up, we squelched through mud one dark summer night. The Arglets drank and cooked only in Tunbridge Wells spa water, which they collected every Monday (his day off), filling whole crates of bottles at the spring in the Pantiles. I can hear them rattling and crashing about now, hear the hiss and recall the smell of their cabbage dinner as she opened up her pressure cooker outside the back door. She was a trenchant, intellectual communist, with her scragged back hair, scrubbed forceful face and unconventional garb. When I heard that their only child, Julia, attended an exclusive, private school (she was collected by car each day), took riding and ballet lessons and that they holidayed regularly in Switzerland, I wondered how this privileged life style added up with their egalitarian ideals. I felt envy that they could give their child so much, but as so often with folk I've felt a flicker of envy for, their life together came to dust and ashes. Phyllis taunted, shouted, and screamed at Ted and finally he knocked her teeth out and she came rushing round to us, shaking all over, nearly out of her mind. It was terrible and they divorced soon after. Over the years I came to notice that those I envied had no more happiness than I, their problems, not always obvious, I came to perceive,   cancelled out any extraordinary luck or possession they may have had that I lusted after. It was more positive to count my blessings.

I cannot leave Sunray Ave. without mention of the Crows who lived next door at 79. Bill was a fanatical member of the T.A., never doing anything in the home, but getting his brother-in-law to do it. He didn't do a lot in the garden either, but he had a military flame-thrower on unofficial permanent loan with which he set about weeding - crawling about on the ground, waving it about, a rare spectacle. However, his main aim was to demolish the air-raid shelter, brick built like ours. To this end he periodically collected up all his household and garden rubbish - bits of carpet, cartons, twigs etc., would build a bonfire deep inside said shelter, throw petrol over it, light it and leap out. Smoke and flames belched forth from the narrow entrance; but he was doomed to disappointment, the walls never even cracked.

The Brockley allotment was given up, of course, but John soon took another, five minutes walk away in Turpington Lane. We didn't keep it for long, it was inconvenient and not greatly productive, having too many large trees around it, so drippy, yet dry and full of insects. In any case, there was enough for John to do without that, for as well as the other extra work he'd taken on, he was now marking Library Association Exam papers, indexing Whitaker's Book List, and in 1958 he started lecturing at evening classes at Gillingham once a week, which he continued to do for a number of years.

Family

A routine of family visitations established itself very soon after we moved. John's Mother came over each Wednesday, usually his afternoon off. An Aunt came on Friday and Mum & Dad on Saturday as Dad had that day free always and John did not. They all came to lunch and usually John drove them home. Unless one was actually laid out with something, they were determined to come, they never missed, and if one were to be poorly in some way, well, of course, I went to see them while the kids were at school. I keenly remember Mill arriving one day, standing in the porch, water pouring off her, soaked to the skin, "Why didn't you phone and cancel?" I wanted to know (our phone number was Hurstway 1575, put in as soon as we moved in, so that we could be contacted any time). "You shouldn't be out in this". (she was nearing 80, but you never mentioned it). She regarded me balefully, "If I plan to go somewhere, I go". As my Mother said, "I never let the *weather* stand in my way". Useless to argue with such pigheadedness; I hung up the streaming garments, stuffed her shoes with newspaper- wet in spite of galoshes. Sitting at the window, she pitched into a pile of mending, purposefully reminiscing. We'd have her favourite lunch, cold mutton - she eating all the fat with bread, and my apple chutney. We remember Helen and Tony making what she called a "Mary, Mary" garden with the bagful of buttons she brought along with her - all colours shapes and sizes? Arranging, rearranging, restful, imaginative.

Mill at Hastings in 1962

When Nell finally decided in the summer of 1954 to do something about the lump in her breast, always a firm believer in homeopathy, she settled on the Homeopathic hospital, London, for the operation. She'd left it three years, but at her age, early seventies, it had grown very slowly. Now 76, she said "If ever you find a lump, don't leave it like I have - see about it straight away - I'll show you what it looks like - it doesn't pain, just pricks now and again". Just a small bump, I thought, however, no lumpectomies then - or for several decades - she underwent radical mastectomy, was in hospital 3 weeks and took months to recover. Talking to her about it one day, "Do you want to see it?", she asked. She retained a depth of wisdom and assurance. Nothing daunted, "Yes",

273

I said, curious, repelled. I recall my inner shock, outward calm. Nothing must upset her; the healing was complete, all that remained was a map, a map of a terrible trouble overcome. Not an unknown horror anymore, but one defined, contained. I knew an immense gratitude. (She had left it so long for what at the time she considered good reasons - me with 2 young babies and Dad's severe illnesses).

Special Days

We regularly visited the Chelsea Flower Show, went every year to a rather splendid Mayor's Reception held at the Chenil Galleries (the art gallery next to the Town Hall). We went to the excellent Library Staff Parties and to NALGO Christmas Party held in the Town Hall itself, usually not getting home until midnight. How we danced! and three years running I won a spot prize. It was ballroom dancing mostly - we used to practise to the records bought when we were engaged, e.g. Glen Miller and Joe Loss. 1954 saw (and heard) the advent of Bill Hayley and the Comets, rock and roll had come in with a bang!. In Coronation year ('53) an extravagant party was laid on for the children of all NALGO staff in St. Luke's Church Hall.

By Easter Day morning all the chocolate eggs which had been bought for Tony and Helen were in my care, and the tradition quickly grew that I would hide them all over the garden, and straight after breakfast they would go out and hunt for them. This went on for years, how was it that the weather was always so congenial? bright and dry - perhaps it wasn't; how do others remember it? Then later, older relations would arrive, not altogether, so spread over two days, and we'd drive to the coast or into Kent to see the orchards, sheep with their lambs grazing under the scented clouds of blossom, plum, cherry, apple or pear, Easter being either late or early.

They were all invited for special days, Birthdays (separately from the children's do), then there was Guy Fawkes Day; from 1955 we always made a guy, had a big blazing bonfire and some fireworks - Roman candles, Boyscout rousers, Catherine wheels, golden rain, serpents which shot about all over the ground, rockets, sparklers etc.

Yes, the immanence of relations could sometimes be overpowering, and I wished them further, but the other side of the coin was the bonus of having folk ready and willing to mind two infants under 4 years of age for an evening, occasionally for the day. Once there was a river trip, Westminster to Greenwich organised by the Association of Assistant Librarians and in 1951 we went to the Old Vic to see "St. Bartholomew Fair" - loved it. We managed to get to the South Bank Exhibition (where the Festival Hall now stands), during its last week, after Helen was born, late September, could not manage it earlier, we were glad we went, but I remember being very, very tired. During the 50's we saw several of Priestley's plays, particularly enjoying those concerned with the problem of Time - *Dangerous Corner, Time & the Conways and I have Been Here Before.*

While enjoying the stimulation of becoming acquainted with a whole new set of people, exchanging visits with the Kennerleys, for instance, we kept firm friendship with several of the staff of Deptford Public Libraries. - Hilda Rook, Joan Downar, Jo and Peter Kennett, Pat Mitchell and Mossy of course. When I come to think of it, we were on visiting terms with a wide variety of people, for as well as those mentioned, and our near relatives, we saw a lot of Shan and Blanche, Aunt Flo, Miss Headland, three Quaker couples, and Mavis & Jack and Roy & Joy with whom we exchanged weekend visits.

We visited the Royal Academy Summer Exhibition every year, sometimes we'd go up to London and have supper at a Lyons Corner House, or lunch in the Strand or Villiers Street. We went to the pictures when there was something good on (not weekly), and there were a lot of films we liked - "The Third Man", "The Blue Lamp", "Genevieve", "The Lavender Hill Mob", "Whisky Galore", "War & Peace" and "Limelight", - all 50's productions and mainly British, I think: and we took Tony and Helen to see "Bambi", their first film, they loved it, but I never greatly cared for cartoons and anthropomorphic fantasies.

Before leaving the early 50's I must mention a really exhilarating trip we took to London in 1953 to see the practice parade for Coronation day, May 31st. We got up at a quarter to six, arrived at Waller Road by 6.30 where we picked up Nell. She was the only one there interested in the jaunt, and she sat with Tony and me on the back seat of the car, Helen on my lap, Gran in front with John. We were all in festive mood, there was little traffic and we parked easily on the Embankment, where we took up our positions, along with other determined early birds. It was splendid, I see it all in my mind's eye now, the clear air of early morning, us all dressed in our summer best, the cheers as the Coronation Coach rolled by; just forty

277

years ago. Gran loved every minute of it, Nell was in her element, (was she remembering the excited crowds in London 50 years earlier when they had danced at the Relief of Mafeking?). However that may be, we were all steeped in enjoyment of the present. Gran and Nell provided a picnic, we walked by the Thames, then up to Trafalgar Square and the Mall to see the decorations. Finally we made our way home; we'd really achieved something. By contrast the weather two days later, on Coronation day itself could hardly have been worse, so cold, wet and grey it was. A public holiday, like everyone else (except the very few who'd bought T.V. for the occasion) we had the wireless on all day listening to commentaries on the ceremonies   Richard Dimbleby - and the magnificent service from the Abbey - Parry's "I was glad" and - Handel's "Zadok the priest" - shivers down the spine. By early afternoon it was all over, we 4 donned macs, and just to get some exercise, walked round to a little sweetshop only one open -and bought the babes 5-Boys chocolate bars.

A week later we took our parents up to London one evening to see the illuminations and the following week Nell & Mill, each time arriving back home about 11.30pm. It really was exceptional, everyone was caught up in the magic, the colour, the pagentry of that special occasion. It meant a lot, though had anyone asked us just what it meant, we'd have found it hard to answer.

Tony and Helen mainly had friends in common, at least until they left Princes Plain. A number of boys and girls of similar age lived close at hand, they played in one another's homes and in the street. Quite soon, about 1957, Tony and Helen formed a "gang" called, for some unknown reason, "the Midnight Ghosts" It was all kept pretty secret from me, there were strict orders, rules and complicated projects I know, but they organised it away from us grown-ups, piling into one of their garages if wet, and only calling in for refreshment - a drink or some fresh-baked cake. Weather never seemed to affect their enthusiasm, dressed for all weathers, their eyes shone with excitement, cheeks flushed with exertion, intent on their plans. Their deep involvement in various schemes occasionally led to passions running high, but quarrels were always made up. No neighbour ever complained about this enterprising group of youngsters, they were basically friendly and well-mannered, truly a pleasure to have around.

Tony and Helen started to give birthday parties for their school friends in 1956 and continued about 5 years. Being July/August was a great boon, as they could mostly be held in the garden. I know it was usually very hot and the kids got wild and fractious. Helen enjoyed only her own and Tony's parties; when invited to her friends' I had to drag her along, bawling, all prettied up, wait about embarrassed while she was soothed, then disappear. Usually, 20 minutes later, there she'd be crying her eyes out on the doorstep - someone had brought her back. I never understood that, we knew the families she'd gone to well, and there was no distance involved, all lived within 2-3 minutes walk.

Christmas

It was in 1955 that John and I started to give Christmas. Before then it had been held alternately at St. Norbert or Waller, one Christmas Day, one Boxing Day. Up to 1953 Grandad Homewood always came to the St. Norbert celebration; we remember him singing, upright as ever, nearly blind, voice ancient and quavering, yet determined: "Soon we'll be in London Town See the Queen in her golden crown..." and him teaching the children dominoes. Well, all that was to change, and this year, 1955, at John's suggestion, we left Tony and Helen with his Mother early on Christmas Eve morning and caught the train from Brockley to London Bridge to go to Smithfield to bid for a turkey. It was a tradition, a thing people did. I wasn't too keen, but it was certainly an experience and we returned home triumphant with an excellent hen bird of 17 1/2 pounds for £3. Carried it all the way home, its long neck and little head dangling, drawing amused glances from the busy crowds, all part of the yule-tide fun.

From then on we got into the way of organising the festive season like a military operation. Mincemeat, cake, puddings were all made and put away well before November 30th. It was a matter of interest and pride among us young housewives, a matter of conversation and co-operation, we displayed our products, had tastes, swapped recipes; no-one I knew bought ready made.

The magic of Christmas always began for me as darkness fell on the afternoon of the 24th. - shopping all done, house polished, shining, presents all (meanly) wrapped, I put on the radio (John often at work), and heard the ethereal voice, "Once in Royal David's City", and the choir of King's College, Cambridge, floated out filling the

280

air with glorious sound, as still it does today. As I stood there, rolling out pastry, making mince pies in the enveloping warmth of the kitchen, it crossed my mind to wonder what it must be like to actually be there - to experience the whole proceedings. Not that it really mattered, to hear it was enough.

That evening, the children tucked snugly in bed, we'd stuff the bird with varying forcemeats, sew it up and boil the giblets for gravy and the clamorous cat. Then filling the children's sock - from now on pillowcases - creeping up to their room, they asleep at last - placing them at the foot of their beds.

Excited squeals and chatter would wake us very early next morning, they'd burst into our room in the chilly dark, bare feet stomping, to show us their surprises. I had told them of the real St. Nicholas, so they understood the legend. About 1958 Tony took it into his head to enlighten his friend Philip as to the reality of Father Christmas and began explaining. Not a success, Philip fled home in floods of tears, leaving Tony to make it clear to me that he thought, "It was about time someone told him". Their presents varied, when Helen was four, ('55) Dad completely renovated my old doll's house for her, and we'd bought a number of items to go in it - she was very, very pleased. It was fortunate that that Christmas they were both just fully recovered from chicken-pox, which Tony caught in his first term at school. (I will add that although both had it mildly, Dr. Marmery called in regularly on his rounds to visit them.) Presents, especially for adults, in those days were modest compared with today's flashy geegaws. We always asked surreptitiously for suggestions, so all received something they really wanted, a book, knitting wool, stockings, gloves, socks, tie or braces, a record, scarf, that sort of thing.

Dinner was eaten in the dining room, gaily bedecked with holly and much else, at one o'clock. There were crackers with hats and silly fillings. I need not describe the food, much as we have today, large helpings of everything, large slices of Christmas pudding eaten with lashings of cream, followed by mince pies and coffee. Then some pitched in with the clearing and washing up, others played with Tony and Helen and their new toys and games, music from our modern radiogram cheerful in the background.

And so, into the front room, cluttered and strange with its garlands and real Christmas tree, sparkling with many coloured lights, bringing timeless smells of ancient woodland into that suburban room. 'We'll never have an artificial one again", we said. There'd be carols, Mum playing the piano, maybe new ones learnt by the children at school, certainly all the old favourites still beloved today - and all sung with a will, it was Christmas, we were together, a wave of love swept the room, we had so much to be thankful for.

Great coal fires glowed and flickered in both rooms, while playing paper games was always a tradition of the festive season, Consequences, Birds & Beasts, Pass the Rhyme and Funny people, it could have gone on for hours, it was tremendous fun, we laughed till tears ran down our cheeks. However, we had to pause to eat, and looking back I find it remarkable that we all sat down about 6.0 pm. to a full spread tea including boiled bacon, cold turkey, all sorts of pickles, celery, tomatoes and lettuce, Mill's flaky pastry mince pies, Gran's super trifle, the large rich iced cake and other delicacies. Everyone tucked in with relish, it did you good to see the food disappear. When I consider how, as we played games, the bowls of fruit were passed round, we hardly stopped eating all day - Mum's dish of mixed nuts, Dad' s bowl of dates and chocolate nuts and raisins - were gradually emptied to be refilled next day. Drinks were modest, someone was always making fresh tea (very little coffee, instant coffee · came on the market in 1957), and there was always sherry, Dad's port and Nell's ginger wine.

For three years, until 1958, when Nell died, John made two journeys to take them home, for five was too many to fit into the car and Gran and I would wash up any remaining dirties and clear up generally. Then, incredible to remember, but true, she and I cut a pile of buttery ham sandwiches, nicely seasoned with fresh made mustard, (none other), about then John returned, we had more tea, the sandwiches and pickled onions, or walnuts. Delicious, John drove her home, I to bed,

Boxing Day was to me but a pale imitation of the 25th., a repeat performance I personally could have done without. It was all right, but the mainspring of celebration had lost its momentum, was winding down. I've always found it hard to be festive two days running, let alone a week; we never kept New Year, never had. The food was easy to prepare, tasty though cold, except for mashed potatoes and another large Christmas pudding. Our guests would leave soon after tea, everything tidy and put away, and their departure never failed to touch me, their gratitude and thanks were heartfelt and overwhelming. Mill was usually the last to go, I see her standing in the doorway now grasping my hand, holding my eyes intently with hers, "It means so much to me you know, it was just splendid". The stars shone brightly, an owl hooted in the frosty air, I watched them drive away down the dark and silent street.

So the Christmases passed by, variations on a theme; as I write on this cheerless, grey January day nearly 40 years later, I am struck by the thought that possibly it was in part the tradition our old folks loved. The thought that two terrible world wars and the many violent changes witnessed during their lives had not destroyed this ritual of family get together, this mystical celebration of pagan Yule in the deepest dark of winter, blended miraculously with "Joy, joy for Christ is born", giver of eternal light and love. The thought that our young family enjoyed a Christmas similar in many ways to those of their youth, one that indeed was quite Victorian in its simple, innocent sincerity, made a bond between us, never spoken but deeply felt.

The Christmas celebrations of 1956 were somewhat dimmed by mumps, Tony and Helen both suffered earache which was difficult to assuage. To compensate we took them soon after to their first pantomime at Bromley New Theatre, "Jack and the Beanstalk", a rollicking success.

They were growing fast, while others of our clan aged as rapidly, it was but a few weeks later that Nell got pneumonia, (1957). She was very ill, but rallied and after a month or so recovered well, and her life went on pretty much as it always had. I remember that in the late spring of '58 Tony and Helen developed measles and whooping cough, vaccination was available, but as it was proved meningitis could result, we decided against it. Each had to stay in bed 3 or 4 days, the doctor calling regularly, they were quite ill, but recovered rapidly.

It was soon after this that, on a perfect spring day, John brought Nell over for the day. We sat in the garden and Nell gave Helen my old doll, which had been Mother's, which she had fully dressed in simple late Victorian style - floral petticoat, woolly vest, knickerbockers, shoes and bonnet. She showed Helen how to take them off and put them on again, chatting about the way folk dressed in those days.

However, by summer she began to fail, lost all energy and sparkle, was quiet, accepting that her life was coming to an end. Knowing I'd always wanted a china cabinet she told me to get one, and in October John drove her over to see it. She helped arrange my things in it, although very weak she was relaxed, happy and contented. This was her last visit, for she died 6 weeks later on December 19th. Mum phoned to tell me, I cried, the only time I've wept immediately on hearing of the death of someone close to me. The tears were not for her, of course, but for me. It was irrational for she was "old and full of years". I should not have been surprised, but I was. I went straight to Waller Road, but she had been taken to the mortuary. I was very upset, I felt it right that I should have seen her, said goodbye. (I now know this to be true). However, at the time I could say nothing, as Mill was distraught, in spite of the fact that Nell had just sighed in her sleep and was gone. "We've always been together, 78 years, I've never been without her", and on and on, hysterically. Mum had enough to do calming her down and Dad set about the official business, made more difficult by the approach of this muted, poignant Christmas. Until then, I never really absorbed the fact that she was so old, but death is final. For months after I frequently thought I saw her, getting off the bus she used to come on, walking in Bromley - not an unusual phenomenon, but I've not experienced it since.

Life in General

Occasionally other relatives came to visit, John's Aunt Flo, my Aunts Grace & Lily, Shan & Blanche, John's cousin Jack Teague and family. We drove Nell down to Eastbourne to stay with Lily Sawyer. We had a boat trip and it was at this time that Lily directed us to High & Over and we looked down on the amazing beauty of the Cuckmere Valley for the first time. On another occasion, towards the end of the decade, we took Gran to Broadstairs to see her brother Arthur at St. Peters, he made us all most welcome and more than once we took my parents to Southend and had tea with Aunt Lou.

Now and again in the school holidays I took Tony & Helen by train to Nunhead to spend the day at Waller, (we always got a packet of Refreshers from the machine, 2d., on the return journey). Once, when the children were very small, Mum said, "Here, have you ever heard of someone called Elvis Presley?", I never had. "You will soon", she went on, "He's an American crooner, only 20 and already earned enough money to let his father retire". That was 1956; I listened out for that name, and yes, I heard it, indeed I did.

I know Tony & Helen stayed at Waller Rd., for 2 or 3 days several times from 1957, and that year Mum & Dad took them to Battersea Fun Fair for the day - it cost more than they bargained for, but Dad and the kids had a whale of a time. I was left in no doubt that Mum, typically, had not particularly enjoyed herself!.

John and I took them up to London, to the Zoo, the Kensington Museums, St. Pauls, Westminster Abbey, the great art galleries, and in 1958 we four spent the day in London seeing, in particular, the Sno-Cats in Trafalgar Square, just back from Dr. Fuch's Antarctic Expedition.

The face of London was beginning to be altered, new buildings, modernist, on bomb sites, which were by now seas of willow herb. There were no beggars, ever. However, more often it was to Greenwich or out into the country, picnicking, blackberrying, spending an afternoon at the Roman Villa, Lullingstone, to Canterbury, Penshurst, Tonbridge or at High Rocks and Pantiles, Tunbridge Wells. As before, many days were spent at the coast, Broadstairs, Brighton or Hastings, et al.

I should mention here that we continued to see Mossy regularly, she was still working at Deptford Public Library and was keen to teach the children the piano - which a couple of years later ended in disaster. However, she had early invested in a T.V. ('56), which gave Tony and Helen some inducement to go with us to visit. We arrived at her horrid dump of a basement flat one afternoon to see her waving her fist at a group of rough, muttering, scowling youths. "See them?", she pointed angrily, as they retreated. "They were shouting rude words down my area, I came out and told them to Piss Orf". Good for her; nevertheless, how weird, how unlike her timid, ladylike self. (I dread to think what would have happened to her today).

Towards the end of the fifties, package holidays abroad were becoming popular. I read recently that it was not until 1958 that a decision was made to build a second hotel at the little fishing village of Benidorm on the Costa Blanca. Other villages on the Spanish Mediterranean coast were quick to follow suit, and the entire coastal strip was soon buried under concrete. But, that lay in the future, and Mossy, this unsure, lonely creature, took a great liking to these holidays, was among the first to stay in the new hotels of Yugoslavia - at Bled and Split, horrid names I thought, but lovely places in those days. She took

287

a package holiday every year from then on, each was a success, and she, usually so inept, brought us back pretty, well chosen gifts. By 1958 Helen was already collecting and this year Mossy brought her a charming pair of Norwegian dolls. Realising that her collecting was earnest, John made her her first museum cabinet.

Some time in 1957, when it was usual for both children to be at school all day, the urge came upon me to be mobile - get a bike (The one I had during the War was as good as ever when I became pregnant 8 years later and I sold it). I soon saw one advertised for sale in the newsagents on the Parade -£ 2 from a house in the Fairway. That bicycle, a Raleigh, as far as I could see the same model I'd had before, took me everywhere. It even made the journey to Mavis's at Sidcup, which otherwise involved catching three different buses, far easier. I discovered from a map that a footpath ran from Gosshill Road, off Blackbrook Lane, to Chislehurst, a real discovery. There was very little traffic about in those days. I remember arriving at the start of this path and finding it closed off with a stile. Nothing for it but to lift the bike over and push it up the hill, past a fine Regency house, "Ravenshill", and on through the National Trust Hawkswood Estate, that now I know and love so well. Totally picturesque, isolated and lovely, all seasons, always. Finally, arriving at the Royal Parade, the bike padlocked, I caught the one bus to Mavis's.

For many years we lunched together every other month, alternating the venue. Travelling that way probably took more effort, especially when wet and muddy, than waiting to catch three buses, and when I described it to her, she thought I was mad. Always, however, it was an adventure, something I did alone, and always the stunning, unexpected beauty of that secret hilly woodland invoked in me an instantaneous deeply felt response. By 1958 Mavis and Jack had babes of their own, Julia and Annette, (Viv was not born until 1961). While our husbands were at work, she and I would meet up in one another's houses, or take our brood for a picnic, maybe blackberrying at Hayes or Keston.

By early 1959 we found we could afford to replace "P O" with an Austin Countryman Estate car. Betsy Mk 1 had been breaking down and giving us trouble; we got £25 for her. The Countryman was excellent, started like a dream, was both roomy and reliable. It was a long, glorious summer, we drove to Eastbourne, took Lily for a ride to Alfriston, then back to hers for a nice tea. She was very upset about Nell. "*She* was my friend you know, we went about together a lot; I never knew Mill really". I hadn' t realised at all, all before my time.

Gran loved this vehicle too, her favourite day out was to Hastings, and we spent many great days there. One still, hot summer's day that year we drove Mum and Dad to Camber - a perfect day for such a place - no blown sand, the light across the water clear and beautiful, the sea gentle and warm like a half-set jelly, we bathed, relaxed in a synthesis of sun, sea and air, paddling dreamily for miles on golden sand in rippling water.

Late July, the sun continuing to blaze from a cloudles sky, temperatures in the eighties made us long for the coast, so we made a plan to spend a night in Betsy MK2 at Broadstairs. We got permission to park in a farmer's field for 5/- the night, but Tony and Helen took ages to get to sleep, so did we, it was stiflingly hot and dreadfully uncomfortable lying on the hard floor like that, no room to move (I was never one for camping, I like my creature comforts). On the other hand, it was totally dark and silent except for the startling cry of a fox and the scurrying of some small night animal - not a rabbit for they had been eliminated by the introduction of cruel, man-made myxomatosis in the previous few years. We slept little, but it was good to call in at a local cafe for breakfast at 7.0 in the morning, before anyone else, taking in great gulps of fresh air, before the heat became scorching and unbearable. Quite an adventure, but I think we were all glad to sleep in our own beds that night.

Naturally it was not all high days and holidays, although I may be giving that impression, for it is the outstanding days that linger in the mind. I listened to the radio quite a lot, music, talks, Woman's Hour, sometimes, on a lighter note, Housewives' Choice, and always on a Saturday morning, Children's Choice. How many times was "The Runaway Train" drummed into our ears, or "Champion the Wonder Horse", "The Laughing Policeman", or "Robin Hood", etc. All light music programmes were dominated by the American market, Buddy Holly had arrived, and Harry Belafonte with the "Banana Boat Song", though Cliff Richard appeared on the scene in 1958 and we could not know, but the Beatles and their ilk were only a year or two away.

In the spring of 1957 we redecorated Gran's living room, a few weeks later she was knocked down on a Belisha crossing at Blackheath. As she was housebound I would go and visit her, by 94 bus to Lewisham, then the 144 to Brockley Cross. One of those visits stands out in my memory very clearly indeed. Sitting by her fire, she suddenly told me how she'd got rid of a baby. She'd never told anyone, she said, never dared. I must admit I was astounded, I never knew she had the will power, the sheer guts, she went right up in my estimation. "When I realised I'd fallen for another one, John was at grammar school, things were looking up, I thought I'm not going to have another baby, I don't want one. Syd was out, I got a crochet hook and stuck it in myself sitting over a pail. I had to do it three times, I thought I'd die, it was agony, blood pouring out. Syd was terrified, I don't think he knew what I had done, he got Emm. She was very good, she understood. Never said a word to anyone. She helped me through it. I could have gone to prison". "You could have died", I said. "You don't think I was wrong do you?. We could never have afforded it, it would have pulled us right down again". "No", I said, "I'm jolly proud of you". So I was, and still am. She burst into tears. Compassion overcame any residual antipathy within me. I gave her a hug and made us a fresh pot of tea, musing the while that all that was over and done with nearly a quarter of a century ago, not understanding then, that such things are never, ever, over and done with, for "I am a part of all that I have known".

Helen with Gran, a day out at Brasted, 1958

291

Meeting

Whereas circumstances did not permit us to attend Peckham Meeting at all regularly while living at Brockley, within a month of moving we started the habit of going to Bromley Meeting every Sunday. John, previously a Methodist, considered it best that we go together, rather than split up and worship at different denominations. We were warmly welcomed by this vigorous, strongly motivated group, and were soon drawn into the life of the Meeting, made easier by the presence of several old Peckham Friends, including the Edwards family, who had moved to the Bromley area before us. John joined the Society about this time and I became an overseer, a very green one, but it stretched me somewhat. I learned a lot and was enabled to become involved in things outside the home.

Prominent among this friendly, if diverse, lot were the Barringtons, important here because early in 1959 they gave us Lucky, the only dog we've ever owned. We were not at all sure we wanted her, but one look was enough - blotched black and white descendant of a dalmatian mother and a labrador that she was, she was irresistible. We took this biddable beast to our hearts, and she responded in like fashion, became the darling of the entire family - except poor Sooty, who recoiled, and viewed her with prolonged distaste.

For an hour each Sunday morning then, we experienced in the renewing stillness, a sense of God's purpose, order and design, enriching our inner life, recharging our batteries for the week (and years) which lay ahead.

This flourishing Meeting ran three children's classes, and Tony and Helen soon made friends, the Westwoods, Hendersons, Ellimans and Giles come to mind. I got involved with these classes and helped to organise harvest thanksgiving and the annual nativity play. Moving from Hayes to Bromley town during the war, Bromley P.M. as yet had no premises of its own, using the hall of a private school in Holwood Road (a road no longer there, having been covered by "The Glades"), central, but by the time we joined the congregation plans were afoot to purchase a site and build a Meeting House. This was finally achieved in 1962 at a total cost of £15,000; meanwhile all sorts of money-raising ploys were adopted, friends of Friends were persuaded to give coffee mornings, some venues were historic and beautiful, interesting to visit for their own sake. Great jumble sales were held, and ambitious and successful "Sales of Work". First and foremost of those organising was Winifred Salter, although then over 60, she was inexhaustible, her energy knew no bounds. She contacted estate agents, viewed many plots and properties before the present site was finally agreed upon. For a time, I was on Premises Committee, and can well remember a number of acrimonious gatherings of seething anger, when feathers flew, ending up with one member storming out and resigning.

Winifred Salter also contacted the main shops in the High Street and succeeded in collecting a remarkable number of free gifts for her "charity" - explaining exactly what it was. I know that Boots, Medhursts, M. & S. contributed, and Dunns of the Market Square, high quality furnishers, gave an enormous bundle of off-cuts of Sandersons beautiful fabrics. We women each took some of these pieces of superb quality and design, I made gorgeous cushion covers, and others were made up most imaginatively. When I look back on it I marvel; but commodities were not nearly as readily available in the shops as now, and our goods sold quickly. Aprons, baby clothes, toilet bags, soft toys, homemade cakes and preserves, sweets - several times I made a tray of toffee apples, begging the wooden skewers from our butcher, who was pleased to oblige. All made a colourful and inviting display, with refreshments available all day long. These ambitious, well organised activities enriched the life and fellowship of the Meeting and were carried on for a number of years after the new building was opened, in order to clear our debts.

Being weighty and serious folk, Quakers tend to be continuously bubbling up with "concerns", which is only right and proper; at times, however, it seems to bog them down. Among the many rife at that time, the concern over-riding all others, indeed the cause of deep anxiety and misgiving, not only to all religious bodies, but to all people of sensitivity and goodwill the world over, was that of the Cold War and the nuclear arms race. Much has been written about it, but I will touch upon it here, if only to illustrate how it is that ordinary, humble lives carry on the minutiae of day to day living against the impending horrors of world events.

East-West relations had deteriorated sharply since 1948, our nuclear warning system was ready for use by 1955, thoughts of all that implied were too terrible to be borne. I cannot forget the time notices on how to survive a nuclear attack were issued, we should have left the air-raid shelter the bastion it was, I thought. We must wall ourselves up inside with sandbags at the opening, having laid in stocks of food, water and blankets - and, heart-rending realisation, we must leave Lucky outside. It was fantasy, nothing would survive, we knew, and if by a

294

fluke we did, as we emerged what would we see?. A stricken, burnt out world, with death and decay at every turn?. Fortunately, an aggressive maternal instinct takes over, and that combined with the indestructible will to live and cherish all that makes life meaningful is invincible, engendering faith, hope and courage, against all the odds.

Things were looking pretty black when suddenly, it seemed to me, in 1956 trouble flared up with Egypt. Britain and France tried to stop Nasser seizing the Suez Canal and we joined a Protest Car Drive through Bromley waving banners inscribed *Law Not* War. Meanwhile the Mau-Mau indulged in an orgy of atrocities against whites in Kenya, and Russia invaded Hungary.

Feeling against nuclear arms ran high, manifesting itself in the formation of CND, leaders being Canon Collins, Bertrand Russell, Philip Noel-Baker and J.B. Priestley. Great numbers, from every section of society, marched from London to Aldermaston, we joined them for the first march in 1958, gathering at Trafalgar Square with many from our Meeting and Phyllis Arglet. It was heartening, exhilarating, at last we were able to make a positive statement, to feel we were doing something, however little, to impede the progress of the juggernauts of death and destruction. For that was one of the chief horrors of that situation, permeating all society, the complete helplessness in face of the dynamism of conflict generated by the Cold War.

Maude Teague flies to the States

Although the changes brought about in the 1950's were as nothing compared with what was to come, any world-wide change affects us all. An amazing event to us then, in 1959, was John's Mother's visit to America. She had not seen Ida for 18 years, and when the invitation came was torn with indecision, wanting, naturally, to see her daughter again, yet unable to forget her traumatic departure in 1941, was filled with doubts. Her departure had been traumatic as, to put it briefly, she had married against her parent's wishes; a few years later the marriage foundered, divorce ensued.

Things nowadays could scarcely be more different, fifty years ago the idea of divorce was taboo, spoken of only in subdued whispers. One spoke of one spouse leaving another in shocked, disturbed undertones. It was deadly sin, preferably never, ever mentioned. Certainly, curiosity played its part in the decision to make the visit, glamorous photos, parcels of stylish scarcely-used clothes, costume jewellery excitedly received (like a lucky dip), conjured up a picture of a land of plenty and a life of high living such as Maude Homewood, or indeed, any of us had ever known. Shan went to see her, persuading her to go on the same flight as Blanche, who had already arranged to stay with her son, Arthur and family recently settled in New York. So it was agreed that she go for the statutory maximum period for a visit, three months. John collected her passport and she duly filled in the application form for a visa, stating that she was neither a communist nor a prostitute. Ida sent her return ticket and told her not to bring any luggage as she would buy her a "compete new wardrobe". "Good", I thought, at last Ida is taking some responsibility for her Mother, which up to then John (and I!) had shouldered in full. The prospect appeared dazzling, she stood on the threshold of an irresistible adventure.

I can see us now, that lovely day of June, Gran came to lunch, all dressed in her best - a smart handsome woman, and her sister-in-law, Flo had come over to share the excitement and say goodbye to her. We all sat in the garden, Tony jumping in and out of his new "pool", Helen alternately hanging upside down on the Swiss swing ropes, or, as the current rage demanded, ceaselessly rotating her Hula hoop. John returned from work early, and we all sat and ate our tea in the warm sunshine.

"You say that you're not taking any luggage?" queried Flo, sharing our own doubts. "Only an overnight bag - Ida's getting me all new things", replied Gran happily showing her letter; we felt pretty envious. John drove her to meet Blanche at Victoria Coach Station that evening, the first of our family to fly so far, the first to visit the "New World". She found the flight very long and uncomfortable, for the plane landed in Labrador for a few hours before flying on to New York. There, Arthur met them, exhausted, and drove them to his house, taking Gran back to the airport the next day for the flight to Seattle.

Poor Gran's time with her daughter was a disaster from start to finish. Almost as soon as she arrived, distraught, pitiful letters arrived from her. A black, irredeemable experience for both of them. She was put into smart, fashionable American clothes, her hair cut and dyed and her face made up, but the whole scheme went sour from the start for Ida not only denied that she ever implied her Mother was to arrive luggage-less, but made up a parcel of certain favourite items that Gran was wearing and sent them back to Brockley. That was one thing, there were many other upsetting incidents not worth recalling here. All she wanted was to get back home and no way was that possible, she must perforce stay put until the three months were up.

We four drove to Heathrow early on that day, spent an hour or so looking round and having refreshments and watching the great planes coming in and taking off. We had not been there before, it was a new adventure. I shall never forget how glad she was to see us, later she would talk to me at length about those painful days. Now she was back home in England, all was well, but the distress resulting from that experience lasted for months, only fading with the years.

Holiday 1959

While holidays throughout the 50's continued to be spent at various resorts in Kent, as the decade drew to a close we felt a longing to be more adventurous, and decided to book a caravan on a farm near Bridport. It proved to be one of the most felicitous choices we ever made, we all fell in love with Dorset, its picturesque towns and villages, unique coastline and unspoilt countryside.

It was August 5th., we were up at 5.45 and the car being loaded the night before and all things ready, we set off with despatch, arriving at the Hog's Back for our picnic breakfast at 8.30. The journey was fresh to us, the scenery pleasing, we were all in buoyant mood. I remember we stopped to eat lunch in the New Forest and that as we drove further into Dorset the countryside became hilly and evermore delightful. On the left hand side of the A 35, descending the last steep hill on the approach to Bridport, stood "The Travellers Rest", I thought Hardy must be referring to it in "Weathers": "And we sit outside the Traveller's Rest, And Maids come forth sprig muslin dressed" Maybe he was, I've never been able to find out, but there were worn wooden benches by the pub door, so it pleased me to think so.

A dim old sign suddenly came into view, *Walditch,* we swung off the main road and immediately were journeying into a lost, forgotten backwater of rural England. We were more fortunate than we could possibly have foretold in our choice of accommodation, Mrs. Plenty, the farmer's wife came out to meet us in a most warm and friendly manner, completely at ease, totally natural, a character from half a century before, she and her husband were peasant farmers whom Hardy might have known. Our caravan stood at the side of the farmhouse wall, our car parked beside it on stone paved ground. Among these large stone slabs were several which held embedded great fossils, mainly ammonites found locally in the fields. There were also one or two set in the wall of a double barn close by, others could be seen in various buildings and paths within the village.

Tony and Helen were soon out with daughter Susan collecting eggs from happy scrabbling hens, and searching for the odd broody one - you never knew where one might be nestling in the undergrowth. At night the birds had to be driven up the outer stone steps of the ancient lichen-covered barn, shut in for fear of foxes. One wet afternoon Susan showed us how to tell the sex of an egg by swinging a ring threaded on a cord over it. If it went round and round it was female, if to and fro - a boy. She said they did it over animals' bellies too, for instance cows, to see if a heifer or bull-calf was on the way. I never figured out how the said animal was persuaded to lie still while you performed this jiggery-pokery. You three would go searching for the earliest hazel nuts, pick blackberries, and in the darkening summer evenings ran free chasing bats all round the village.

The Plentys had about 12 cows, all known individually by name, some of which were descriptive - Pansy had a dark blotch over each eye, Snowdrop was pure white, and Buttercup sported a golden patch under her chin. Mr. Plenty got up very early each morning and brought them straggling down Seven Sisters Lane from Five Acre Field to the milking shed, where he and his wife milked them by hand. He then herded them back to the pasture, while Joyce was left to muck out the shed. Walditch Village Street was always caked with cows' muck, for other dairy farms led on to it, mostly much larger concerns than

Plenty's, and the churns standing at the gates awaiting collection by Rax Dairy of Bridport were a feature.

The houses and walls of this village were of honey coloured Hamstone, opposite Plenty's lay Crabbe's long low farm buildings. Their farming methods and life-style identical with Elias and Joyce's, but of interest to us as, "Oldman Crabbe, his brain do turn at the full moon. Alright other times mind, but they do lock him in then, and still he breaks china and throws furniture at the windows. Ah, we stay in then, mind." A pity, but we never managed to witness that particular phenomenon. These village dwellings harmonised with their setting, for they were constructed of this weather-beaten stone, quarried from the hillside. This quarry, long since disused, now formed a steep, dark ravine, completely over-hung with trees, whose roots clawed into the loamy Ham stone beneath. Enormous ferns flourished, rare ones and common, gross in size. When in later years we came at Easter, we'd find the trees bare, the whole ravine light and glowing with giant clumps of primroses, lush violets, the crowns of ferns ready to uncoil the current season's fronds; the whole untrammelled, alive with birdsong, rich in country smells.

To the west, south and east of the village, high, green conical hills rose sharply, here and there crowned with a clump of trees, others deeply stepped by ancient lynchets. Walditch Street formed a long and winding crescent, it was unfrequented for it led nowhere, except, in both directions on to the A 35. A lane looping round from it had also once, generations ago, been a quarry, but was now a narrow tarmacked road of sharp incline, whose vertical sides of hewn rock formed a gloomy gorge of gothic aspect, at evening alive with bats.

The village comprised a number of houses, farms, a general store, a pub and a mid-Victorian church, St. Mary's, and was served by a bus four times? a day. However there was also an Elizabethan mansion, the Hyde, a wonderful building of the mellow local stone, standing serene in an idyllic setting, reached by a short tree-lined drive from Walditch Street. The strange ecclesiastical-looking building in the grounds which excited curiosity was an indoor tennis court said to have been erected on the occasion of an impending visit by Edward VII, which in fact never materialised.

Mrs. Plenty was immensely kind and open hearted; I can recall her one day sitting on a rickety stool in the kitchen crying her eyes out. "What ever's the matter?", I asked with some trepidation, knowing their marital position was none too stable. "Oh poor Snowdrop, she'm been ailing and Dad's taken her to be slaughtered. I know I'm stupid crying like this, but I do get so fond of them all, it's always the same, I can't help it". She calmed down, but I thought how rotten it was that she had to be involved in dairy farming; there was no way out now. However, someone has to do it, and far better they be over-tender than harsh and insensitive. As was the custom, the hens, and eggs were her domain, she gathered them up for collection weekly. There were invariably a lot of cracked ones which she scrambled, omletted or used in cakes. How she managed to cook I don't know, the scullery was rudimentary and the equipment antediluvian. They inhabited the big kitchen/living room, stone-paved right through the scullery to the back door, a few tatty mats dotted around. On rare occasions she'd, "Pull the (almost bald) broom through", dirt swept straight out the back door - all she had time for. There was an ancient, greasy, black iron gas oven, a big wooden table and that's about it. Bowls, empty jam-pots, packets and jars of ingredients were stacked higgledy-piggledy on rough wooden shelves. There were rows of bottles of home-made wine, concocted from every fruit and flower here flourishing freely, and crocks of it stood about on the floor. They had a hot-water system, but chose not to use it, instead lit a fire in the living room every day, composed mainly of sticks and logs, which was surrounded by trivets - hooked on and standing, on which heavy old iron saucepans continually stood, simmering and heating water. To "hurry up", a little tin kettle, entirely smothered in soot, was rammed on top. Another thing which springs to mind is the antique wooden butter maker, yes, she sometimes still made butter and showed me how to do it, very hard and boring it was. When younger she always kept a pig, and in her youth at Cheddar was a champion cheese maker. She showed me her certificates, maybe City & Guilds, and she frequently made a soft cheese now.

As we talked, she knitted, fine, pretty garments for the grandchildren, there was never a moment when she and "Dad" were not working. Dawn to dusk; "Time is money", he'd say. Saturday was market day in Bridport, and there she'd be selling any spare fruit or vegetables and pretty bunches of the flowers she'd grown purposely and made into posies at sunrise that morning.

Mr. Plenty had little to do with us, brief time to talk, which perhaps was just as well, his accent being so broad made it difficult for us to understand him. The Milk Marketing Board had recently set up a local office in the village and he got part-time employment there, yet he never allowed this to affect his agricultural labours in any way. (What did he do there?) An orphan, brought up by a harsh uncle who forced him to work all day on his farm, he had next to no schooling, he was thin, small and bent, walked staring at the ground, but on looking up the sharp blue eyes glinted from the leathery wrinkled face, he'd give a wry grin, raise his moth-eaten cap to us, and greet John as, "Sirrr". Plenty's land was composed of tiny fields, those attached to the house resembling a market garden, beds of lettuce, cabbage, carrots, potatoes, runner beans, peas and so on, all thriving in the rich moist loam, sheltered by the surrounding hills. Set apart only by narrow grassy paths were 2 or 3 small orchards of aged fruit trees, twisted knarled and green with layers of moss, choked with grass and weeds, long past their prime, and yielding only a fraction of the crop once harvested for marketing and the cider press.

At that time the government was offering grants for land improvement, and old Plenty put in for as many as possible. In this way he got much of his land, including the various fields and plots he owned in the vicinity, cleared and drained and most of the now useless fruit trees grubbed up. However, to a large extent the Plenty's remained self-sufficient, the double barn heaped with cooking and eating apples, strings of enormous onions, shelves of gross marrows, clamps of potatoes - an unusual and delicious variety he had grown for half a century, now, (1959) unobtainable and for which he kept all his own seed. We always bought a sack of them to take home, in fact we loaded the car with so much local produce I don't know how it all fitted in - Dorset knobs from Morecombelake, generous segments of Dorset Blue Vinney Cheese, Lardy cake, and from Plenty's a cornucopia of delights, eggs, fruit, vegetables, and we were always given a big bunch of flowers. But then everywhere hung vegetable seeds drying in paper bags and near this barn he'd erected 2 large, ramshackle glass-houses, which he kept packed with heavy-cropping tomato plants. Self-sufficient, yes, but at what cost? Not exactly "The Good Life" was it? "What is this life if full of care" etc. It turned out later that Plenty's were much better off money-wise than we were!

We were out all day, everyday, absorbing the total beauty of this area. Some of those places I recall most clearly, two or three I had been taken to 20 years before when on holiday with my parents at Weymouth, Portland, Abbotsbury, Swanage and Lulworth. Others I visited from Poole during the war, Wimborne, Dorchester, Maiden Castle and Wareham; but now I was to see these places with a clearer vision, an enlarged perception, now I was to come to know Long Bredy, Eggerdon Hill, Loders, West Bay with its crashing tides, where mountains of tiny pebbles form the beginning of Chesil Beach. Charmouth where we spent hours hunting fossils in the soft grey oolite cliffs. I see us now walking the Cobb at Lyme Regis buffeted by a light sea breeze, Tony swimming strongly and Helen floating the shallow waters on her new Lilo, deflected sunlight glinting across the bay.

I saw it through Hardy' s eyes, saw where ships of the Napoleonic era sailed past Portland Bill, where the Melstock choir and musicians made their way along the snowy lanes, saw where the effigy of the mayor's body floated down river to Casterbridge. They "flash upon the inward eye" - what a blessing that can be - and clear and sharp I see Little Bredy, as it was the following Easter, so perfect its beauty caught your heart strings. (Mentioned by Mother as the place where her cousin Ros settled when she married a native of this village - like going to the moon then, she disappeared from their lives). Entering the ancient church, where men had worshipped from time immemorial, we found it dressed for Easter, incredibly pretty, while on a central windowsill shone out in primroses, "GOD IS LOVE"

Thereafter we were to stay in Walditch many times, remaining close friends of the Plenty's until Joyce's death. The 60s and 70s brought great change to the village, as they did to all England. It has been scrubbed clean, polished bright, no cows now, none of their muck on that pleasant rural road. It's gentrified, "Chocolate Box", attractive "Country Life" style, "Homes & Gardens" pattern, set about with desirable residences.

For all that it remains uniquely beautiful, and here in this village, epitomising, as it does for me, "England's green and pleasant land", I will close the curtains on my memories of the nineteen fifties.

Postscript

At first I found it difficult to recall details of the 50s, to get them into some semblance of order, much like trying to unravel a great knotted bundle of many coloured wools, when suddenly the various strands loosen, and all fall into place.

I was fortunate in being able to check certain dates with John's engagement diaries (I was too preoccupied then to keep one). It is noteworthy that frequently he writes:- "the babies are queer", or, "we are gay" - how the meaning of words has altered in the intervening period.

I have written only that which I could readily remember of our lives in that decade, mentioning only those outside events which concerned us, or had some impact on our lives.

Life is a continual challenge; health is largely essential, wealth - a fair proportion (neither more nor less) of the nation's wealth is vital. Happiness is a most creative asset (more than misery ??) and commonsense a blessing.

(1991-1993)

Summing Up

Now I have come to the end of the 50s, a decade which saw the stabilising of the new nations of India and Pakistan (47) and Israel (48), seen the establishment of apartheid, the signing of the Treaty of Rome (57) and the first influx of immigrants into Great Britain from the West indies. Other world-shaking events have already been mentioned, the Korean War, the fast escalating war in Vietnam and the nuclear arms race. Many notable people died, including Orwell, Shaw, Vaughan Williams, Einstein and Picasso.

At home how did we keep up with the changing times? Suburban life suited us admirably, we could be completely private when we chose; on the other hand we made staunch and lasting friends. From our marriage we had an electric iron, a vacuum cleaner, bought our first television set in September 1959, deliberately delayed, but put to good use once purchased (one of John and my favourite series then was "Maigret" - Rupert Davies). Our first fridge arrived in 1960, I was not desperate about this, having an excellent tiled, north-facing larder, but once we got it, I wondered how I'd ever done without it. That year the first freezer foods began to appear, but were slow to catch on, and it was another 10 years before we bought a freezer. However, the washing machine was purchased soon after the fridge - one of the modern inventions which, together with man-made fibres, saved literally hours of work. Central heating was put in in 1965 (we were early) and fitted carpets first came on the market about the same time.

All this is average, and it meant that when I started going out to work in 1962 my housework was considerably lessened. However, in comparison expectations remained lower than today's, the "acquisitive society" had not arrived, and on the whole life was simpler. Of course there was as yet no notion of "convenience foods". From the outset I made all soups, cakes, pastry and pies every week, all jams and marmalade much as my female forbears before me, and found it both creative and satisfying. The throwaway consumer society, the violent social changes of the 60's, including the ability of women to have control over their own fertility, loomed on the horizon, unthreatening as yet, clouds no bigger than a man's hand.

I mentioned the smog and floods of the early 50's, the winter of 62-63 was equally abnormal, Arctic conditions prevailing from Boxing Day to early March, the sea froze for miles out, birds froze on their perches and snow covered the land for 65 days.

The succeeding years would bring significant changes to all our lives. Six months on (June '60) John became College Librarian at Chelsea College, London University, thus we became acquainted with the Jellises and Eatwells. Tony and Helen both gained scholarships, and we would spend wonderful holidays in Scotland.

It would have been about 1960, when the idea of women going out to work became generally accepted, that vague thoughts of returning to librarianship floated through my mind. However, it would be a great effort to emerge from the pattern of routine in which I was so happily settled, it would take a big jolt to shift me from the entrenched comfort of my present well-organised life. The jolt came that year, when three close acquaintances of ours, three husbands, were killed violently in road accidents. The effect on their wives, none of whom had paid employment, was devastating. While fully realising that these bereaved women would be no less devastated

309

initially if they had professions of their own, it was, nevertheless obvious to me that having a regular income of one's own would at least ease the financial loss which must follow the loss of the breadwinner. I decided then and there to look for suitable work - part-time school librarian, but such jobs being strictly limited in number, it was two years before I obtained the post at Bromley Grammar School for Boys in Hayes Lane. It was a start, I thought, I found it exhilarating, and my intention was, as the children grew older, to go back to full-time librarianship.

I suppose I am bourgeois, I value harmony, routine, order, little things, ordinary days when nothing much happens (as well as those sparkling and splendid). I actually look forward to unbusy days, savour them; there is time, there is space. With my life in that decade then so completely humdrum and banal, why did I persist in writing it up?

The family may appreciate it later on from a family history point of view.

To show as clearly as possible how much, and how little life has changed in 40 years.

"Apologia pro vita sua" - an attempt to show that as a mere housewife my life was far from boring, but fulfilling, interesting and as far as I can judge, useful. (I hope).

Although we did not know it at the time, it is now acknowledged that between the late 40's and 60's most people in Britain lived in an age of certainty. This post-war age of certainty lasted as long as the period between the two World Wars. People came to regard it as normal, imagined it would never end, we were confident in mind and spirit, believed that life's continuities would be preserved. The threat of nuclear war, and Britain's relative decline we felt to be world affairs. There was very little unemployment, jobs were for life, promotion likely. Marriage was generally for life too, which meant that most people came from a stable, if not always happy, background. Retirement had to be planned for, but the future was assumed to be foreseeable. Many things contributed to ending this age of assurance. Thatcher's government's emphasis on individualism, the threat to global environment, confusion of morals, gross unemployment, lack of meaning in so many peoples' lives, denial of the spiritual side of life, accent on the vicious, violent and brutal. Enormous problems developed; alcohol, drugs, promiscuity and lack of beauty and culture.

Whereas the 30's ended in war, and the 40's for me in marriage, the 50's came to an indefinite end, life for us flowed on without interruption into the 60's. One could take any ten years, a decade is convenient; however, it can only be but a shadow of the experience - not being Proust I cannot, could not bear, to spend my present life writing of my past - or I lose the here and now.

APPENDIX
Prices and Comparison Statistics

In order to assess our standard of living I quote:

1950	Me: Coat £8, Shoes (good ones) £2-15-0 John: Suit £11 -18-0
1951	Festival of Britain:- A cup of coffee cost 9d. (approx. 3 1/2p.) Lunch cost 7/6d. (approx. 36p.) Afternoon tea cost 3/- (approx. 15p.) Dinner cost 10/- (approx. 50p.)
1952	Average housewife shops Fridays and spends 10/- to £2. One household in three has no bath
1953	TV licence rose to £3 John's salary was £45-10-0 monthly after deduction of tax and superannuation contribution
1957	Average couple (married of course) lived in 2 bedroom rented flat with 3 children. He worked 48½ hours per week and earned just under £12 per week. No vacuum, no wall to wall carpet- not around, no fridge etc. NHS was a boon, but at this date no ECGs, hip-replacements, heart surgery, organ transplants, no facilities for keeping ailing tiny babies alive – nor any artificial fertility.
1958	Radio Times 4d., Observer 5d., (six News Chronicles 1/3d.), John haircut 3/- Piano tuned 14/- 2 shirts (sale) £2-0-0d. 4 white collars 10/- China cabinet twenty guineas (£21) reduced from £25

1959	Sold Betsy Mk.1 car for £25 Austin Countryman £335 John light cotton jacket and shorts £3-2-6 Hula hoop 5/-
1967	Car - Mini cost £579 Weekly state pension for single person £4 per week Loaf of bread 1/4d. Can of baked beans 1/3d. Pint of beer 1/7d.
1975	The change to metric currency was 1971 Marks & Spencer prices:- Brown woven skirt and waistcoat £8 Raincoat £10 Blue & white dress £10 Blue corduroy velvet suit £18.50p. Kay shoes (sale) £5 Clark's Navy blue sandals £5.40 Clark's Brown lace-up shoes £5.50p. Littlewoods:- Pink jumper £2 Littlewoods:- Pantie girdle £2 Perm. £6 All from my own notes

	1957	1987
Litres of wine drunk by the average person	1	11
Percentage of households owning a car	24%	65%
Percentage of households owning a fridge	2%	98%
Percentage of households owning a washing machine	25%	85%
Percentage of households owning a TV set	60%	97%
Percentage of households without hot water system	25%	2%
Millions of people taking holiday abroad	1.5	16

Family Allowance first paid Aug 1946 for every child beginning with the 2nd; 5/- (present 25p.) per week, so I got it for Helen.

> *"Between 1910 and 1930 alcohol consumption halved, a trend that continued into the 1950's and its decline marked a critical social change: as alcohol consumption decreased so did acts of violence. during that period Britain was probably a safer place to live, the Blitz excepted, than at any time before or since. From the 1960's onwards, there has been a rise in alcohol consumption which has been closely linked with a similar rise in violence".*

(From:- *The Nineties* by G. Wood and P. Thompson. B.B.C. 1993.)

I understand that 1940 to the early 60's there was full employment, but low inflation.

To Grammar School

Family Tree

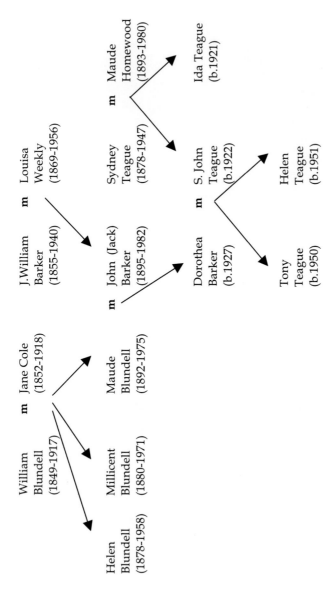

William Blundell (1849-1917) **m** Jane Cole (1852-1918)

Helen Blundell (1878-1958)

Millicent Blundell (1880-1971)

Maude Blundell (1892-1975)

J.William Barker (1855-1940) **m** Louisa Weekly (1869-1956)

John (Jack) Barker (1895-1982) **m** Dorothea Barker (b.1927)

Sydney Teague (1878-1947) **m** Maude Homewood (1893-1980)

Ida Teague (b.1921)

S. John Teague (b.1922)

Tony Teague (b.1950)

Helen Teague (b.1951)

316